GOOD FOOD
❦ SERVED RIGHT ❦

Traditional Recipes & Food Customs
From New York's North Country

Bon appétit!
Lynn Ekfelt

Lynn Case Ekfelt

TAUNY

Traditional Arts in
Upstate New York

Research and publication of Good Food, Served Right has
been partially underwritten by generous contributions from
the ALCOA Foundation and The Sweetgrass Foundation.

First Printing, June, 2000

ISBN 0-9678774-0-7

LCCN 00 131195

Front cover photo:
"Sunday Dinner," memory painting, oil on masonite by
Edna West Teall (1881–1968), Lewis, Essex County, 1957.
Courtesy of the Teall Collection of Mr. and Mrs. Albert Gates.

Back cover photo:
Painted wooden sign from former Sara's Kitchen diner,
Hopkinton, St. Lawrence County, by Kenneth Greene,
ca. 1990. Mike Shufelt Photo/TAUNY Archives.

Printed in the USA by

WIMMER
The Wimmer Companies
Memphis
1-800-548-2537

Contents

Introduction 10

Nature's Bounty

Apples 15
Cheese 27
Fish 39
Game 51
Maple Syrup 63
Wild Foods 73

Who We Are

African Americans 87
Amish 103
Armenian Americans 115
French Americans 127
Greek Americans 137
Homesteaders 155
Hungarian Americans 171
Italian Americans 183
Jews 195
Korean Americans 211
Lebanese Americans 225
Mennonites 241
Mohawks 251
Yankees 263

Building Community

County Fairs 277
Church Suppers 291
Fundraisers 301
Firemen's Field Days 313
Ice Cream Socials 317

Bibliography 325

Equivalents and Substitutions 329

Index 333

The following recipe was reprinted with permission from *Bill Saiff's Rod & Reel: Recipes for Hookin' & Cookin'*. Watertown, NY: Rod & Reel of WNPE-TV, 1990. Dilled Pike and Pea Pods.

The following recipes have been reprinted with permission from *Cornwall Recipe Book*. Alexandria Bay NY: Alexandria Township Historical Society, 1994. Pebble Island Pickled Pike, Lawrence Senecal's Fish Chowder, Ola Lowe's Doughnuts.

The following recipes have been reprinted with permission from *Friends of Croghan Mennonite Cookbook*. Croghan NY: the Friends, 1997. Kuchen bread, Sauerkraut Salad, Scalloped Peas and Onions, Apple-sauce Cake, Whoopie Pies, Pie Plant Pie, Shoo-fly Pie, Raisin Nut Pie, Apple Dumplings, Mincemeat, Ezra Widrick's Barbecue Chicken Sauce.

The following recipes have been reprinted with permission from *Hopkinton Maple Festival Cookbook*. Hopkinton NY: Hopkinton Bicentennial Committee, 1976. Jack Wax, Maple Cream, Maple-Candied Sweet Potatoes, Maple Ham Loaf, Maple Pickled Beets.

The following recipes have been reprinted with permission from *Landmarks and Lemon Crackers: A North Country Cookbook*. Canton NY: St. Lawrence County Historical Association, 1979. Dandelion Salad, New England Boiled Dinner, Indian Relish, Cheese Pudding with Creole Sauce, Lemon Crackers, Corn Chowder, Steam Pudding.

The following recipes have been reprinted with permission from *"Take the Gray Basin. . ."* Canton NY: Mary Hadlock Biondi, 1976. "By Guess and by Gosh" Bread Pudding, Lemon Crackers, Baked Apples with Maple Sugar, Apple Brown Betty Baldwin, Maple Hard Sauce.

Credits and Acknowledgements

Good Food, Served Right was made possible because of the encouragement and cooperation of countless people in the North Country who contributed in so many ways to the development and completion of such a major project for a small arts organization like TAUNY. While we are very grateful to all, we are especially indebted to the following:

We have been truly blessed to have Lynn Ekfelt undertake the compiling and editing of this publication. Her background in folklore studies, her personal skills as a cook, her competence in research and writing, her high standards in editing, and her good cheer through the whole long process have made all the difference. This committed friend of TAUNY and longtime personal friend may never know how much we appreciate what she has done here.

We thank Nils Ekfelt for his painstaking editing and proofreading of several drafts of essays and recipes, and for cheerfully sampling and critiquing dishes from a variety of cuisines.

While we thank the dozens of individuals and some publications who have been credited for their contributions of recipes within the text, we especially thank these individuals for contributing information from oral interviews used in the essays and historical sketches: Nora Akiki, Shirley Aldous, Nevart Bogosian, Sebouh Bogosian, Jessie Bonno, Maria Booras, James Brabant, Magda Breg, Walter Cade, Florence Cook, the Reverend Max Coots, Patreesha Endres, Janet Favro, Roger Favro, Judith Glasser, Madeleine Gray, Helen Holcomb, Judy Hoyt, Dr. Karen Johnson-Weiner, the Reverend John Jordan, Harriet LaFrance, Joan Masterson, Scott McRobbie, Chrisoula Mesires, Mary Mesires, Addie Miller, Ira Miller, Sr., Frank Mitchell, Odessa Mitchell, Rosalind Morgia, David O'Neil, Beverly Sabad, Capril Serabian, Eunice Southworth, Kelly Southworth, Jennie Spaziani, Rosemary Spozato, Shin Tupper, and Emily White. We particularly thank Ellen Maroun, Samuel Thomas and Peter Van de Water for contributing essays to the collection.

We thank Beverly Hickman, Lamar Bliss and North Country Public Radio for their part in recording hours of oral interviews for the Home Cooking series of short documentaries that was broadcast in the early 1990s. These recordings, now in the TAUNY Archives, were very useful in preparing essays for this book.

We thank Martha Cooper, Mark Sloan, and photographers from the *Watertown Daily Times* for their fine images, and thank the *Watertown Daily Times* for their permission to reproduce selected photographs in our book.

We particularly thank the Alcoa Foundation, and especially Michael Cooper of the Alcoa Massena Operations, for support of the initial research and writing of the book; and Kate and Allan Newell and the Sweetgrass Foundation for partial underwriting of the book's publication. We also acknowledge ongoing support for the Folk Arts Program at the New York State Council on the Arts whose grants made possible our research on and documentation of foodways of the region several years ago. Their faith in and encouragement of TAUNY projects made accomplishing our organization's mission possible.

TAUNY

Traditional Arts in
Upstate New York

Celebrating the Customs and Creativity of Everyday Life in Northern New York

Welcome to Traditional Arts in Upstate New York (TAUNY), an organization devoted to recording and presenting the rich living heritage of customs and folk arts in the fourteen counties of New York's North Country. Long before the age of electronics and space exploration, residents of the hills and valleys of the Adirondacks, the St. Lawrence River, and Lake Champlain region told stories and sang songs about local life. They marked the passing of time with celebrations and crafted objects for their own use. Over the years people from many parts of the world settled in the region and contributed to the mosaic of local cultural expressions. Through memory, mastery, and legacy, they and their children helped to shape the North Country way of life.

While times have changed, there are individuals families and communities today who remain committed to some of the old ways and pass them on to the next generation. Because they are part of the fabric of everyday life, these customs and traditions are sometimes taken for granted, even by the people who practice them. TAUNY's mission is to focus attention on the traditional knowledge, skills, and creative expressions of local life, to gain a better understanding of their importance, and to encourage their careful stewardship into the future.

Among the variety of activities TAUNY undertakes are:

Folk Art Exhibits

The North Country Wall of Fame

The North Country Folkstore

Regional Folk Culture Archives

Publications on Local Culture

Music, Storytelling and Dance Performances

Crafts Demonstrations and Workshops

School Programs

Elderhostels

Audio and Video Productions

Folk Arts Marketing Resource Center

Consulting and Planning

Research and Documentation

The current Board of Directors is Paul M. Fischer, Esq., Canton, President; Varick A. Chittenden, Canton, Vice President; Dr. Peter C. vanLent, Dekalb Junction, Secretary; James Barrick, Canton, Treasurer; Judy C. Chittenden, Canton; Sam Hendren, Lake Placid; Allan Newell, Hammond; Linda Pettit, Hannawa Falls; Stanley Ransom, Plattsburgh; Dr. Laurie W. Rush, Clayton; Bill Smith, Colton; and Emily Tarbell, Akwesasne.

The current staff of TAUNY includes Varick A. Chittenden, Executive Director; Jill R. Breit, Assistant Director for Operations; and Amalia Abanto-Denesha, Administrative Assistant.

***

TAUNY is a membership organization, open to anyone who wishes to contribute to general operating support or program costs of the organization. Several levels of membership offer a variety of benefits to donors. Contributions by individuals, foundations, or businesses are tax-deductible. Please write or call for more information.

Foreword

For several years during the 1990's I drove into my small hometown of Hopkinton, on the eastern side of St. Lawrence County, past the convenience store I remember from the 1950's as Dwight and Mary Yentzer's Shell station and barber shop. Next door a neat, clapboarded building housed a homemade diner called "Sara's Kitchen." Mounted on the side of the little restaurant was a handmade wooden sign, painted solid black—a silhouette of two people sitting at a diner table. Below the figures in simple script were the words GOOD FOOD, SERVED RIGHT. No matter what the time of day, I found the lot full of local cars. I was always amused, since just a few hundred yards farther into town is my own mother's house—herself a Sara—and I was most likely headed for her kitchen.

With some degree of guilt, I would occasionally stop at the restaurant instead of Mother's house, because I have always had a kind of love affair with diners and wanted to know more about Sara's. I remember I could get good beef stew and cole slaw or meatloaf with mashed potatoes there, and on one occasion, I even found peasoup and johnny cake as the daily special. "Peasoup and johnnycake makes a Frenchman's belly ache," I used to hear the old men joke in my father's store in that same town. Hearty food for lumberjacks and plenty good enough for me. I love that stuff! My lunch that day was good (although not as good as I remember it at home!)

A few years before spotting Sara's sign, I had worked on a series of short documentary pieces about regional foods and food customs for a collaborative venture of TAUNY and North Country Public Radio. We called the series HOME COOKING: THE FOLK ART OF GOOD FOOD. It featured regional specialties like cheese, apples, and maple products, as well as ethnic favorites like Mohawk corn and Greek pastries. Instead of resorting to a "cooking show," with recipes for home use, we featured the contexts for the preparation and uses of the foods. The events and the people involved were highlighted in our shows; recipes were sketchy or non-existent.

While we were researching our radio series, I was observing all the interesting sites of food-related activities in the region—farmers' markets, church dining rooms, gardens, firemen's halls, general stores, and family kitchens, to name a few. Soon after, we began an extensive photographic documentation of such spaces, the result of which was an exciting photographic essay in the form of a traveling exhibition. During that search for images, we found the sign on Sara's Kitchen. The simple message was too good to pass up. We gave the exhibition the title GOOD FOOD, SERVED RIGHT, and that is how we get to this book.

At TAUNY we have done many other things with local food customs since the beginning of our research over a decade ago. A teacher's resource guide to accompany the exhibition to schools; aprons and T-shirts featuring a long list of local foods; and public lectures, college classes and Elderhostel courses are just a few. TAUNY has even presented North Country Heritage Awards to Franklin County Fair Grand Champion Cook Bea Reynolds of Burke—her carrot cake and lemon meringue pie are great!—and to the annual bullhead feed sponsored by the Brier Hill Volunteer Fire Department, probably the oldest and one of the biggest in the whole area. All through this time, we have frequently been asked, "Why don't you do a cookbook?" Great idea, but we knew that we wanted it to be special, to be more than a collection of recipes and to contribute to a much better understanding and appreciation of the diverse cultures and customs of our North Country. And that would take time.

This book—GOOD FOOD, SERVED RIGHT—is the culmination of all these previous efforts. The title is a natural for this selection of recipes and customs. The food is neither high style, nor elegant, nor chic. But it meets the high standards of most traditional home cooks, meaning it's hearty, plentiful, good-tasting and good-looking. And that means it is served right, too. No tuxedoed waiter or wine stewards here. Instead, it's family or community celebrations in local church halls or family dining rooms, often with expected menus and seating plans, heirloom china and special platters or bowls reserved only for favorite foods. It's the familiar, friendly atmosphere of home and hometown.

We at TAUNY hope you truly enjoy having and using this book. In fact, we hope it will even become an heirloom itself, as you use it to bring some of the warmth of local traditions into your gatherings of family and friends. We wish you "Good eating!"

Varick A. Chittenden
Executive Director
Traditional Arts in Upstate New York

Introduction

"Well, that should keep body and soul together for a while," my grandfather would say, pushing himself back from the table, replete with one of my grandmother's enormous Sunday dinners. As a child I always laughed, as he meant me to, at the incongruity of anyone's possibly starving to death while stuffed with Ma's fried chicken, corn on the cob, creamed new peas, apple/grape/Jello salad, and apple pie with ice cream. Now that I am older, I look back on those dinners and see another meaning to his joking words—one I'm sure he never consciously intended. For those family meals helped give me a strong sense of who I was, where I came from, and how I fit into my universe— satisfying and anchoring my spirit as they nourished my body.

What we eat and with whom; how we prepare and preserve our food— these help define our culture and ourselves. From the time we are small we connect various nationalities with specific food specialties: Italian lasagna, German sauerkraut and sausage, Greek baklava, and Chinese won ton soup. In fact the eating of certain foods helps give people a feeling of unity with other members of their own culture; foodways are a visible badge of identity. For that reason, they are one of the most persistent of ethnic traits. Often families who have lived in a culture other than their own for generations and have become indistinguishable from their neighbors in terms of language, dress, and occupation still consider "home cooking" to be the recipes brought by their grandparents from the old country.

In addition to everyday foodways, every culture has special holiday occasions which usually include the preparing and eating of food as part of the festivities. In the United States, family Thanksgiving dinners and July 4th reunions use food as a central point around which to build family identity. Similarly the church or community covered-dish supper helps to draw a whole town together. In fact sharing a meal is one of the universal ways of indicating fellowship. In times of sorrow our first thought is to take food to the bereaved, only partly because we think they may actually need it to feed visiting relatives. The casserole or cake we take a grieving friend is also a way of acknowledging our commitment to our relationship with him or her.

Because food is so closely related to our concepts of nurturing, food preparation and eating is an important time of apprenticeship—a time when new members of a family or community learn how to take their place as contributing members of the group. Children begin by watching their grandmothers, mothers, and aunts, (and more recently in our culture, fathers) then slowly, over the years, begin to help, absorbing not only the hands-on skills needed to roll a pie crust or stuff a turkey, but also the community values defining "good cook." Finally, the older generation surrenders pride of place to the younger, secure in the knowledge that the tradition will continue. More than food-related values are passed on during these sessions; they are also a time for retelling of family legends and establishing a communal response to events both within and outside the family. The listening child effortlessly learns his or her history and picks up the family and community morality.

Our families and communities do not exist in a vacuum. We are part of the natural world around us—more so in the North Country than in more urban areas—and our food traditions reflect that. Even though nationwide grocery chains bring out-of-season fresh foods to our towns, the high cost of certain foods often prevents our taking advantage of this bounty. The diets of most people still depend very much on what is native to the area in which they live. In the North Country our short growing season puts many foods out of our reach. Most fruits, for example, prefer a warmer climate and an earlier spring than we can offer. However, apples of many varieties thrive in our cold area, so they have become a staple of the North Country diet. The many dairy farms in the region provide a wealth of cheese—from cheddar so sharp it stings the mouth to the mild, rubbery deliciousness of fresh cheese curd. There are many who feel that a meal in the North Country is simply not complete unless it has cheese in it somewhere! Our warm early spring days and cold nights provide the perfect environment for the production of maple syrup. Like apples and cheese, syrup shows up constantly in the local diet. North Country cooks have been very inventive in discovering new ways to use these products, as well as the abundant game and fish native to our area.

The idea of depending primarily on local products is only part of traditional cookery. Another important aspect can be summed up in the old adage "Waste not, want not." This guiding principle is behind the cooking of all traditions and has led to the creation of such diverse dishes as bread pudding and head cheese. It also has contributed to the development of a great variety of methods of food preservation—pickling, drying, salting, preserving in jams and jellies, freezing, and canning. Although different cultures emphasize different choices among these methods, the underlying principle never varies.

It has been said that "You are what you eat." Most often this phrase is used by mothers urging carrots onto unwilling offspring or dentists lecturing on the evils of candy and soda, but clearly the truth of the statement goes much deeper than its purely physical implications. I hope that this book will give readers a picture of what it means to be a part of the North Country community and of some of the smaller communities that help to make it up.

* * *

Lynn Ekfelt

Adapted from an essay which I wrote for the program booklet of the Second Festival of North Country Folklife in September 1979.

About the Author:

Lynn Case Ekfelt earned her M.A. in Library Science from the University of Denver in 1970 and her M.A. in Folklore from Indiana University in 1977. During her 28-year career at the St. Lawrence University Library in Canton, NY, she served in various capacities, ending her tenure as archivist. Lynn is an experienced and accomplished cook herself, particularly known in her community for the fabulous desserts she turns out. In addition to cooking, she likes to hike, travel, and read, especially cookbooks!

Using flashlights, buckets and nets, boys search for enough bullheads for supper in a culvert near their home in Norwood, St. Lawrence County.
David Duprey Photo/Watertown Daily Times

NATURE'S
BOUNTY

APPLES

Apple orchards on the farm of S.W. Hemenway, Dekalb, St. Lawrence County, from Evert's 1878 *History of St. Lawrence County*.

Apple Tasting
East DeKalb

Floors scarred by years of feet encased in "Sunday-go-to-meeting" shoes, walls revealing strips of lathe where plaster has fallen away, the Meeting House of the Methodist-Episcopal Society at Dewey's Corners looks every one of its hundred fifty-nine years. It's easy to see that this shell is no longer home to a living congregation, though patches of new wood hold promise of an impending rebirth as the home for a historical society. On this glorious fall day, though, the building's ghosts have plenty of company. Outside, Brian Thompson hand-presses cider for eager crowds of children and wasps. Inside, we are torn between the blandishments of a small side table of apple-based baked goods and those of the huge u-shaped set of tables in the center of the room presenting their apples unadorned.

We opt to start with the basics and pick up our tasting sheets and pencils. The North Country Garden School is holding an apple tasting— 80 different varieties—for those who might hope to restore the North Country to its former status as a prime apple-producing region. When I first came to Canton in 1970, the local groceries offered customers a choice between Delicious, Cortland, or nothing; now I know my way around Granny Smiths, Empires, and even a few exotic Japanese imports. Still, the variety in this room is mind-boggling. Chenango Strawberry, Swiss Gourmet, Westfield Seek No Further, Black Gilliflower, Belle de Boskoop, Colvis Spice, Zabergau Reinette, Kidds Orange Red, and the mysterious NY75413-30—intriguing names entice us to sample slices of them all.

It becomes obvious as we move around the table that I lack the proper vocabulary. I envy the wine connoisseurs their "silky tannins" and "cherry-scented nose." All I seem to be able to manage is "tart," "mushy," and "yuck—tastes like a pear." When we find ourselves spending more time chatting with friends and less concentrating on tasting, Nils and I decide we have arrived at taste-bud overload. We grab a piece of cider pie* for "dessert" and hop on our bikes to work off the morning's excesses. As we ride, I daydream our yard transformed into a springtime bower of apple blossoms.

16

Crow's Nest

Apple Layer

6-8 Tart apples (to fill an 8-inch square pan)	Dash nutmeg
	Dash cinnamon
½ cup water	1½ tablespoons lemon juice, if
⅔ cup sugar	needed

Cobbler

1 cup flour	2 teaspoons baking powder
½ teaspoon salt	¼ cup soft butter
2 tablespoons sugar	1 cup milk

Lemon Sauce, optional

1 cup water	2 tablespoons vinegar or
1 cup sugar	lemon juice
2 tablespoons flour	Dash salt
1 teaspoon vanilla	Lump butter the size of an
Dash nutmeg	egg

To make the crow's nest, peel and slice enough apples to fill an 8-inch square pan. Remove the apples to a saucepan. Add the water, sugar and spices. If the apples are not tart, add lemon juice. Cook slowly, stirring frequently, until the apples are very hot and nearly tender. Pour the apples back into the 8-inch square pan.

To make the cobbler dough, combine the flour, salt, sugar and baking powder in a bowl. Cut in the butter until the mixture is crumbly. Stir in the milk.

Spoon the cobbler dough over the apples and smooth the top. Bake at 375 degrees until the biscuit top is done (approximately 30 to 40 minutes).

Serve crow's nest with whipped sweetened cream or the optional lemony sauce—or both! To make the sauce, cook all the ingredients except the butter in a saucepan, stirring constantly, until they have thickened. Add the butter and pour the sauce over the crow's nest.

Apple Dumplings

Dough

2	cups flour	6	tablespoons fat
1	teaspoon salt	⅔	cup milk
4	teaspoons baking powder		

Filling

4-5	apples, peeled and sliced	½	teaspoon cinnamon
1	teaspoon vanilla		Dash salt

Sauce

4	tablespoons butter, melted	2	tablespoons cornstarch
1	cup brown sugar	4	cups milk

To make the dough, put the flour, salt and baking powder into a bowl. Cut in the fat until the mixture is crumbly. Add the milk and lightly stir the mixture until it forms a stiff dough. Pat it out on a floured board until it is about ½ inch thick. Cut it into four squares.

To make the filling, slice the apples quite thin and mix them well with the other ingredients.

To make the sauce, melt the butter in a heavy pan and heat it slightly with the brown sugar. Stir the cornstarch into the butter mixture until it forms a smooth paste. Add the milk and bring the mixture to a boil.

Center some filling on each square. Bring the edges together over the filling and seal the edges. Gently place the dumplings into the boiling sauce and cook them for 20 minutes, moving them occasionally so that they do not stick to the bottom of the pan. If the sauce does not cover the dumplings, turn them over halfway through the cooking time, or baste them occasionally to ensure that they cook uniformly. Makes four dumplings.

These also taste good, but have a very different texture, if you bake them instead of boiling them in the syrup. For this version, place the dumplings in a greased baking dish. Bake in a preheated 425 degree oven for 10 minutes, then turn the heat down to 350 degrees and bake for another 30 minutes, basting every 10 minutes with the hot sauce.

Paul Lyndaker
Croghan

Just Like Grandma's Apple Pie

This pie won the third annual Hometown Proud Homemade Apple Pie Contest, sponsored by the Canton Jubilee IGA.

Crust

5 cups flour	1 tablespoon white vinegar
1¾ cups butter-flavored solid vegetable shortening	Cold water
1 teaspoon salt	1 egg, beaten
1 egg	White sugar

Filling

8-10 apples, peeled and cored	¼ cup flour
1 cup white sugar	1 egg white, optional
¼ cup brown sugar	3 tablespoons butter or
½ teaspoon cinnamon	margarine
1 teaspoon vanilla	

To make the crust, mix the flour, shortening and salt until they are crumbly. In a one-cup measuring cup beat the egg. Add the vinegar and enough cold water to make one cup, then stir them together well. Mix the egg mixture into the flour mixture. Divide the dough into six equal portions. Roll out the dough on a floured surface.

This crust recipe makes three double crusts. The dough will keep up to two weeks in the refrigerator or three to four months in the freezer. Just bring it to room temperature before rolling it out.

To make the filling, cut the apples into large chunks and mix them with the sugars, cinnamon, vanilla and flour. Place the filling in the bottom crust. (If you brush egg white onto the bottom crust before filling it, then it will not become soggy.) Dot the filling with butter. Top with the top crust and seal the edges. Brush the top with beaten egg, then sprinkle with sugar. Bake in a preheated 425 degree oven for 15 minutes, then turn down the heat to 350 degrees and bake 40 to 45 minutes more.

Use an assortment of apple varieties for a more interesting flavor.

Cheryl Bell
Canton

Apple Cider Pie

5	cups cider		Sugar, optional
10	tablespoons cornstarch	1	(9-inch) pie crust, baked
1	teaspoon cinnamon, optional		

Boil the cider and cornstarch together (with the cinnamon and sugar, if desired) until the mixture looks clear and is thickened. Pour it into the pre-baked crust. Allow the pie to cool before serving.

Sally Thompson
Gouverneur

Apple Cinnamon Muffins

Muffins

½	cup margarine	1	teaspoon salt
¾	cup sugar	1½	cups diced apples
1	egg, beaten	¾	cup whole wheat flour
1	cup buttermilk (or 1 cup milk combined with 1 teaspoon vinegar)	1	teaspoon baking soda
		1	teaspoon cinnamon

Topping

1	teaspoon cinnamon	2-3	teaspoons sugar

To make the muffins, blend the margarine with the sugar and the egg. Add the buttermilk, salt and apples; mix well. Combine the flour, soda and cinnamon. Stir them into the apple mixture just until the flour is moistened.

To make the topping, stir the cinnamon and sugar together until they are well mixed.

Spoon the batter into greased muffin cups and sprinkle with the topping. Bake at 375 degrees for 20 minutes.

Becky Van de Water
Canton

Baked Apples with Maple Sugar

Apples—one for each person
Maple sugar, crumbled

Water
Cinnamon
Heavy cream

Core one apple for each person and fill the holes with crumbled maple sugar. Place the apples in a baking dish with a little water in the bottom. Bake at 400 degrees until the apples are soft (approximately 30 to 45 minutes), basting frequently with the pan juices. Serve the apples hot, sprinkled with cinnamon and drizzled with cream.

Richard Perry
Hammond

Apple Walnut Cake

Cake
4 cups apples, peeled and shredded
2 cups sugar
2 eggs
½ cup vegetable oil
2 teaspoons vanilla

2 cups sifted flour
2 teaspoons baking soda
2 teaspoons cinnamon
1 teaspoon salt
1 cup chopped walnuts

Icing
2 cups maple syrup
3 egg whites

⅛ teaspoon salt

To make the cake, combine the apples and sugar and set them aside. In a large mixing bowl beat the eggs slightly, then beat in the oil and vanilla. Sift together the flour, baking soda, cinnamon and salt. Gently, but thoroughly, stir the flour mixture into the egg mixture, then add the walnuts and sugared apples. Pour the batter into a greased Bundt pan and bake at 350 degrees for 1 hour.

To make the icing boil the syrup in a medium saucepan over medium to high heat without stirring until it forms a thread from the spoon (242 degrees). Beat the egg whites with the salt until they are stiff but not dry. Beat the syrup into the egg whites in a thin stream.

Becky Van de Water
Canton

Apple Brown Betty Baldwin

1½ cups fine dry bread crumbs
¼ cup melted butter
2½ cups Baldwin apples, peeled, cored and sliced
¾ cup brown sugar
1 teaspoon cinnamon
¼ teaspoon nutmeg
¼ teaspoon cloves
½ teaspoon salt
1 teaspoon finely grated lemon rind
2 tablespoons water
1 tablespoon lemon juice
¼ cup raisins, optional

Mix together the crumbs and the melted butter. Place one third of the mixture in the bottom of a greased baking dish. Distribute half the apples evenly over the crumbs in the baking dish. Mix together the brown sugar, cinnamon, nutmeg, cloves, lemon rind and salt. Cover the apple slices with half this mixture and sprinkle with the water and lemon juice. Add another third of the crumb mixture and, if desired, the raisins. Repeat the layers, ending with the remaining crumb mixture. Bake, covered, at 350 degrees for about 40 minutes. Remove the cover, raise the temperature to 400 degrees, and allow the mixture to brown for about 15 minutes. Good served with hard sauce.

Alanson Perry
Oswegatchie

Microwave Apple Crisp for One

1 tablespoon margarine
2 tablespoons quick oats
2 tablespoons brown sugar
1 tablespoon flour
1 apple, peeled and sliced
Nut meats
Cinnamon

Melt the margarine in a small bowl. Stir in the oats, sugar and flour; mix well. Sprinkle this mixture over the apple slices in a small buttered baking dish. Top with nuts and cinnamon. Bake 2½ minutes, turning the dish once.

Susan Lyman
Norwood

Indian Relish

This family recipe came to Susan Lyman over 65 years ago.

12	ripe apples	1	teaspoon cloves
12	ripe tomatoes	1	teaspoon cinnamon
6	onions	1	teaspoon ginger
5	cups sugar	1	teaspoon red pepper
¼	cup salt	1	teaspoon turmeric

Peel and grind the apples, tomatoes and onions. Put them into a large kettle. Add the remaining ingredients and mix well. Cook the mixture very slowly until it thickens. Seal it in sterile jars and use it as a relish with meat.

Susan Lyman
Norwood

Kidney Bean Casserole

This recipe comes from the Ursuline Nuns, for whom Celeste Sweet used to be a cook. She says "It seems like an odd combination of ingredients, but it is one of my most requested recipes."

2½	cups raw cooking apples, sliced and peeled	8	ounces tomato sauce
3	large onions, sliced	½	cup brown sugar
½	pound raw bacon, diced	1	tablespoon salt
3	pounds and 3 ounces red kidney beans	½	teaspoon pepper

Combine all ingredients in a 3-quart casserole or crock pot. Cook at 350 degrees for 1½ to 2 hours, stirring occasionally.

Celeste Sweet
Bangor

Yoghurt Fruit Salad

Tart apples, chopped but
   not peeled
Bananas, sliced

Raisins
Vanilla or lemon yoghurt
Cinnamon to taste

Mix the chopped fruit (the amounts and proportions will vary with the number of servings desired and the preferences of the cook) with enough yoghurt to coat it well. Add cinnamon to taste.

Denise Dingman
Richville

Scalloped Sweet Potatoes and Apples

6   medium sweet potatoes
1½ cups apples, sliced
½   teaspoon salt

½   cup brown sugar
1   teaspoon mace
4   tablespoons butter

Boil the sweet potatoes until they are tender, then slice them into ¼-inch pieces. Butter a baking dish and put a layer of sweet potatoes in the bottom, then a layer of apples. Sprinkle them with salt, sugar and mace; dot with butter. Repeat until the dish is filled, finishing with a layer of apples. Bake at 350 degrees for about 50 minutes.

Ruth Trudell
Lisbon

The book Rural New York by Cornell Professor Elmer Pippin, published by Macmillan in 1921, has a map showing St. Lawrence County with approximately 25,000 acres in apple orchards in 1910. The dots indicating orchards on the map appear mostly along the St. Lawrence River.

According to Jeanine Anderson, writing in the St. Lawrence Plaindealer of November 1, 1978, Atwood Manley of Canton recalls the time when "almost every farmer had an apple orchard out back." Manley is quoted as saying "George Crary used to pack apples in barrels and send them to Boston." Crary's grandson, Mahlon Bullis, remembers hitching up the horses to take barrels of Snowapples and Russets to market.

What happened to the old orchards? Bill MacKentley, successor to Fred Ashworth as propagator of local apple varieties, thinks the deep freeze that hit the North Country in December of 1933, wiping out most of the trees, was the main culprit....Is the pendulum swinging to create a situation where a backyard orchard again makes sense?....Several homeowners in St. Lawrence County have already begun setting out backyard orchards of the new varieties. Who knows? Perhaps in another ten years our eminences may once again be crowned with the glory that is the blossoming orchard in spring and the fruited orchard at harvest.

John Van de Water
"Backyard Orchards: Past and Future," SLCHA Quarterly, October 1980, p.7

The North Country Garden School recommends the following varieties to those who would like to see local hills white with apple blossoms again in the spring. These apples are particularly suited to our short growing season and cold winters.

Alexander	Milton
Haralson	St. Lawrence*
Cortland	Honeycrisp+
St. Johnsbury*	Freedom+
Tolman Sweet*	McIntosh*
Fameuse [Snow apple]*	Minnesota 1734
Loko	Sharon

*=old variety   +=new variety

CHEESE

Jim Marrilley continues to cut wedges of extra sharp cheddar cheese from 40 pound wheels kept at room temperature at his family general store in Croghan, Lewis County. *Mark Sloan Photo/TAUNY Archives*

Heritage Cheese House Heuvelton

It's the kind of morning that makes your nose hairs stick together. When I arrive at the Heritage Cheese House, I am the sole customer in the tiny shop—a good thing, for now I can browse to my heart's content without feeling I am blocking anyone's access to the shelves of pickled vegetables (everything from broccoli to okra), shoe-fly pie mix, all sorts of honeys, jams, sausages, home-cured bacon, candies, and, of course cheese: green cheddar, mild cheddar, medium cheddar, sharp cheddar, extra sharp cheddar, super sharp cheddar, bacon-horseradish cheddar, green onion cheddar, and that North Country favorite, cheese curd. I load a bag for tomorrow's Super Bowl party; pickled cauliflower will be a perfect addition to our usual menu of pizza and ice cream.

Now that I have provisions enough to feed both teams as well as the two couples who will be viewing their titanic struggle on the gridiron, I slip on an extremely unattractive hair net and move beyond the shop to the factory in back where the cheese is made. There I meet the O'Neil family and hear about the birth of this family-run business. When the Amish first moved to the North Country in the 1970s, the O'Neils, who live near Watertown, developed a fascination with their culture. Weekend rides often ended up on the back roads around Heuvelton and Rensselaer Falls, where there was always something interesting to see: a row of horse-drawn buggies returning from church, a clothes line with a row of solid blue or brown shirts, and maybe even a barn-raising. As time went on, the family got bolder and began stopping at roadside stands where Amish families sold vegetables and baked goods, talking to the proprietors and becoming acquainted.

Soon they learned that their new-found friends had a problem. This growing community of farmers had no secure market for their milk. Because the Amish sell their milk in cans rather than in bulk tanks, the Kraft plant will not purchase it. A small cheese plant in Heuvelton was buying the milk, but the owner was not interested in expanding, and the Amish community was growing. Tentatively, the farmers asked David O'Neil Jr., then in college, if he would be interested in running a cheese plant that would provide an outlet for their milk. David, a finance major, agreed to consider their proposal and used a cheese plant feasibility study as his independent study project. At the end he told his friends that he would run the plant and agreed to buy as much milk as they produced, provided they would help with finances and construction. The Amish raised enough money to enable David to get a bank loan. He and his dad used chain saws (forbidden to the Amish themselves) to cut the trees, then the farmers dragged the logs out of the woods with their horses and sawed them into lumber in their mills. At that point, the O'Neils took over again and trucked them to the site of the new plant. On October 22, 1994, 125 Amish men and boys showed up for a giant barn-raising and chicken barbecue; by the end of the day, the building was up. And on January 11, 1995, the first load of milk arrived at the plant. Today the plant buys the milk of 49 Amish farmers, three of whom always sit on the board of directors.

While we talk, I keep an eye on the huge tank of butter-yellow liquid beside us. At 9:30 this morning this vat was filled with milk—some brought in by horse and buggy, the rest collected by truck. (Amish milk is kept cool with water and meets all state safety and purity requirements.) Rennet and culture have been added and it is about to be cooked. Two men work their way slowly down the length of the gleaming metal vat with wire frames that look like square harps, cutting the yoghurt-like mixture into cubes so that it can cook more uniformly. That done, they give a Clorox bath to four large paddles resembling square draining spoons and start them slowly agitating the hot liquid, creating a yellow whirlpool where creamy blobs circle frantically. It's hard to believe that by 2:30 this afternoon, this tank of liquid goop will have become cheese and the curd will be on sale in the store.

David Jr. takes a break to deliver a load of whey to the Heuvelton Whey Company where it will be dried and sold as animal feed. The rest of the whey will go to the Amish to feed their pigs. While he is gone, I chat with his mother and his sister, both conveniently named Linda. They explain that they come up from Watertown to help on weekends. David Jr. has moved to this area to avoid the commute, but his father makes the drive up most days to give a hand. The plant makes only cheddar—300 to 600 thousand pounds per year— which they sell to local stores and also by mail order to tourists who have become addicted. They have mailed cheese to such exotic places as England and Australia, as well as to cheese-deprived areas of the U.S.

By now the miniature store is packed with customers. An Amish man discusses the purchase of a horse with a local "English" farmer. The dripping icicles promise a warmer ride home. Lunch beckons—I think it will be sesame crackers with horseradish cheddar.

Fish and Cheese Chowder

1	pound fish fillets, fresh or frozen	¼	cup flour
2	tablespoons butter	½	teaspoon salt
6	tablespoons chopped onion		Dash paprika, optional
1	cup chopped carrot	20	ounces chicken broth (either homemade or 2 10-ounce cans)
6	tablespoons chopped celery	3	cups milk
		1	cup grated cheddar

Thaw the fish fillets if they are frozen. Cut the fish into 1-inch cubes. Melt the butter in a large saucepan; add the onion, carrots and celery. Cook them until the onion is transparent. Blend in the flour, salt and paprika. Cook for one minute, stirring constantly. Gradually add the chicken broth and the milk, then cook the mixture, stirring constantly, until it is thickened. Add the fish; simmer until the fish flakes easily (5 minutes for fresh fish, 10 for frozen.) Add the cheese and stir until it is melted.

Nancy Alessi
Russell

Cheese-Topped Biscuits

2	tubes refrigerated biscuits (or 20 homemade ones)	2	tablespoons light cream
1	cup sharp cheddar, shredded (about 4 ounces)	½	teaspoon poppy seeds
			Dash dry mustard

Overlap 15 uncooked biscuits around the edge of a well-greased 9 x 1½-inch round pan. Place the remaining biscuits in the center of the pan. Mix the remaining ingredients and crumble them over the top of the biscuits. Bake at 425 degrees for 15 minutes. Remove the biscuits immediately from the pan.

Melissa Hicks
Antwerp

This recipe appeared in the Kitchen Exchange section of the Watertown Daily Times.

Cheese Pudding with Creole Sauce

This favorite old family recipe was handed down to Dot Mackey by her mother. It resembles cheese soufflé, but does not fall so quickly when the cooking stops.

Pudding

4	eggs, separated	1½	cups milk
2	cups shredded sharp cheese	1	cup sifted flour
		1	tablespoon butter
2	teaspoons salt		

Sauce

1	onion, sliced	1	(10½-ounce) can tomato
½	green pepper, cut in strips		soup
1	large clove garlic, minced	¼	cup water
1	tablespoon oil		

To make the pudding, beat the egg yolks and mix them well with the cheese, salt and milk. Add the flour and beat just until it is moistened. Beat the egg whites until stiff and fold them into the cheese mixture. Grease a 2-quart baking dish well with the butter and pour in the batter. Cover the dish tightly with aluminum foil or its own lid. Place on a rack in a kettle on top of the stove. Fill the kettle with boiling water so it comes up about halfway on the casserole dish. Boil for 1¾ to 2 hours, adding water as needed to keep making steam. Do not peek at the pudding itself. Serve topped with the sauce.

To make the sauce, brown the onion, green pepper and garlic in the oil. Add the soup and water and simmer for 15 minutes.

Be sure that some steam can escape between the baking dish and the container holding the water so it will not blow up.

Dorothy Mackey
Potsdam

Sesame Sticks

1½	cups unsifted all-purpose flour	1	cup shredded sharp cheddar
½	teaspoon salt	½	cup margarine
2	tablespoons sesame seeds, toasted	2	teaspoons cold water
		3	tablespoons Worcestershire sauce

Combine the flour, salt and sesame seeds. Cut in the cheese and margarine until the mixture is crumbly. Sprinkle the water and Worcestershire sauce over the flour mixture and stir everything together with a fork until the mixture clings to the side of the bowl. Shape it into two or three balls, handling it lightly. On a lightly floured board, roll the dough to a thickness of ¼ inch. Cut it into 3 x ½-inch strips. Bake the strips on an ungreased cookie sheet at 450 degrees for 8 to 10 minutes.

Becky Wilson
Potsdam

Cheddar Pepper Crisps

1¾	cups flour	1½	cups shredded cheddar cheese
½	cup cornmeal		
½	teaspoon baking soda	½	cup cold water
½	teaspoon sugar	2	tablespoons vinegar
½	teaspoon salt		Black pepper, coarsely ground
½	cup cold margarine		

In a large bowl, combine the flour, cornmeal, baking soda, sugar and salt. Cut in the margarine until the mixture is crumbly. Stir in the cheese. Sprinkle the water and vinegar over the top of the mixture, then toss it with a fork until a ball forms. Wrap the dough tightly in plastic wrap and refrigerate for one hour or until the dough is firm. Divide it into six portions. On a lightly floured surface, roll each portion of dough into an 8-inch circle. Cut each circle into eight wedges and place them on greased baking sheets. Sprinkle ground pepper over the wedges and lightly press it into the dough. Bake at 375 degrees until golden brown and crisp (approximately 10 to 14 minutes). Cool the crisps on wire racks, then store them in an airtight container.

Darlene Leonard
Canton

Cheese Hash Browns

1	can cream of chicken soup	1	small onion, minced
6	ounces (1½ cups) shred-ded cheddar	1	(20-ounce) package of shredded hash browns
½	cup sour cream		

Combine all ingredients except the potatoes and mix well. Fold the potatoes into the cheese mixture. Place in a greased 1½-quart baking dish. Bake at 350 degrees for 45 to 50 minutes.

Darlene Leonard
Canton

Welsh Rarebit

8	ounces grated extra sharp cheddar	2	teaspoons flour
			Twist black pepper
1	tablespoon butter	4	tablespoons beer (or milk or sweet white wine), approximately
2	teaspoons Worcestershire sauce		
1	teaspoon dry mustard	4	slices bread, toasted on one side only

Put the cheese, butter, Worcestershire sauce, mustard, flour and pepper into a saucepan. Mix them together well, then add enough beer to moisten the mixture without making it too wet. Stir over a gentle heat until all is melted. When it is a thickish paste, stop stirring and swivel it around the saucepan; it will move quite easily. Leave it to cool a little while you toast the bread on one side only. Spread the rarebit over the untoasted side and brown it under a hot grill. This mixture can be made and kept in the refrigerator for several days.

Mickie Williams
Canton

Mickie Williams, whose husband Bob is Welsh, found this recipe for the quintessential Welsh dish in A Taste of Wales in Food and Pictures by Theodora FitzGibbon, published in London by Pan Books. It is an old family recipe of the author.

Cheese Strata

8	buttered slices of bread, cubed	4	eggs, slightly beaten
		2½	cups milk
2	cups (½ pound) cheddar, cubed	1	teaspoon salt
		1½	teaspoons dry mustard

Layer the bread and cheese in an 11 x 7-inch dish. Mix the eggs, milk, salt and mustard and pour them over the top. Cover the pan and refrigerate (overnight if you're making it for lunch, or from morning until evening if you're going to eat it for supper.) Uncover the dish and bake the strata at 325 degrees for 50 minutes. Let it stand a few minutes before serving.

Josephine Mentley
Canton

Four-Cheese Macaroni

3	cups uncooked elbow macaroni	6	ounces processed cheese, cubed
2	onions, finely chopped	2	ounces cream cheese, cubed
1	tablespoon vegetable oil	½	cup extra sharp cheddar, shredded
¼	cup flour		
⅛	teaspoon ground pepper	2	ounces (½ cup) Parmesan cheese, grated
2½	cups skim milk, divided		Bread crumbs, optional

Cook the macaroni according to the package directions and drain it. Sauté the onions in the oil and set them aside. Combine the flour and pepper in a saucepan. Add ½ cup of the milk, whisking until the mixture is smooth. Gradually add the remaining milk while stirring briskly. Cook the mixture over medium heat for five minutes or until it comes to a boil. Cook one minute, stirring constantly. Reduce the heat, then add the cheeses, stirring until they are melted. Remove the pan from the heat and stir in the macaroni and the onion. Pour the mixture into a 9-inch square baking pan. Sprinkle the top with bread crumbs if desired. Bake at 350 degrees until brown and bubbly (approximately 30 minutes).

Ruth Trudell
Lisbon

Cheese Tea Crackers

2	cups flour	¼	teaspoon mustard
2	cups shredded cheese		Cayenne pepper to taste
2	sticks margarine	2	cups crisp rice cereal

Mix the flour, cheese, margarine, mustard and cayenne thoroughly. Mix in the cereal—gently, so it doesn't get squashed. Make the dough into balls about ¾ inch in diameter. Place them on a greased cookie sheet, then flatten them with your fingers, again trying not to break the cereal too much. Bake at 350 degrees for 10 minutes.

Lynn Ekfelt
Canton

Italian Three-Cheese Macaroni

2	cups uncooked elbow macaroni	¾	cup (3 ounces) cheddar, shredded
4	tablespoons margarine or butter	¼	cup Parmesan cheese, grated
3	tablespoons all-purpose flour	1	(14½-ounce) can diced tomatoes, drained
1	teaspoon dried Italian seasoning	1	cup (4 ounces) mozzarella, shredded
½-1	teaspoon black pepper	½	cup dry bread crumbs
½	teaspoon salt		Butter-flavored cooking spray
2	cups milk		Fresh chives and oregano, optional

Cook the pasta according to the package directions until it is al dente, then drain it and set it aside.

Meanwhile, melt the margarine in a medium saucepan over medium heat. Add the flour, Italian seasoning, pepper, and salt, stirring until the mixture is smooth. Gradually add the milk, stirring constantly until it is slightly thickened. Add the cheddar and Parmesan cheeses and stir until they melt.

Layer half the pasta, tomatoes, and cheese sauce in a greased 2-quart casserole; repeat each layer. Combine the mozzarella cheese and bread crumbs in a small bowl, then sprinkle them evenly over the casserole. Spray the bread-crumb mixture several times with butter-flavored cooking spray.

Bake, covered, at 350 degrees until hot and bubbly (approximately 30 minutes), then uncover the dish and bake five minutes more to brown the top. Garnish with chives and oregano if desired.

Ruth Trudell
Lisbon

Chicken Breasts with Cheese

3   whole chicken breasts, skinned and boned
    Salt and pepper to taste
½   cup room temperature butter, divided
2   tablespoons parsley
1   teaspoon marjoram
2   teaspoons thyme
¼   pound mozzarella cheese
½   cup flour
2   beaten eggs
1   cup bread crumbs
½   cup dry white wine

Cut each chicken breast in half. Place the six pieces between sheets of wax paper and gently pound them with a mallet or the side of an empty bottle until they are about ¼-inch in thickness. Sprinkle the flattened halves with salt and pepper and spread them with half the butter. Blend the remaining butter with the parsley, marjoram and thyme and set it aside. Cut the cheese into six sticks and place one in the center of each breast piece. Roll up the breasts jelly roll fashion, tucking in the edges as you go so the cheese is completely enclosed. Roll the breasts first in the flour, then in the eggs; finish by coating them thoroughly with the crumbs. Place them in a well-buttered baking pan. Melt the butter and herb mixture then pour it evenly over the chicken. Bake at 350 degrees for 30 minutes. Pour the wine into the baking pan and bake 25 minutes longer, basting frequently.

Judy Chittenden
Canton

Before the Civil War farmers processed their milk at home by necessity; it would have spoiled before they could get it to a central location. By the 1860s, however, roads improved enough that farmers were able to transport their milk to small factories, thus reaping the economic benefits of pooling labor and raw materials. Since refrigeration technology was not yet good enough to permit shipping milk to down-state markets in liquid form, the resourceful farmers settled instead for sending it in the form of cheddar cheese.

The first cheese factory in St. Lawrence County was opened at Richville in 1863, and by 1880 farmers were delivering over 125,000,000 pounds of milk to local factories.[1] In the 1880s there were twelve cheese and butter creameries in the town of Dekalb, sixteen in the town of Canton, fifteen in Potsdam, ten in Gouverneur, eight in Hermon, seven in Hammond, seven in Morristown, and six each in Madrid, Waddington, and Massena.[2] In order to market dairy products, cheese boards were set up in Canton, Gouverneur, and Ogdensburg; buyers from all parts of the nation came to this area to bid for North Country cheese.

Those days are past, but we still produce a lot of cheese—our historic specialty, cheddar, and other varieties as well. And it's still made pretty much the same way as it was in the past in those little Mom and Pop factories. The biggest difference is in the size of the operations: the Heritage Cheese House, a present-day version of those local plants, handles 18,000 pounds of milk a day; the Canton Kraft plant handles one million.

Supposing you wanted to start a cheese plant, the actual list of ingredients you'd have to buy would be short. First you would need milk—10 pounds for every pound of cheese. Then you would have to get some rennet and a bacterial culture. The culture (along with the type of milk used) is what determines the type of cheese you will produce—Swiss, cheddar, mozzarella. Heritage House buys theirs frozen; big factories like Kraft can keep a pot of their own going, much as one might keep a container of sourdough starter for baking. These three ingredients, along with salt, constitute your total shopping list for a basic block of cheese.

Depending on how strongly flavored you want your final product to be, it can take anywhere from half a day to 18 months to make your cheese. The process begins when the milk, along with the rennet and the bacterial culture, is dumped into a large vat with a v-shaped bottom.

The rennet coagulates the solids in the milk into a creamy, yoghurt-like consistency. This mixture is what will eventually become the cheese. (The liquid portion of the milk that is left, called the whey, will be sent off to become animal food or an ingredient in human packaged foods.) Frames with wires across them are dragged through the vats in three different directions to cut the custardy mixture into small cubes so it will cook more evenly. The mixture is agitated while it cooks. Because the vat is pitched toward one end as well as toward the middle, the whey can be drained off and suctioned out by a hose. The slippery slabs that remain on either side of the drainage groove are held together by heat and by their own weight into two blocks. These are then "cheddared," or cut into 8-inch strips, a process which releases more whey and helps maintain an equal temperature for the cheese. While this is going on, pH readings are taken to determine whether the bacterial culture is growing as desired. If so, the agitating of the pieces continues and salt is added to bring out the flavor and push out even more whey.

At this point the little pieces can be taken out and sold as cheese curd. Alternatively, they can be placed into forms, or "hoops," which will eventually produce 40-pound blocks of cheese. The hoops are put under air pressure for five hours to press the curds into a firm block. The resulting block is placed in a plastic bag and vacuum sealed, then put in a cardboard box in the cooler. It could be sold the next day as green cheddar or allowed to age and ripen into super sharp cheddar 18 months later.

[1] Thomas, Kenneth. "Agricultural History of St. Lawrence County," *Farm Economics*, No. 209, March 1957, page 5555.

[2] Webster, Clarence. *St. Lawrence County: Past and Present.* 1945. p. 26.

FISH

Tinted postcard view of 1000 Islands Fishing Guides Shore Dinner, ca. 1900. *TAUNY Archives*

Shore Dinner
Clayton

5:15 a.m. is pretty much tempus incognitus for a confirmed night owl. Fortunately our friends Lamar and Susan chatter cheerfully with Nils as we drive to Clayton, giving me the opportunity to accustom myself gradually to the idea that for some folks, morning starts before 8 o'clock. By the time we are ready to set off with guide Jim Brabant on our fishing excursion, I am even able to appreciate the blue haze over the perfectly still water and to look forward to the day's adventure.

Pulling out of the harbor, we find ourselves sharing the river with a massive ship, the Lake Carling. Even at a distance the sharp angle of her bow to the water identifies her as a "salty," an ocean-going ship, since a fresh water "laker" has a bow that is almost straight up and down. Having duly admired this behemoth, we spot another vessel, much smaller and flatter, carrying two Niagara Mohawk trucks. Jim tells us that she is an old LCM, or Landing Craft Mechanized, left over from World War II, now metamorphosed into a delivery boat for the residents of the 1000 Islands. Aside from these ships, we pretty much have the river to ourselves; there's something very peaceful about the slight rocking of the boat and the wide-angle view across both distant shores.

But we're here to catch lunch, not to admire the view. Harboring visions of a prize fish mounted over the fireplace, we ask Jim about our prospects for the day. "Wind from the east, fishing's the least," he replies, adding that the best days for fishing are those with a southerly wind. Prophetically, he promises us "small-mouth bass and maybe a perch or two."

This is the way to fish! When we need bait, we simply pass our rods to Jim and he puts on a minnow for us. We drop our lines overboard, letting the lead weights pull our hooks to the bottom. When the line stops going out, we reel it in about four feet or so, allowing our minnows to wiggle their tails enticingly. Once a fish of any size takes the bait and we slowly reel it to the surface, Jim nets it for us and removes it from the hook, adding it to the growing cache in the live well. When there's a lull in the fishing, he whisks us off to try our luck elsewhere, announcing—with the help of his depth finder—that we are now fishing in 25, 60 or 75 feet of water. All that is required of us is to hold our rods overboard and reel in such fish as volunteer for the frying pan.

We find that we are not the only ones interested in our fishing success. Sleek white terns, black accents making the rest of their bodies seem even purer white by contrast, circle the boat waiting to snap up any bait fish that die and are discarded before they succeed in attracting anything to our lines. The pleasure of watching the terns plummet toward the water, rarely missing the tiny, two-inch floating corpses, makes up for any disappointment we feel at not catching a big fish. Even more comforting somehow is the news that they are carrying the minnows away to feed their nestlings. It's good to know the little fish did not die in vain.

Slowly, the live well fills up with our "keepers"—7 perch and 8 bass— the rest of our catch returned to the river to grow for next year or, sometimes, to provide a meal for the gulls which have joined our tern escort party. Nils shouts in frustration as his line snaps, allowing a 13-inch bass to swim away with his hook. Minutes later, I triumphantly reel in the same fish, Nils' hook still stuck in his lip. Nils and I decide that he deserves to be awarded an assist on that catch.

As we fish, we ply Jim with questions. He's been guiding for 33 years, so his hands have no trouble taking over the mechanical tasks, leaving the rest of him free to tell us about his life growing up on Grindstone Island, one of the biggest of the 1000 Islands. During much of the year, he hires out as a pipe-fitter wherever there is work so that he can spend two months in the summer "having a good time and getting paid for it" three days a week. It was his former father-in-law who got him started fishing, and the old guides, then in their late 70s, who showed him the best spots. He shows us proudly how many parts of his boat and pieces of his cooking equipment have been passed down to him from these mentors. Almost every one of his pots and pans has been given to him by a predecessor; softly he says that he enjoys thinking about the old guides while he uses their things. Lamar asks him if he's now passing on secrets and equipment to younger men. He shakes his head and replies that times have changed. There's only one young guide in the association now; everyone else wants to work only part-time on weekends.

Finally we have enough fish to feed our group of six. We head for land, to a wooded spot rented by the Clayton Guides and outfitted for their shore dinners with a large grill, a wood pile, and two picnic tables with benches. Before we ever leave the boat, Jim plugs in an electric knife and cleans the fish in minutes—so deftly that not a trace of skin remains on the fillets and no flesh clings, wasted, to the skin or bones. The whole idea of filleting—let alone with an electric knife—is one the old guides scorned. Jim says that when he worked with them, they refused to cook fish that had been filleted, declaring that it would not hold together. Instead, they sliced the fish into serving pieces, then pulled the skin off with pliers, leaving the backbone to anchor the meat.

Each of us grabs a box, cooler, or pail to carry up to the picnic area, then our work is done, except for setting the table. No electric ax— Jim starts his meal by chopping kindling in the time-honored way. In a much shorter time than I would have imagined possible, he has sliced onions and tomatoes, broken up lettuce and cleaned corn, and started the potatoes cooking and the fatback frying. While we munch on fatback sandwiches*, Jim batters the fish filets* and drops them into the fatback oil; takes the potatoes out of their pot and replaces them with the corn; chops peppers, onions, cucumbers and tomatoes, and tosses the salad. Perhaps it's the fresh air that has given us such prodigious appetites; perhaps it's just that Jim is a great cook. Eventually, even we are satiated—but we stagger down anyway to watch our French toast* bubbling in the fatback/fish oil. One look at this scrumptious dessert, made elegant by the addition of Grand Marnier, and we miraculously find one more empty spot in our over-stuffed stomachs.

Our dinner has taken about three hours from fish cleaning to box re-packing. Jim tells us that in the days of the old guides, life was even more relaxed. Then dinners often took many hours; now everyone is in a hurry to get back to the river. He casts a suspicious eye at the bank of dark clouds approaching, and suggests that we, too, might want to begin a retreat—not to further fishing but to find shelter. We outrun the rain, and I sleep soundly all the way home. Nils and I decide we'll skip dinner.

Fatback Sandwich

Vegetable oil
Fatback (not salt pork) May
  need to be ordered
  specially from your
  butcher.

Tomatoes, sliced
Sweet red onion, sliced
  thin
Butter
Bread

Heat ½ inch of oil in a frying pan over an open fire. Slice the fatback into strips about ½ inch wide. Fry it until it is very crisp. Remove it from the pan with a draining spoon, reserving the oil and the rendered lard for cooking the fish (see below). Butter the bread lightly, then make sandwiches with crisp fatback, onions and tomatoes.

Jim Brabant
Clayton

Fried Fish

Italian seasoned bread
  crumbs
Pancake mix
Fish fillets (about ½ pound
  per person)

Frying pan of vegetable oil
  and lard left from cooking
  the fatback (see above)

In a plastic bag, combine equal amounts of bread crumbs and pancake mix—enough to coat the amount of fish you are planning to cook. Pat the fillets dry with a paper towel, then toss them in the bag until they are well coated. Place them carefully in the hot oil. Fry them until they are crisp and golden brown—4 to 6 minutes, depending on the heat of the oil and the size of the fillets. Place the fish on folded paper towels to soak up any excess fat before serving.

Jim Brabant
Clayton

French Toast

2	pints heavy cream, divided		Grand Marnier, Scotch, or
4	eggs		bourbon
	Cinnamon to taste		Frying pan of oil and lard
	Crusty Italian bread		in which the fish was
	Maple syrup		cooked (see above)

Whisk together 1 pint of heavy cream, the eggs, and the cinnamon. Slice the bread 1 inch thick. Dip the bread slices into the cream mixture, turning them over so both sides are well soaked. The longer you leave the bread in the mixture, the more pudding-like it will be in the center. Place the bread slices in the hot fat and cook them, turning occasionally until they are golden brown and crisp on the outside (about 3 to 4 minutes.) Serve topped with a drizzle of the remaining heavy cream, then the maple syrup and the liquor to taste.

Jim Brabant
Clayton

Pebble Island Pickled Pike

Valarie Zammiello says that this is a great recipe because she can use the usually discarded strip of bones obtained when skinning and deboning her husband's catch of a large Great Northern, thus wasting not a bit. The bones dissolve during pickling. She says it is a wonderful appetizer to enjoy while sitting around watching a beautiful St. Lawrence sunset, discussing the day and the ones that got away.

1¼-1½	pounds pike (or any firm-fleshed fish)	½	cup water
2	large onions, sliced thin	1	cup sugar
		3	tablespoons salt
1¼-1½	cups white vinegar	1	tablespoon whole pickling spices

Clean and scald a 1½-quart jar with a lid. Alternate 1- to 2-inch pieces of fish with thinly sliced onion. In a small bowl, combine the vinegar, water, sugar, salt and pickling spices; mix them well and pour the mixture over the fish and onion in the jar. Shake the jar to combine the ingredients, then refrigerate it. Shake the jar daily. Once they are pickled, the fish and onions may be removed. Pour out the juice and spices and add sour cream.

Valarie Zammiello

Black Lake Pan Fish with Almonds

2 pounds small fillets (Suggested fish: crappie,
  sunnies, or perch)
  Flour

Butter and vegetable oil
½ lemon, juice only
½ cup slivered almonds

Dredge the fillets in the flour. Brown them in a skillet in equal amounts of butter and vegetable oil. Let them simmer for about 8 minutes, or until they flake apart easily with a fork. Lay the fillets on a serving dish; add the lemon juice to the butter and oil mixture and sauté the almonds for a few seconds. Pour them over the fish and serve.

Carol Musser
Canton

Zesty Grilled Fillets

2 pounds fish fillets
¼ cup French dressing
1 teaspoon lemon juice

1 tablespoon grated onion
2 teaspoons salt
1 dash pepper

Cut the fillets into serving-size portions. Combine the remaining ingredients and baste the fish with the resulting sauce. Place the fillets in a well-greased hinged wire grill. Cook about 4 inches from moderately hot coals for 8 minutes, basting with the sauce. Turn and cook until the fish flakes easily with a fork and is white all the way through. The time will vary depending on the thickness of the fillets and the heat of the fire.

Emil Michalik

Lake Champlain Smelt

Smelts—about ½ pound
per person

Heavy cream
Bread crumbs or cornmeal
¼ cup butter

Clean the fish, but do not remove the heads. Rinse the fish and pat them dry. Roll them in cream, then in bread crumbs or cornmeal. Heat the butter in a frying pan. Sauté the fish in the butter until they are brown on both sides.

Stanley Ransom
Plattsburgh

Fish Chowder

1 pound haddock fillets (or northern pike or walleye)
1 cup water
2 cups potatoes, cut into ½-inch cubes

1 (1-inch) cube of salt pork, diced very small
1 small onion, diced
2 cups milk or a combination of milk and cream
Salt, pepper, butter to taste

In a saucepan boil the fish in the water until it flakes when it is tested with a fork. Remove the fish and separate it into flakes. Add the potatoes to the cooking water and cook them until they are tender but still firm.

Place the salt pork in a frying pan and cook it slowly until the fat melts. Add the onion and cook it slowly until it is soft and slightly browned. Add the onion and fish to the potatoes in the saucepan.

Pour the milk (or milk and cream) into the frying pan where the onions were cooked. Heat the milk and stir it to get all the flavor of the pork and onions from the pan. Add it to the chowder. Heat the chowder, but do not boil it. Add salt, pepper and butter to taste. (If you used cream as part of the liquid for the chowder, you will not need to add butter.)

The chowder is improved if you cook it one day and serve it the next.

Phil McMasters
Canton

New Orleans-Style Pike Fillets

½	stick butter	1	pound northern pike fillets
1	large onion, minced		(or other similar fish)
2-3	cloves garlic, minced		Salt, black pepper, cay-
1	teaspoon Worcestershire sauce		enne pepper to taste

Melt the butter in a saucepan. Add the onion, garlic and Worcestershire sauce. Lay out the fillets in a glass baking dish. Sprinkle them with salt, black pepper and cayenne. Spoon the sauce over the top of the fillets. Bake at 450 degrees for 10 minutes per inch of thickness. The fish is done when it flakes easily and is white all the way through.

If you make rice to go with the fish, you can spoon any excess sauce over it.

Nils Ekfelt
Canton

Lawrence Senecal's Fish Chowder

According to Gay Millett, this recipe dates back to the early 1900's. Her grandfather served it every Christmas Eve to his family and friends.

Note: quantities depend on the size of the kettle, as does the cooking time.

Salt pork, cut in cubes
Potatoes, sliced
Onions, sliced
Fish, cut in small pieces
(this is easier if the fish is
slightly frozen)

Crackers
Tomatoes
Celery or celery salt
(optional)

Put the ingredients in layers in a kettle starting with salt pork and ending with tomatoes. Add water to fill the kettle. Simmer on slow heat and do not stir. (That's Grandpa's secret—don't stir the chowder.) A large pot will take all day to simmer until it is done.

Gay Millett
Alexandria Bay

Manhattan Clam Chowder

1   (1½-inch) cube of fat salt
    pork, diced
1   onion, sliced thin
1   cup cubed potatoes
1   teaspoon salt
2   cups boiling water

2   cups stewed or canned
    tomatoes
1   pint fresh or canned clams,
    chopped fine
¼   teaspoon dried thyme
    Salt and pepper to taste

Put the salt pork in a deep saucepan (even better is the bottom of a pressure cooker, as it is thicker). Cook it slowly until it melts. Add the onion and cook it, stirring, in the fat for 5 minutes. Add the potatoes, salt and boiling water and boil for 10 minutes. Add the tomatoes and cook the mixture until the potatoes are soft (approximately 5 to 10 minutes). Add the clams, thyme, salt and pepper. Simmer the chowder for three minutes.

Serves 4.

Phil McMasters often varies this by cooking ½ cup chopped celery, ½ teaspoon caraway seeds, and a bit of bay leaf with the onion. He always tries to make it one day and eat it the next.

Phil McMasters
Canton

Trout with Vegetables

Note: Amounts will vary, depending on how many fish you catch.

Small trout—6 to 9 inches
    long after the heads are
    removed
Olive oil

Green peppers, sliced
Onions, sliced
Mushrooms, sliced
Salt and pepper to taste

In a large skillet (preferably cast iron), put three tablespoons of olive oil, then the sliced vegetables. Lay the trout on top of the vegetables and drizzle a little more olive oil over them. Cook on medium to medium-high, turning the trout occasionally until they flake easily. By then, the vegetables should be cooked as well. Just before serving, sprinkle the fish with salt and pepper.

John Hall
Canton

Dilled Pike and Pea Pods

8	pike fillets, ½ to 1-inch thick	¼	teaspoon dill weed
2	teaspoons flour	1	medium carrot, thinly sliced
⅓	cup plain yoghurt		on the diagonal
¼	cup milk	1	cup pea pods
1	teaspoon instant chicken bouillon	1	tablespoon oil

Cut the fish into 1-inch pieces, discarding the skin and bones. Blend the flour with the yoghurt in a small bowl. Stir in the milk, bouillon and dill. Spray a wok or skillet with nonstick cooking spray and preheat it to medium-hot. Stir-fry the carrot pieces for 2 minutes. Add the pea pods and stir-fry until they are tender-crisp (approximately 2 to 3 minutes). Remove the carrots and pea pods to a bowl. Pour the oil into the wok and add the fish. Stir-fry the fish pieces until they are cooked through, taking care not to break them up (approximately 3 to 6 minutes). Remove them gently to the bowl with the vegetables.

Reduce the heat and pour the yoghurt mixture into the wok. Cook, stirring constantly, until the mixture has thickened and is bubbly. Continue cooking for 1 minute more. Add the vegetables and fish; toss them lightly to coat them with the yoghurt.

Makes 2 servings.

Diane Hiles
Watertown

The Shore Dinner

When you hire a fishing guide, you expect that he'll provide a boat, probably with a fish finder, a live well to hold your catch, and plenty of bait and tackle. You also assume that he'll know the best places to catch fish. But if you hire a guide from the Clayton Guides Association, you get all that and more. For generations, the Clayton guides have filled their customers' stomachs as well as their bait buckets. Mornings they pilot their charges to those special weedy places beloved of bass and pike, then dispense advice, bait, encouragement, and cheerful conversation as needed. Come early afternoon, they change from fishing cap to chef's hat and transform the morning's catch to that bountiful feast known as a "shore dinner."

The menu is unvarying. Its history is vague; according to Jim Brabant, member of the Guides Association, an old hotel in Clayton produced the first such meal. Guides in other towns along the St. Lawrence also do shore dinners, but subtle differences in menu make the Clayton meals unique. Should you feel inspired to produce a shore dinner yourself after a successful day's fishing, here is what you will need to cook over your wood fire:

fatback sandwiches

fried fish

corn on the cob

boiled new potatoes

tossed salad

French toast

GAME

Hunter, guide and decoy carver Frank (Goldie) Coombs and Abbie Coombs with day's catch of ducks, ca. 1917, Alexandria Bay, Jefferson County. *Photo courtesy of the Alexandria Township Historical Society.*

Wild Game Feed
Dockside Pub (Alexandria Bay)

"Bewildering array" seems to be the watchword for the day. Ducking through the door of the Dockside Pub to escape the rain, we are greeted by five TVs hanging from the ceiling. On two of them New England battles Minnesota on the gridiron; on the third Chicago goes head to head with Washington; on the fourth, TNN Motor Sports presents cars speeding around a track—location unknown. The fifth is dedicated to Quick Draw and seems to be the screen of choice for most of the tiny bar's patrons. We grab the last table, then turn our attention to the raffles to benefit minor hockey in Alex Bay. Again, the choice is over-whelming—a bucket for the 50-50 raffle, one for the carved duck decoy, and one for everything else from a Capt. Morgan Rum jacket to a gift certificate from the Thousand Islands Bait Store. Having taken several chances on the beautifully carved duck, we settle down for the main event—a drink or two and a feast of the area's wild game.

Various crockpots and heated serving dishes shoulder each other on the serving table; taking even a dab from each would overwhelm our small plastic plates and bowls. The hostess, Rosemary Spozato, hovers anxiously, looking for a bare spot large enough to accommodate yet another pot and wondering where to plug everything in. Each dish is helpfully labelled and we graze, piling our plates and filling our bowls with venison jerky, moose chili*, pot-roasted beaver, wild turkey lomaine (sic), duck egg rolls, and trout-leek soup. A lone dish of cole slaw in the center of the table reminds us that there are other food groups than MEAT, but we pass it up, not wanting to take up valuable space with something so prosaic. Replete, we lean back but find that we can't resist the lure of duck barbeque, rabbit stew*, venison ribs, and moose sausage with peppers and onions. So, it's back to the table with a fresh plate. As we eat, we enjoy the lively cribbage game going on between the sales of raffle tickets—much more intriguing than the bunch of helmeted packing cases charging up and down the fields over our heads.

After we finish eating, I head to the rear of the pub to thank the cooks, Rosemary and her able henchpersons Nina Walts and Ron Ogden, and to inquire about the history of this annual event. Rosemary explains that she and her husband began the feed in 1989 when they were owners of the bar. It started purely as a "thank-you" from the owners to the bar's regular customers—the regulars brought in the meat; Rosemary cooked it. Then, last year their son took over the bar, continuing the feed, but adding the idea of holding a concurrent benefit for a local person or organization. Most of the customers hunt and fish to feed their families over the winter, so Rosemary avoids asking for specific contributions; she cooks what can be spared—with one exception. Everyone liked the beaver pot roast so well when it joined the line-up several years ago that Rosemary admits that she breaks her "don't request" rule every year now in order to ensure that she has one beaver for the pot. In the past there's been muskrat stew, too, but the price of pelts has gone down to the point that no one bothers to trap them anymore.

Rosemary and her team have been cooking for two days to prepare for this moment, and she eyes the downpour outside nervously, hoping it won't keep the crowd away. I can't believe it will; this spread is worth a few drops of water down the neck. As we turn to leave, one of the cribbage players yells over to Ron Ogden, "Did you tell her you poached everything you cooked?" Without missing a beat, Ron fires back, "No, some of it I fried." We walk out the door to the accompaniment of hearty laughter and seductive aromas.

Wild Game Meatballs

½	loaf or more Italian bread	¼	teaspoon oregano
1½	pounds ground meat	¼	teaspoon parsley
	(venison, moose, elk, etc.)	¼	teaspoon basil
½	pound ground pork or	¼	cup grated Parmesan
	ground chuck (to provide	½	teaspoon garlic powder
	fat to keep meatballs from	½	teaspoon onion powder
	being too dry)	2-3	eggs

Soak the bread under running water, then squeeze the water out and break the bread into small pieces. Mix the bread well with all the other ingredients. The mixture should be soft. Shape it into balls and bake on a large flat pan at 375 degrees for 20 to 30 minutes.

Dry bread crumbs will make the meatballs hard.

Rose Mary Sposato

Wild Game Chili

4	onions, diced	1	(28-ounce) can tomato
1-2	pounds ground meat		purée
	(venison, moose, elk, etc.)	1	(28-ounce) can crushed
1	teaspoon minced garlic		tomatoes
1	teaspoon basil	2	tablespoons dark brown
2	teaspoons cumin		sugar
1½	teaspoons oregano	2	(2-pound) cans dark red
2	tablespoons chili powder		kidney beans
1	small can tomato paste		

Sauté the onions. Add the meat and brown it. Stir in the garlic, basil, cumin, oregano and chili powder. Add the tomato paste, purée and crushed tomatoes. Cook this mixture for 20 minutes. Add the beans and brown sugar. Cook the chili for 30 minutes more.

The seasonings can be adjusted to taste.

Rose Mary Sposato

Wild Game Stew

2	pounds meat (venison,	1	tablespoon Worcestershire
	moose, elk, etc.), cubed		sauce
5	tablespoons lard, melted	1	tablespoon parsley
2	large onions, chopped	1	teaspoon thyme
2	stalks celery, chopped	4	bay leaves
2	cloves garlic, crushed		Salt and pepper
1½	cups beef broth		Vegetables (potatoes,
1½	cups water		onions, carrots, rutabaga,
1	(15-ounce) can stewed		turnips), cut into thick pieces
	tomatoes	1	tablespoon dark molasses
			Flour to thicken if needed

Brown the meat in the melted lard. Remove it from the pan and sauté the onions, celery and garlic in the same pan until soft. Add the rest of the ingredients except for the meat, and cook them together until the vegetables are done. Add the meat. Thicken if necessary.

Rose Mary Sposato

Rabbit Stew

2	rabbits, cooked in water and boned	2	bay leaves
4	carrots, sliced	¼	teaspoon cinnamon
4	onions, chopped	¼	teaspoon ginger
1	cup celery, sliced	¼	teaspoon nutmeg
6	potatoes, cut into bite-sized pieces	¼	teaspoon ground cloves
2	cans beer	½	teaspoon marjoram
2	teaspoons Worcestershire sauce	6	tablespoons butter or bacon fat (optional)
2	cloves garlic, minced		Salt and pepper
		6	tablespoons flour

Cook the vegetables in the water in which the rabbits were cooked. Add the beer, Worcestershire sauce and seasonings. Put in the rabbit meat. Mix enough water into the flour to make a smooth paste; stir this into the stew to thicken it.

Rose Mary Sposato

Magnolia Lane Roast Duck

2	wild ducks	½	teaspoon ground ginger
½	can orange juice concentrate	1	teaspoon Dijon mustard
½	orange juice can of honey	2	tablespoons lemon juice
		1	tablespoon brandy

Place foil in the bottom and up the sides of a baking dish. Put the ducks on the foil and prick their skins with a thin-tined fork. Combine and heat the remaining ingredients until they are hot. Brush the resulting sauce onto the ducks. Place the pan in a preheated 425 degree oven for about 1½ hours, brushing frequently with the sauce. The duck is done when no blood comes out when it is pricked with a thin-tined fork.

Carol Musser
Canton

Partridge or Pheasant in Wine Sauce

4	partridge or pheasant breasts, skinned and boned	6	tablespoons butter, divided
1	onion, sliced thin	3	tablespoons flour
1	tablespoon chopped celery	½	teaspoon salt
¼	teaspoon tarragon		Dash pepper
½	cup white wine or vermouth	1	egg yolk, slightly beaten
		3	tablespoons heavy cream

Place the breasts, onion, celery, tarragon and wine in a large saucepan. Add just enough water to cover them. Cover the pan and simmer the mixture for 30 minutes, or until the breasts are tender. Remove the breasts and keep them warm.

Strain the liquid and boil it to reduce it to two cups. Melt 4 tablespoons of the butter. Stir in the flour, salt and pepper. Gradually add the 2 cups of reduced broth. Cook, stirring constantly, until the mixture is smooth and thickened. Add the remaining 2 tablespoons of butter and simmer gently for 5 minutes, stirring occasionally. Combine the egg yolk and the cream; stir them into the hot sauce.

Serve the breasts covered with the sauce. There's enough sauce to spoon it over rice or noodles to accompany the breasts.

Mabel Jenkins
Canton

Good and Easy Rabbit Casserole

1-2	rabbits, cut into serving pieces	1	tablespoon rosemary
	Flour, seasoned with salt and pepper	1	clove garlic, pressed
		½	cup dry white wine
⅓	cup cooking oil	⅓	cup meat broth
		1	teaspoon wine vinegar

Dredge the rabbit pieces in the seasoned flour. Heat the oil, rosemary and garlic together in a frying pan, then brown the meat in that mixture. Place the rabbit in an ovenproof casserole. Add the wine, broth and vinegar to the frying pan and bring the mixture to the boiling point. Scrape the pan and pour all the juices over the rabbit. Cover the casserole and bake in a preheated 350 degree oven for 1 hour.

One rabbit will serve three people.

Carol Musser
Canton

Rabbit Baked in Tarragon Mustard, Garlic and Cream

2	rabbits, cut into serving pieces	⅓	cup minced parsley
3	tablespoons tarragon mustard (or Dijon mustard to which you add ½ teaspoon dried tarragon per 3 tablespoons mustard)	3	tablespoons red wine vinegar
		1	cup chicken broth
		¾	cup heavy cream
			Pepper, freshly ground
			Salt
2	tablespoons minced garlic	1-2	tablespoons chopped parsley for garnish

Coat the rabbit pieces with the mustard. Mix the minced garlic and minced parsley together with a little salt and sprinkle half over the rabbit. Combine the vinegar and broth and pour into a large baking dish. Sprinkle the remaining garlic and minced parsley over the liquid, then put the rabbit pieces on top. Bring to a boil, then cover the baking dish and bake in a preheated 350 degree oven until tender. Turn the pieces of rabbit after 45 minutes. When they are tender, remove the rabbit pieces and keep them warm.

Pour the cream into the juices in the casserole and boil to reduce the liquid by half or more; it should have the consistency of a light cream sauce. Salt and pepper the rabbit pieces and return them to the casserole. Spoon the sauce over the meat and taste to correct the seasoning if necessary. Sprinkle a little chopped parsley on top and serve.

June Latimer
Bucks Bridge

Black Jack Barbecue Sauce

1	cup strong black coffee	2	teaspoons salt
1	cup Worcestershire sauce	2	cups chopped onions
1	cup catsup	¼	cup minced hot chile
½	cup cider vinegar		peppers
½	cup brown sugar	6	cloves garlic, minced
3	tablespoons chili powder		

Combine all the ingredients in a saucepan and simmer them for 25 minutes. Strain or purée the cooked mixture in a blender or food processor. Store the sauce in the refrigerator.

This sauce is especially good on venison or beef ribs.

Makes 5 cups.

Greg Howe
Canton

Greg Howe found this recipe years ago in a little cookbook put out by the Philip Morris company entitled Chuckwagon Cooking from Marlboro Country *and has been using it ever since.*

The Original Stillwater First and Last Weekend Venison Jerky

¼	cup salt	1½	teaspoons garlic powder
7	cups soy sauce	3	ounces bourbon
4	(12-ounce) bottles of dark beer	8	teaspoons ginger
2	large onions, diced	1	large apple, diced
5	teaspoons grated orange peel	1½	cups brown sugar
			Cayenne and chile peppers to taste
10	whole cloves	20-25	pounds venison

Combine all the ingredients except the meat in a good-sized bowl and mix them well. There should be approximately 2 gallons of liquid.

To prepare the meat, cut it into strips or chunks approximately ¼ inch thick. The length doesn't matter, but you don't want thick chunks as they won't dry properly.

In two or three large tubs (dishpans work well) combine the marinade mixture with the meat, trying to distribute all the mix evenly. Cover the containers and soak the meat in the marinade for two to three days, stirring at least once a day.

Now you're ready to smoke the meat. Using a smoker or Weber-type barbecue grill, set up your smoker with one full pan of smoking chips, either hickory or alder. Distribute the meat over the mesh rack, trying not to overload it. Smoke the meat on high until all the chips are gone. Turn the heat down and dry the meat until it is black on the outside. Check frequently to be sure it doesn't dry beyond that just-right point. When twisted, the meat should form white lines on the outside and should be the consistency of a rubber eraser. This process may take a long time (8 to 10 hours), but it's worth the wait. Store the meat in an airtight container or bag. It may be frozen as well.

Joe Siematkowski
Canton

Chef Locy's Country Venison Pâté

½	yellow onion	30	pistachio nuts, broken in half
2	medium leeks		Thyme to taste
6	cloves garlic, chopped	½	teaspoon black pepper
½	stick sweet butter	¼	teaspoon white pepper
2-3	pounds lean hindquarter		Dash of Cajun spice
	venison—no fat	1	bay leaf
1	pound chicken livers	¼	cup cognac
½	pound ground pork		Bay leaves and parsley for
1	can beef consommé		garnish
2	eggs, beaten	8	strips prosciutto ham

Cook the onion, leeks and garlic with the sweet butter until the onions are translucent; set them aside to cool. Put the cooled mixture into the food processor and blend until it is smooth.

Put the venison, livers, and pork into the food processor in small batches, each with a little bit of the consommé. Using the pulse button, blend each until it is smooth, transferring each batch to a large mixing bowl as it is finished. Add the beaten eggs, the onion mixture, the nuts, the spices, the cognac and the remaining consommé, if any, to the bowl and blend everything together well.

In the bottom of a regular bread pan put a design of parsley and bay leaves. Line the pan with the prosciutto, letting any extra drape over the sides. Put the blended meat mixture into the lined pan, pressing it in well, then flipping the edges of the ham over the top. Bake at 325 degrees for 1 to 2 hours.

Put a heavy weight (about 1 ½ pounds) on top of the pâté to squeeze it down. (Put a cookie sheet under the pan before you begin, as this step can be messy.) Let it cool overnight. Flip the pan to remove the pâté so your parsley design is on top for serving.

William Locy
Canton

The Stillwater Club

For many North Country residents hunting camp is akin to the Promised Land. Traditionally this idyll entails bonding across generations by the men of the family while their wives wait at home to cook the game their heroes bring back. But not all camps are family-owned. Other hunters prefer to join clubs of like-minded sportsmen, buying or leasing land on which they can meet to pursue outdoor interests by day and card games by night.

The oldest such deer-hunting club in the Adirondacks is Canton's Stillwater Club. Located in the Town of Clare, it occupies a tract of approximately 15,000 acres, roughly the size of Manhattan Island. The founders were all Canton men, led by Judge Ledyard Hale, in whose office the first meeting of the group was held on May 13, 1893. At that time they decided to rent the Hepburn Tract, the piece of land which had made the fortune of the North Country's lumberman/philanthropist A. Barton Hepburn. They also hired James O'Brien to serve as warden and guide "at the rate of one dollar per day." They were a dedicated group, for in those days the trip to camp involved a half-day stage ride to Clare, then a two-mile, gear-laden hike into the woods. The original camp was built on the North Branch of the Grasse River; in 1896 a second camp was added seven miles away on the Middle Branch.

Unlike many such groups, the Stillwater Club was really founded as a canoe club. One of the moving spirits behind its establishment was J. Henry Rushton, canoe-maker and born organizer. He had already helped found the American Canoe Association, the St. Lawrence Canoe Club, the Canton Gun Club and Canton's first public reading room, the forerunner of the present public library. The club took its name from the stretch of smooth river above the Hepburn wing dam on the North Branch of the Grasse. Members did their fishing and hunting from Rushton cedar canoes, though they did keep a few rowboats for "greenhorn guests."

Over the years the club has boasted many noted members and guests. Norman Rockwell visited in October, 1927, leaving behind him a signed sketch of the club's guide with whose craggy, Lincolnesque visage he had been greatly impressed. Colonel Theodore Roosevelt, relative of the president, was a regular visitor and avid-to-a-fault fisherman. Apparently he even wore out the guide, who hated to see him arrive. In 1898 Canton's famous son, novelist Irving Bacheller, joined the club. Those in the know later found traces of guide Jim O'Brien in some of Bacheller's characters.

As long ago as 1910, the Stillwater Club developed an interest in conservation, taking measures to limit the take of fish and deer on their property, requiring their warden/guide to patrol for forest fires, and restocking their streams with trout fingerlings. The club today is as lively as it was in the past, having rebuilt the Middle Branch camp after a disastrous fire in 1988.

* * *

This information was gleaned from the papers of Atwood Manley in the St. Lawrence University Special Collections.

MAPLE SYRUP

Using a wide mouth dipper, Ira Miller of Hopkinton tests boiling maple sap to see if it comes off in sheets rather than droplets— "aproning," he calls it—to indicate if it is ready as maple syrup. *Mark Sloan Photo/TAUNY Archives*

Sugaring Off at Roger and Janet Favro's Canton

It's a long walk from our car back into the woods to the sugar shack, and my boots get heavier with each step. Not for nothing is March known as "mud season." We push open the door to the shack and are met by a gust of fragrant steam. Wow! I feel as if I could eat the air if someone would just hand me a spoon. The shack is mainly taken up by the huge evaporating pan, about 12 feet long, made of sheet metal and presently filled with rapidly boiling sap. The pan looks like the sort of maze that cries out for a little white rat. Intricate patterns of interior walls allow as much heat as possible to reach the sap. As the sap cooks down and becomes more dense, it moves through the maze by gravity. At the top end Roger occasionally starts more sap on its journey. Under the pan is a roaring fire with an insatiable appetite. Our conversation is punctuated by the clang of the metal door as Roger feeds yet another log into the wood stove.

My friend Peter vanLent and I have arrived in time for the day's gathering of sap. We hop on the wagon behind the tractor and begin our slow journey through the sugar bush, emptying the buckets on the trees into the big tub we have brought with us. Back at the sugar shack, we pour the contents of the big collecting tub into a holding tank with other sap awaiting a turn in the evaporating pan.

Inside, Roger checks to see whether the sap has thickened enough to become syrup. He dips a wooden paddle into the evaporating pan, then holds it up to see whether the liquid runs off as individual drops or whether it "aprons" off in one thick sheet, the sign that it is ready. Then he grades the new syrup by comparing its color to a row of little bottles, each containing a different grade of syrup. As he prepares to strain the syrup into cans for sale, we munch on eggs hard-boiled in the sap. Enough sap has found its way through the shell to impart a mild maple flavor—tasty, but not spectacular.

Other friends and neighbors have found their way to this steamy oasis, and the shack is filling up. It's an off season for farmers, indeed for everyone except tax-preparers. People are freer than sometimes to take an hour or so off to catch up on neighborhood gossip. What better place to gather than this warm, sweet-smelling haven from early spring's chill? Peter and I say our farewells, making room for the newcomers. We head back downhill to the car, each of us carrying a can of syrup, with visions of much tastier treats than sugar-plums hastening our descent.

Jack Wax or Wax on Snow

Maple syrup   Fresh white snow or
                                     cracked ice

Boil the maple syrup to 238 degrees. Pour it at once over fresh white snow or cracked ice. Twirl up a layer of wax with a fork.

You can eat more if you alternate the sweet treat with bites of pickle.

Maple Cream

Boil maple syrup to 232 degrees. Pour the syrup into a flat dish set in a larger pan filled with ice water to cool the syrup quickly. When it cools to below 199 degrees, stir it continuously with a spoon for 15 to 20 minutes.

Addie Miller
Hopkinton

Maple Pecan Pie

2   large eggs   ¼   teaspoon salt
⅓   cup sugar   ¾   cup pecan halves
¼   cup butter, melted   1   (8-inch) unbaked pie shell
1   cup maple syrup

Beat together the eggs and sugar until they are creamy. Add the melted butter, maple syrup and salt to the sugar mixture; mix them well. Add the pecan halves. Pour the filling into the pie shell. Bake the pie in a preheated 375 degree oven for 40 minutes. Cool and serve with whipped cream.

Iona Brewer
Canton

Grand-Pères au Sirop d'Érable (Dumplings in Maple Syrup)

1½	cups maple syrup	¾	teaspoon salt
¾	cup water	3	tablespoons shortening
1½	cups sifted flour	¾	cup milk
3	teaspoons baking powder		

Combine the maple syrup and water and bring them to a boil. Sift the flour, baking powder and salt together. Cut in the shortening until the mixture resembles coarse bread crumbs. Stir in the milk to make a soft dough. Drop by tablespoons into boiling maple syrup. Cover the pot tightly and boil the mixture gently for 20 minutes without removing the lid. Serve immediately.

Makes 6 servings.

Francine Poulin
Massena

Maple Popcorn

1	cup maple syrup	½	cup sugar
½	cup light corn syrup	1	large bowl popped corn

Boil the maple syrup, corn syrup and sugar together until they form a thread when the spoon is lifted from the pan. Pour the syrup mixture over the popcorn and stir them together.

Marion Thomas
South Colton

Maple Johnnycake

2	eggs	1	cup flour
½	cup milk	1	cup cornmeal
½	cup maple syrup	3	teaspoons baking powder
½	cup butter, melted	½	teaspoon salt

Beat the eggs; add the milk, maple syrup and melted butter. Combine the flour, cornmeal, baking powder and salt. Add the flour mixture to the egg mixture, beating until they are well blended. Pour the batter into a greased 8-inch cake pan. Bake at 400 degrees for 25 to 30 minutes .

Iona Brewer
Canton

Hot Buttered Rum

¼	teaspoon cinnamon		Boiling water to fill a
1	tablespoon butter		coffee mug
1	tablespoon maple syrup	1½	ounces rum

In a coffee mug, stir together the cinnamon, butter, syrup and enough water to fill the mug, but still leave enough room for the rum. Add the rum to the mixture, but do not stir it again. Drink it as soon as the water has cooled enough not to burn your mouth.

By adding the rum at the end, you avoid boiling off the alcohol.

Josephine Mentley
Canton

Pralines

2	cups powdered sugar	1	cup maple syrup
½	cup cream	2	cups pecans, partly broken

Boil the sugar, cream and syrup to the soft ball stage (238 degrees on a candy thermometer). Remove the pan from the heat and beat the mixture until it is creamy. Add the nuts and drop from a spoon onto waxed paper in small clusters.

Madeleine Gray
Helena

Maple Syrup Squares

2	cups brown sugar	1	tablespoon butter
1½	cups maple syrup	⅛	teaspoon salt
½	cup light cream	½	cup chopped nuts

Heat the sugar in a heavy saucepan until it dissolves. Add the maple syrup and cream. Cook until the firm ball stage (245 to 250 degrees), stirring occasionally. Add the butter, salt and nuts. Pour the mixture into a shallow buttered pan. When it has cooled, cut it into squares.

Florence Tasetano
Madrid

Maple-Candied Sweet Potatoes

6	large sweet potatoes, unpeeled	2	tablespoons melted butter
⅔	cup maple syrup	1	cup apple cider
1	teaspoon salt	⅓	cup water

Wash the potatoes, then boil them until they are nearly tender. Drain off the water. When the potatoes have cooled to the point that you can handle them, peel and slice them about 1 inch thick, placing the slices in a greased skillet. In a saucepan, add the salt and butter to the maple syrup, then add the cider and water. Bring this mixture to a rolling boil, then pour it over the potatoes. Bake them about an hour at 300 degrees, basting occasionally.

Sara Chittenden
Hopkinton

Maple Pickled Beets

¼	cup maple syrup	1	tablespoon mixed whole pickling spice
½	cup cider vinegar	2	cups sliced or whole baby beets, cooked
½	cup water		
½	teaspoon salt		

Bring all the ingredients except the beets to a boil; simmer them together for five minutes. Add the beets. Return the mixture to the boiling point. Before serving the beets, let them stand in the refrigerator at least 12 hours.

Addie Miller
Hopkinton

Quick Baked Beans

1	(22-ounce) can baked beans	½	teaspoon salt
2	tablespoons maple syrup	⅛	teaspoon minced onions
2	tablespoons water	2	tablespoons bacon, sausage or ham drippings

Mix all the ingredients together and heat them at 375 degrees for 35 to 40 minutes.

Marion Thomas
South Colton

Maple Ham Loaf

4	cups ground ham	1	teaspoon dry mustard
1	cup bread crumbs	½	teaspoon ground cloves
½	cup maple syrup, divided	¼	cup vinegar
½	cup milk	¼	cup brown sugar
2	eggs		

Combine the ham, bread crumbs, ¼ cup maple syrup, milk and eggs. Bake the mixture in a loaf pan for 45 minutes at 350 degrees. Mix together the mustard, cloves, vinegar, brown sugar and remaining ¼ cup maple syrup. Baste the ham loaf frequently with this mixture.

Grace Powell
Hopkinton

Maple Fluff Frosting

1	cup maple syrup	⅛	teaspoon salt
2	egg whites	1	teaspoon vanilla

Cook the syrup until it forms a firm, but not hard, ball when tested in cold water. Let it stand off the stove while you beat the egg whites with a pinch of salt, until they form stiff peaks but are not dry. Add the syrup in a fine stream, beating constantly with an egg beater. Continue beating until the frosting holds its shape. Add the vanilla and frost the cake.

Marion Thomas
South Colton

Maple Fruit Salad

1	bowl of your favorite fresh fruit (mixed berries, melons, peaches, etc), chopped for salad	2-4	tablespoons maple syrup

Gently stir the syrup into the chopped fruit for sweetening and flavor.

Marion Thomas
South Colton

Sugaring Off

by Ira and Addie Miller and their daughters,
Jessie Bonno and Joan Masterson

as told to Lynn Ekfelt and the production staff of TAUNY's
radio program "Home Cooking"

There's a lot of walking involved in sugaring. You have to go once around the bush to drop off the buckets, once to drop off the lids, once to drill the holes, and once to pound the spiles. We used to tap our trees with an awl. Now we use a chain saw with a special attachment. A good tree gives a full bucket twice a day. We put out 3000 buckets this year.

Years ago we used a tractor pulling a sled to collect the sap, but now we have a wagon with wheels. Some people use plastic tubing to collect the sap nowadays—it goes right from the tree by gravity down to a holding tank at the sugar shack. We don't like to do that, though; some of the customers say they can taste the difference.

Our evaporator is made of sheet metal—it holds the steam down and makes the sap cook faster. We use a mixture of hard and soft wood to heat it. If the sap starts to boil over, you can sprinkle a little milk in it. The fat content stops the boiling over. Or you can use spray-on PAM.

We use a hydrometer to measure the weight per gallon. If it's more than eleven pounds per gallon when you put it in the can, it candies in the bottom—turns crystal just like glass. And then, it'll keep on candying until it gets below the legal standard of eleven pounds to the gallon in the can. And then when it gets weaker than that it will ferment and sour. But you can bring it back to flavor pretty good by bringing it to a boil.

Once the syrup is ready to go into the cans, we filter it through orlon in order to get the nitre, or "sugar sand," out of it. That precipitates out of the sap while it's boiling.

A good season is two or three weeks. You need daytime temperatures in the 40's and nights below freezing to get the sap running. The longer you tap, the more the trees dry up. There's no way to affect the grade of syrup you make; you just take what you get. You can tell when the season's winding down. The syrup starts getting darker and stronger and then it gets buddy. When the buds come out, the sap will still run sometimes if you have the right weather, but it's buddy—strong like molasses.

Ira Miller's family has been making maple syrup and other maple products on their farm in Hopkinton for over a century.

Maple syrup was the only sweetener known to North America, aside from dried berries, until honey bees were introduced in the colonies in the 1630s.[1] The Iroquois and Ojibways notched tree trunks, then drove in wooden sticks to allow the sap to flow into containers made of bark. They taught this skill to European settlers, and maple sugar became an integral part of the diet of all of us fortunate enough to live where there are sugar maples and frosty spring nights.

A sugar maple tree is usually 30 years old and at least ten inches in diameter before it can be tapped. Depending on its size, a tree can have up to four taps, each of which yields an average of ten gallons of sap per season. When the sap comes out of the tree it is mostly water. During the boiling down, this water is boiled away, leaving a thicker and sweeter liquid, the maple syrup. It takes about 40 gallons of sap to make one gallon of syrup.

The grading system still used today for maple syrup dates from the time when Northern maple sugar manufacturers were competing with Southern cane-sugar growers for the national sweetener market, according to gardener and cook Martha Rubin.[2] The goal was a bland, flavorless sweetener for use in coffee and tea and for baking. The darker grades of syrup acquired their reputation as less desirable at that time. In fact, these grades may actually be better for some uses as they are more strongly flavored and less sweet. New York State assigns five grades to syrup, only the first three of which are available to retail consumers. Grade A syrup can be made only by the evaporation of pure maple sap. It must contain no less than 66 percent sugar by weight. Grade A Light Amber is the lightest. It has a very mild and delicate flavor. Grade A Medium Amber is a bit darker in color, with a fuller flavor. Grade A Dark Amber is the darkest of the three and has the strongest maple flavor. Grade B syrup can not be sold in small containers; it must be marketed in bulk for reprocessing and for the manufacture of commercial table syrups where it will be mixed with other ingredients. Extra Dark is marketed in bulk for cooking and for flavoring chewing tobacco.

[1] Gay, Kathlyn and Martin. *Encyclopedia of North American Eating and Drinking Traditions*. Santa Barbara CA: ABC-Clio, 1996. p. 159.

[2] Rubin, Martha. *Countryside, Garden and Table: A New England Seasonal Diary*. Golden CO: Fulcrum, 1993. p. 39.

WILD FOODS

In a marsh near his camp on the Raquette River at South Colton, St. Lawrence County, Russell Hendrik picks the leaves of marsh marigolds—locally called "cowslips"—to be boiled as a vegetable dish in early May. *David Duprey Photo/Watertown Daily Times*

Berrying
Murphy Islands

Passing boaters glance askance at our diminutive flotilla as we slowly make our way from the mouth of Brandy Brook to the Murphy Islands. Objectively, I must admit we do make a rather odd picture—two canoes roped together, a tiny electric motor on the first one slowly powering both boats across the wide expanse of choppy water that is the St. Lawrence River. In the first boat, Nils sits with his hand on the tiller, directing us slightly upstream so that the current will carry us in a parabolic curve to our destination. His mother, her head shielded from the July sun by a wide-brimmed hat, keeps a lookout for the loon family we saw here last year. In the second boat, I help the plucky little motor by paddling a bit while my father-in-law leans eagerly forward, begrudging the minutes consumed by our slow passage.

We stop first at the smaller of the islands and leave Linda with her book on the sand. She has declared that she's done enough berrying in her life and would rather recline under a tree with Barbara Pym and her *Excellent Women* for company. The remaining three of us hop into the larger canoe and within minutes are tying up on the shores of the bigger island, a dome-shaped mound totally covered with raspberry canes. Around our necks we tie children's sand pails, leaving both hands free to pick. Then we spread out and begin to work in a silence broken only by the sound of our feet trampling down the old canes. Near the shore I find two large eggs floating. I hope they do not belong to our loon family, but I worry. I have heard that loons nest very near the water and the wake from power boats and jet skis often washes their eggs away.

After a couple of hours of slowly filling my pail—one here, one there, remembering always to look behind me for the ones hidden by leaves on my forward progress, I hear Nils hallooing to announce that it's lunchtime. Knowing what's going to happen, I reluctantly join the two men for the hop over to picnic with Linda. Fearing the worst, I peek into Fred's pail. He's done it again—his pail overflows, while mine is a scant half-full. It's so humiliating to be consistently outpicked by an 85-year old man! I take some comfort in the fact that we have different picking styles. Mindful of the kitchen work that will follow our day on the island, I pick cleanly—no leaves and twigs, as few stems as possible, and only bright red, fully ripe berries. Fred, on the other hand, attacks the patch. So many berries; so little time—he's a picking machine, heedless of the occasional trash and unripe berries which mar the perfection of his collection. We dump our pails into a large plastic container in the cooler, mercifully erasing the humiliating evidence, and munch our sandwiches.

Long before I'm ready to face thorns, sun which sends wet trickles down my back, and bugs which find my sweaty body irresistible, Fred is urging us back to the canoe. We return to our respective sections of the island and settle in for the afternoon. Suddenly the silence is broken by some powerful swearing from Fred. He has disturbed a nest of yellow-jackets who are making painfully clear their resentment of his intrusion. By the time Nils and I reach him, he has been stung eleven times. We look around for spotted touch-me-not, but the island is bare of much but raspberries. "Perhaps we should go on home," Nils suggests, mindful of the dangers of wasp venom. But no, ripe berries remain on the vine, so Fred soldiers on. When at last we do dump the result of our afternoon's work, he's again picked twice as many berries as I have.

Back home, Linda concocts a cobbler* for Nils' birthday that would easily feed a family of ten, Fred takes a bath and dabs his stings with juice from my aloe plant, and Nils and I begin the long process of washing and picking through the remaining berries, preparing them for the freezer. The next day in the grocery store we calculate the value of our plunder in terms of the half-pint cartons on sale at P & C— roughly $40.00. That night at dinner, the subject of Christmas comes up and Fred says dreamily, "You know what I would really like for Christmas? A big burlap sack to use when I gather black walnuts."

Wild Greens

Wild greens fall into two basic groups: the ones sweet enough to eat as is and the ones that require parboiling to remove the bitterness.

Sweet Greens

Wintercress
Gather wintercress as soon as the snow is off the ground. When the nights stop being cold, the leaves are too bitter to eat. They are good added to a salad.

Fiddleheads
Gather fiddleheads when they are just a few inches off the ground and still tightly coiled. (It's good to identify a patch of ostrich fern or bracken the year before since those have the best-tasting shoots and you might have difficulty distinguishing them in the spring.) They will be sandy and hairy, so they need much cleaning to remove the grit and hairs. Steam and serve with butter.

Dandelion crowns
These are the blanched leaf stems between the top of the root (about 2 to 3 inches below the surface of the earth) and the green leaves. Wash the grit off. Boil the crowns for five minutes, then drain and serve buttered and salted.

Young green leaves can also be used raw or cooked, but once the blossoms have come, the leaves are too bitter to eat. Grace French uses these young leaves to make the following salad: Dice and fry ½ pound bacon, reserving the drippings. Chop up one onion and cook it in the drippings. Add ½ cup vinegar and ½ cup water to the pan and mix well. Boil and dice four potatoes. Hard-boil 4 eggs and dice them. Cut 4 cups of young dandelion greens into strips. Gently toss together the greens, potatoes, bacon and eggs with the vinegar sauce.

The blossoms can be made into wine. Madeleine Gray of Helena provides this recipe: boil 1 gallon of dandelion blossoms with 1 gallon of water for five minutes. Strain the liquid and add 2 pounds of sugar for each gallon. Allow the mixture to ferment for nine days, then strain it through a woolen cloth and bottle it.

Pigweed
Gather young, tender plants, less than one inch high. These can be found from mid-spring until frost. According to Max Coots, these are one of the best cooked greens.

Pusley (purslane)
Gather the young tips and add them to salads. These tips may also be steamed or boiled lightly and eaten with butter. However, like okra, purslane

tends to get slimy when it is cooked, so some people might find the texture objectionable. This very quality makes it a good thickener for soups and stews—again like okra.

The stems can be pickled. Euell Gibbons offers the following recipe: Strip off the leaves and clean the grit from the stems. Stir together 1 cup white vinegar, 2 cups cold water, ¼ cup salt, and ½ teaspoon alum. In each of two pint jars, place a flower of dill, a clove of garlic, and a small red pepper. Pack the jars, but not too tightly, with the pusley stems. Put another flower of dill on top. Fill the jars with the liquid and seal them. (No cooking or processing is required.) Store in a dark place at least one month before using the pickles.

Watercress
To gather watercress, pinch off the plant at the surface of the water; don't pull up the roots. Then your patch will live to produce again. Euell Gibbons says that the leaves make a good sandwich teamed with cucumber or with a chopped hard-boiled egg and one tablespoon of chopped chives per ¼ cup of chopped cress with just enough mayonnaise to moisten the mixture.

Gibbons also stir-fries his watercress in the following manner. Cook a tablespoon of grated fresh ginger in 2 tablespoons of hot cooking oil for 2 minutes. Add one pound of well-washed watercress. Cook, stirring, for four minutes or until the cress is wilted and coated with oil. Toss with 2 tablespoons of soy sauce to serve.

Bitter greens
Bitter greens must be parboiled to leach out the acid in order to be palatable. To parboil, cover the greens with boiling water (don't start with cold water and bring it to a boil). Boil one minute. Drain off the water. Repeat the process two or three times before cooking the greens. Unfortunately, all the boiling also leaches out the vitamins, so these vegetables are enjoyed more for taste than for nutrition.

Cowslips
Gather the leaves before the plants blossom. Parboil the greens twice. Serve with butter and salt.

Milkweed
You can cook many parts of the milkweed: young shoots (8 inches or less), leaves before the plant flowers, flower buds (light colored and tightly closed), or pods (young and hard.) For all of these, parboil the greens three times. Boil them for 10 minutes after the parboiling, then season and serve.

Max Coots
Canton

Wild Garlic

These are gathered like scallions. They are very pungent when raw, so most people prefer to cook them like any other onion. They are good sautéed or slivered and inserted into slits in meat which is to be roasted.

Max Coots
Canton

Wild Leek

These should be picked early in the spring while the leaves are a tightly rolled cylinder. (They are easy to find since you can smell them as you walk by.) They are good chopped fine in a salad, or boiled for 20 minutes in salted water then served with butter or a cream sauce.

Max Coots
Canton

Burdock Roots

Gather the roots in June or early July; after that they become too woody. For that reason you should use only first-year roots of this biennial plant. You can recognize a first-year plant because it puts up a flower shoot. The roots can not be pulled. Instead, you must dig a hole 2 feet deep beside the plant and pull the root out into your hole from the side. Peel the root and cut off the hair root. It can then be boiled or baked like a potato.

Max Coots
Canton

Cattail Pollen

With a sharp knife, scrape the yellow pollen off the cattails in the spring. You can substitute pollen for up to half the wheat flower in pancake or muffin batter.

Max Coots
Canton

Sumac

Gather the red blossoms. Put them into a large container, covered with cold water. Using a stick or potato masher, crush the berries, then strain them through cheesecloth to get rid of the hairs and other garbage. The remaining liquid, sweetened with sugar, makes a good drink, much like lemonade.

Max Coots
Canton

Mushrooms

BE VERY CAREFUL when gathering mushrooms. The varieties listed here are quite recognizable, so are reasonably safe to enjoy. Most mushrooms give off a considerable amount of juice when cooked, so any method of cooking comes to resemble boiling. This richly flavored juice should not be discarded, but rather used in the recipe or thickened with flour to make a sauce.

Puffballs

Any puffball that is white all the way through when sliced is safe to eat. (But make sure that the inside is a solid white mass, not a coiled-up embryonic mushroom.) They can be sliced into slabs and french-fried or sautéed with butter and garlic.

Shaggy Manes

These must be gathered when they are fresh. As they age, they become black, slimy, and unpalatable. Refrigeration does not stop this process; cook them soon after picking. Sauté them in a heavy skillet, turning them gently so they don't break. They are ready when they are brown around the edges.

Max Coots
Canton

Blackberry Cake

When my grandmother was a little girl in Ohio, her mother would send her out to pick berries for this cake armed with a long hatpin. "In case a black snake tries to wrap himself around you, just stick him with the hatpin and he'll let go" was her sage advice. I prefer my berry picking in our black-snake-free North Country, but this cake is so good I might almost brave an Ohio berry patch.

1½	cups sugar	1	teaspoon cloves
¾	cup shortening	1	teaspoon nutmeg
3	eggs	2	teaspoons baking soda
3	cups flour	8	tablespoons buttermilk
1	teaspoon cinnamon	1½	cups blackberries
½	teaspoon salt		

Cream the sugar with the shortening. Add the eggs one at a time, beating well after each addition. Combine the flour, cinnamon, salt, cloves and nutmeg. Dissolve the baking soda in the buttermilk. Stir ⅓ of the flour mixture into the sugar mixture, then ½ of the buttermilk mixture, then ⅓ of the flour, then ½ of the milk, then finally the last of the flour mixture. Fold the blackberries in lightly. Bake in a 9 x 13-inch pan at 375 degrees for 30 to 45 minutes. (The cake is done when a toothpick inserted near the center comes out clean.) Serve the cake topped with a dusting of powdered sugar or a sliver of vanilla ice cream.

Lynn Ekfelt
Canton

Blackberry Pudding

1	cup sugar	1	teaspoon salt
½	cup butter	1	cup milk
2	cups flour	2	cups blackberries
2	teaspoons baking powder	2	cups boiling water

Cream the sugar with the butter. Combine the flour, baking powder and salt. Add them to the creamed mixture and mix well. Stir in the milk. Put the resulting dough into a greased 9 x 13-inch baking pan and put the berries on top. Pour the boiling water carefully over the berries. Bake at 350 degrees until the top is golden (approximately 50 minutes).

Regina Willette
Canton

Raspberry Cobbler

This is the dessert my mother-in-law always made when she visited for Nils' birthday and we made our berry-picking excursions.

2	rounded cups flour	½	teaspoon nutmeg
½	teaspoon salt	⅓	stick of margarine
¾	cup shortening		9 x 13-inch pan of berries,
½-¾	cup ice water		mounded gently in the
1½	cups sugar		center, just slightly lower
			than the sides of the pan

Combine the flour and the salt; cut in the shortening. Toss enough ice water in with a fork to allow you to form a ball of dough. Roll out a rectangle of dough bigger than the top of the pan. Cut off the edges for dumplings. Mix a little more flour into that extra dough, then roll it out as thin as possible. Cut it into thin strips.

Mix the nutmeg and the sugar. In a 9 x 13-inch glass pan, put a little of the sugar on the bottom of the pan, then a layer of berries, then a layer (one-deep) of dumplings, then more sugar, more berries, more dumplings, more berries and more sugar. Cut the butter into pieces and dot on top of the berries. Cover with the crust. Bake at 425 degrees for 15 minutes. Turn the oven down to 350 degrees, then cook about an hour more until the cobbler is bubbly.

Lynn Ekfelt
Canton

The next two recipes came to Arline Wolfe from her friend Howard Hinman of Parishville. Mr. Hinman had a huge black notebook that was a treasure-trove of recipes, some dating back to the early 1900s.

Raspberry Crisp

1	quart raspberries	⅓	cup flour
½	cup white sugar	⅓	cup brown sugar
¼	cup butter	¾	cup rolled oats

In a 9-inch square pan, sprinkle the raspberries with the white sugar. Blend the butter, flour, brown sugar and rolled oats. Sprinkle this mixture over the raspberries. Bake at 350 degrees for about 30 minutes.

Arline Wolfe
Hermon

Open-Faced Raspberry Pie

1	tablespoon lard	3	eggs, very well beaten
2	cups milk	1	quart raspberries
1	teaspoon salt	1	cup sugar
2	cups flour, sifted		

Put the lard into a 9 x 12-inch metal pan and heat it until it is sizzling hot. Stir the milk, salt and flour into the eggs to make a very thin batter. Pour this batter into the sizzling hot pan. Spread the berries over the top, then sprinkle it with the sugar. Bake at 425 degrees for about 45 minutes. The batter will rise, then fall.

Arline Wolfe
Hermon

Unlike their city neighbors, whose food is usually at a remove from nature equal to at least two middlemen, most North Country residents appreciate the bounty that surrounds them in the woods and by the roadsides. Few of us have the time to be a Euell Gibbons, preparing entire meals consisting solely of foods gathered in the wild. But most of us have at least one specialty which draws on foods we ferret out ourselves, whether it be watercress sandwiches from the patch in the stream behind camp or wild leek soup made from leeks we literally nose out on an early spring hike. There's something particularly satisfying in making a delicious dish with no cost except "sweat equity." Money considerations aside, wild foods have usually not been sprayed with pesticides, bird songs make a better accompaniment to food acquisition than Muzak does, and there are no long checkout lines on a forest trail.

Max Coots, minister emeritus of the Canton Unitarian-Universalist Church, spent many years gathering physical as well as spiritual sustenance from nature. I asked him to give me a calendar of his collecting year. These foods are all readily available in the North Country. To save the effort of describing each plant in enough detail for a novice to identify it, I've given the Latin names along with the common ones. Should you want to do some searching yourself, it will be easy to find detailed descriptions and illustrations of the plants in a field guide.

Spring:

Wintercress (Barbarea vulgaris and Barbarea verna)

Cowslips, or marsh marigolds (Caltha palustris)

Dandelion greens (Taraxacum officinale)

Wild leeks (Allium tricoccum) and wild garlic (Allium canadense)

Wild asparagras (Asparagras officinalis)

Fiddleheads, or ostrich fern (Matteuccia struthiopteris)

Milkweed sprouts (Asclepias syriaca)

Violets (Viola—any of the various species are good to eat)

Staghorn sumac (Rhus glabra)

Cattail pollen (Typha latifolia)

Summer:

Burdock roots (Arctium lappa)

Milkweed blossoms (Asclepias syriaca)

Pigweed, or lamb's quarters (Chenopodium album)

Pusley, or purslane (Portulaca oleracea)

Wild berries: raspberries, blackberries, black caps, blueberries

Wild grapes

Wild ginger (Asarum canadense)

Watercress (Nasturtium officinale)

Fall:

Hickory nuts (Carya ovata)

Butternuts (Juglans cinerea)

Black walnuts (Juglans nigra)

Morel mushrooms (Morchella esculenta)

Shaggy mane mushrooms (Coprinus comatus)

Puffballs (Lycoperdon and Calvatia—each has several species. Any with white flesh is good to eat.)

* * *

An excellent guidebook and recipe book for those who would like to explore further the idea of gathering food from nature is Stalking the Wild Asparagus *by Euell Gibbons (NY: David McKay, 1962.)*

Members of the Spaziani-Morgia-Alteri families are invited to share a meatless meal in silence each spring in observance of the Feast of St. Joseph, patron saint of Sicily, at the Morgia home in Watertown, Jefferson County. *Varick Chittenden Photo/TAUNY Archives*

WHO
WE ARE

AFRICAN AMERICANS

Walter Cade and Sylvester Harrison volunteer to fry chicken in the basement kitchen of the Thomas African Methodist Episcopal Zion Church in Watertown, Jefferson County, for the annual Southern Fried Chicken Dinner. *Varick Chittenden Photo/TAUNY Archives*

Southern Black Cooking in Watertown

by Varick Chittenden

"When I first married my husband," Odessa Mitchell remembered, "he was used to biscuits every morning, but I'm a northern girl, and I couldn't make biscuits, so he had to eat toast!" That's what she told me when she sat with her husband Frank in their living room in the summer of 1990. "And, " she added, "up here, I never heard of collard greens*. My mother never cooked 'em. She cooked scalloped potatoes and baked macaroni and cheese* and spaghetti. Now Frank never saw spaghetti. We had turkeys at Christmas time, he never had turkey as a kid."

I learned about Frank and Odessa when I went earlier in that June day to the annual fried chicken dinner at the Thomas Memorial African Methodist Episcopal Zion Church, just a few doors away from their home. They had lived for over forty years in a well-kept small house on Morrison Street on Watertown's old north side. At the dinner, everyone told me I must go to see Frank's garden. When I got there, I was amazed by some things I had never before seen growing in the North Country. I needed Frank to guide me through: alongside the neat rows of potato plants, green onions and yellow wax beans were collard greens, okra, turnip greens, and mustard greens. Next to the tomatoes were sprawling young vines that would produce plenty of cantaloupes later that summer. Cabbages were growing where the strawberry crop had flourished a few weeks before. In the middle of it all was a five foot tall scarecrow with a hint of a black face, topped by a bright yellow Kodak baseball cap—Frank's gift from his son-in-law who lives in Rochester. All in all, it was a great sight, and I was in for a very interesting afternoon.

Odessa told me that her great-grandfather, a former slave "somewhere in the South," had raised his family in Barnes Corners. When they moved into the city for work in Watertown's factories, they found a few other black families already there. These families had formed the Young African Christian Association which later became affiliated with the African Methodist Episcopal Zion Church. They had been worshipping in family homes since the 1870's; finally, in 1909 a few of them enjoyed enough prosperity to undertake building a church.

The church was named for Odessa's grandfather, Frank Thomas, a mechanic and brick mason who was instrumental in its construction. It was built of cement bricks made by hand in the backyard of his house on Water Street. Working by the light of lanterns late into each night, Thomas—who was also chairman of the church's board of trustees at the time—and his neighbors and friends hurried to finish the job in time for a cornerstone-laying ceremony that summer.

Frank Mitchell first came to Watertown early in the 1940s, when he was driving trucks loaded with oranges and other fruits and vegetables to deliver to local markets. A native of rural north Florida, he grew up on a "large farm"—eight acres of tenant land—with a big family. They chopped cotton for a living and raised most of their own food. "We had everything but black pepper and flour and sugar. We made our own cane syrup and raised white potatoes, yams, sweet potatoes, everything," Frank explained. They even butchered 25 to 30 pigs each winter and smoked the meat. He loved church back home and soon found the small congregation in Watertown to his liking. He also met Odessa there.

In the forty-plus years since they were married, Frank had done a lot of the cooking at home. "If you had one sister and eight brothers," he joked, "you'd better learn how to cook somethin'. I used to stand right behind my mother's apron strings and watch everything she'd do. She was one of the best; *I* think one of the best." Fried fish, lean ham, peas ("black-eyed peas, butter beans, snap peas, wax beans, any kind"), and corn bread*—the things he grew up with—were some of his favorites. A "boiled dinner of ham, beans, and potatoes served with *real* corn bread", he said, "that is one beautiful meal!" But in Watertown, and in the AME Church in particular, Frank was best known for his fried chicken*. That was from the 1940s to the 60s at least, when the whole Thomas family was involved in the church. Fund-raising was an important volunteer activity for this small congregation and they came up with a fried chicken dinner to help out. Because the black population was so small at the time, many people from other churches and other neighborhoods became regular customers.

Frank always prepared and fried the chicken; his sister-in-law supervised the kitchen; his mother-in-law was in charge of the dining room.

The menu was standard from year to year: a chicken half, dredged in flour seasoned simply with salt and pepper, then fried in hot oil; mashed potatoes and gravy; cole slaw; green beans cooked with ham hocks; baked macaroni and cheese; biscuits with butter; and apple pie. Odessa always baked and served the pies—all forty of them.

When her mother was responsible for the dining room, most of the dinners were served in the church basement. With room for about eighty guests at a time, that was quite a task. Odessa remembered her mother's strict rules for the volunteer servers: white uniforms and aprons, no arguments, and "smile at the people; ask to help them." In those days, as many as five hundred came to several sittings of the meal, often having to wait in line around the edges of the room until their turn came. Odessa remembered, "We used to fill the place, and it was fun."

At the dinner I attended a few years ago, I found that the meal was the same, but many other things were quite different. The little church building was abuzz with activity, but the dining room was not full. In fact, only about a dozen of us actually sat down to eat at the red vinyl cloth-covered tables. Down in the small basement, a regular assembly line of volunteers was packaging the food in styrofoam boxes for takeout. The phone rang frequently, and each time the booming, rich voice of Buster Crabbe greeted the caller and took the order that a volunteer would deliver. I couldn't help overhearing that most callers were living on post at Fort Drum or in military housing developments in nearby towns. Between calls, Buster, a retired Army civilian employee, told us a little about the dinner and the building fund for the church. He also introduced us to the helpers. The menu—advertised around town as "Southern fried chicken with all the trimmings," was about the same as the Mitchells remembered. That day, however, only a handful of workers were actual members of the church. Most were young men from a black Masonic lodge at Fort Drum who had come because a fellow mason, the church's pastor, the Reverend Clate Borders, had invited them to help.

The hub of the activity was the small kitchen. Mrs. Borders was in charge that day. According to Buster, "The Reverend's the Reverend, but his wife is the boss!" Giant, institution-sized pans of boiling oil were tended by Sgt. Sylvester Harrison, a burly fellow from North Carolina and by Walter Cade, a native of Cleveland, Ohio. Stockpots of beans and ham simmered on the kitchen stove, and large pans of mashed potatoes and of macaroni and cheese sat alongside. Mrs. Hattie Welch, a church member in her eighties, was firmly in control of the apple pies.

One of my favorite memories of the day was meeting Walter. As a child in suburban Cleveland, he watched his mother and father prepare all kinds of "Southern food" at home. Ribs, roasts, and sweet potato pie were favorites. And fried chicken was the predictable choice for Sunday dinner. As a young man he had a number of jobs in restaurants and became interested in cooking as a profession. After a false start in engineering college, Walter enrolled in the celebrated Culinary Institute of America, where he trained to be a chef. Following several positions in restaurants, he became a civilian employee of the United States Army and, in 1986, was sent to the newly-expanded Fort Drum's Officers Club to be in charge of food operations. Walter knows food and knows how to serve it.

I was intrigued by his story, and by his presence in the church basement that day. Since American regional foods were back in style in trendy restaurants in the early 90s, I couldn't resist asking him, "If you were featuring 'Southern fried chicken' on the menu of a five-star restaurant today, what would you do differently with today's meal?" His reply: "The only thing that would be different would be the price. I would charge you a little bit more because of the restaurant, but the technique for cooking everything is the same. If you have a good recipe, you stick with it... I'd take my mashed potatoes and pipe them out in a pastry bag on the plate. Then I'd place the fried chicken in the center, take the gravy—or in a five-star restaurant they'd call it the 'sauce'—and drizzle it around the potatoes like a little border, then take the plate and heat it and brown the potatoes in the broiler on the top side. Then I'd place my vegetables and a little garnish like a piece of watermelon, and serve it up. The meal you got for a five dollar donation to the church would be at least twenty dollars in a five- star restaurant. Same meal! That's just the way it is... People eat with their eyes. Nine times out of ten they're gonna think that's the best meal they've ever had!"

The foods in this section were described by the Reverend John Jordan. The actual phrasing of the recipes is from the indicated cookbooks.

Fried Chicken

1 (2½-3 pound) frying chicken	Pepper
¼ cup lemon juice	Paprika
Onion powder	Cayenne, optional
Garlic Powder	Flour
Salt	Vegetable oil for frying

Rinse the chicken and cut it into quarters or smaller pieces. In a large bowl mix the lemon juice with enough water to cover the chicken pieces; soak the chicken in the water for 1 hour. Remove the chicken from the water and season it to taste with the onion powder, garlic powder, salt, pepper, paprika and cayenne. Place the chicken in a plastic bag in the refrigerator overnight—or at least two hours if you are in a hurry.

Mix flour and a little salt in a plastic bag. Shake the chicken pieces in the bag until they are thoroughly coated. Heat ½ to 1 inch of oil in a frying pan. Put the chicken pieces into the hot oil and cook them, covered, for 30 to 40 minutes, turning them so that both sides turn golden brown.

For crispier chicken, remove the lid after the first side has browned.

William and Patricia Carson

This recipe came from *The Smithsonian Folklife Cookbook.*

Barbecued Ribs

Sauce

1 (8-ounce) can tomato sauce	¼ cup firmly packed brown sugar
1 (14-ounce) bottle ketchup	1 onion, sliced thin
2 cups water	1 green pepper, diced
½ cup Louisiana hot sauce	1 lemon, seeded and sliced

Ribs

2 slabs pork ribs (2½-3 pounds each)	1 teaspoon freshly ground pepper
2 teaspoons salt	1½ cups cider vinegar
1½ teaspoons red pepper flakes	

To make the sauce, combine all the ingredients in a medium saucepan. Cover the pan and simmer the sauce over low heat for 45 minutes, stirring occasionally. Refrigerate the sauce in a covered container for 24 hours.

To prepare the ribs, pat them dry with paper towels. In a small bowl combine the salt, red pepper flakes and pepper. Rub both sides of the ribs thoroughly with this mixture, cover them loosely, then refrigerate them overnight.

Place the ribs in a 16 x 11-inch roasting pan and pour the vinegar over them. Bake them in a pre-heated 425 degree oven, turning them two or three times, until they are fork-tender and beginning to come away from the bone (approximately 1 to 1½ hours). Drain off the pan juices. Bake the ribs until they are browned (approximately 25 to 30 minutes more).

Reheat the sauce over low heat and spoon some over the ribs before serving them.

This recipe came from *The Food Lover's Guide to the Real New York.*

Southern Macaroni and Cheese

1	(16-ounce) box macaroni, cooked according to package directions		Garlic, optional
		2	sticks of butter
2	eggs	4	ounces yellow cheddar, shredded
1	teaspoon pepper	4	ounces white cheddar, shredded
2	teaspoons salt		

Drain and rinse the macaroni. Beat the eggs with the salt and pepper, and the garlic if desired. Add the butter and cheeses. Stir the resulting mixture gently, but thoroughly, into the macaroni. Bake in a greased 1½-quart dish at 300 degrees for 30 minutes.

This recipe was served at the SUNY Canton multicultural feast in 1998.

Hoppin' John

1	pound dried black-eyed peas	1	medium onion, peeled but whole
1	2-inch piece (about ¾ pound) fatback	2½	cups long-grain white rice
			Salt and pepper to taste
1½	quarts water		

Wash the peas in cold water. Place the fatback in a large pot of water and boil it over medium heat for about 30 minutes. During this process much of the water will boil away; what remains will be well seasoned with fatback flavor. Add the peas and onion and enough water to cover the peas. Cook on low to medium heat for about 1 hour.

When the peas are soft, season them with salt and pepper, remove the onion, and add the rice. Add more water if necessary to cook the rice (about five cups total is needed). Cook the peas and rice for another 30 minutes.

Anna Gilliard

This recipe came from the *Smithsonian Folklife Cookbook.*

Collard Greens with Ham

6	pounds collard greens, trimmed and coarsely chopped	5	cups water
		2½	teaspoons salt
		½	teaspoon freshly ground pepper
1	meaty ham bone (about 1½ pounds)	2	tablespoons distilled white vinegar

Combine the greens, ham bone, water, salt and pepper in a 5-quart Dutch oven. Bring them to a boil, then reduce the heat and simmer them uncovered for 1½ hours, adding more water if necessary. Remove the ham bone. Shred the meat, discard the skin and bone, and return the meat to the Dutch oven. Stir in the vinegar. Serve seasoned with salt and pepper.

This recipe is from the *Food Lover's Guide to the Real New York.*

Candied Yams

4	pounds (before peeling) fresh yams or sweet potatoes—can also use 6 (17-ounce) cans, drained	¾	cup sugar
		½	teaspoon nutmeg
		1	cup water
		2	teaspoons vanilla
6	tablespoons butter, cut into small pieces		

If you are using fresh yams, peel them, cut them into quarters lengthwise, them boil them for 30 minutes.

In a greased baking dish, gently toss the cooked yams (or drained canned yams) with the butter, sugar and nutmeg until they are thoroughly combined. In a small bowl, mix the water and vanilla; pour them over the yams. Bake them uncovered, basting occasionally, until they are tender (approximately 1½ hours). If you are using canned yams, bake them covered for 45 minutes, then uncovered for 45 more.

This recipe comes from *The Food Lover's Guide to the Real New York.*

Stewed Tomatoes

1	can tomatoes	½	large green pepper, chopped fine
6	heaping tablespoons brown sugar	½	large onion, chopped fine
¾	stick butter		Salt to taste
			Buttered crumbs, optional

Combine all ingredients in a sauce pan. Cook slowly over low to medium heat until the mixture is thick (approximately 1 hour), stirring often to keep it from sticking. If desired, it can be served topped with crumbs and browned in the oven.

Mary Anne Kernan

Hush Puppies

2	cups cornmeal	1	teaspoon baking soda
¼	cup flour	1	egg, lightly beaten
2	teaspoons baking powder	1	cup finely chopped onion
1	teaspoon salt		Vegetable oil for frying
1¼	cups buttermilk		

Combine the cornmeal, flour, baking powder and salt. Combine the soda with the buttermilk. Stir together all the ingredients only until they are well moistened. Heat 1 inch of oil to 370 degrees in a heavy skillet. Drop the batter by teaspoonfuls into the hot oil. Fry the hush puppies until they are golden brown. Drain them on paper towels, then serve immediately.

This recipe comes from *Cooking Texas Style*.

Golden Corn Bread

1	cup flour	¾	cup cornmeal
1	teaspoon salt	2	beaten eggs
3	teaspoons baking powder	1	cup milk
2	tablespoons sugar	½	cup vegetable oil

Sift together the flour, salt, baking powder and sugar. Combine them with the cornmeal. Beat together the eggs, milk and oil; add them to the dry ingredients and stir until the mixture is smooth. Bake in a greased 9-inch square pan at 400 degrees for 20 minutes.

Florence G. Santangini

Sweet Potato Pie

8	large or 10-12 small yams or sweet potatoes, peeled	2	cups sugar
		¼	cup brown sugar
1	stick of butter	1	tablespoon cinnamon
4	eggs	¼	cup condensed milk
¼	cup corn syrup	3-5	unbaked pie shells

Boil the yams until they are soft. While they are hot, mash them with the butter, eggs, syrup, sugar, brown sugar, cinnamon and condensed milk. When everything is well mixed, pour the filling into the pie shells. Bake at 400 degrees for 10 minutes, then reduce the heat to 350 and continue baking until the filling is set (approximately 30 to 35 minutes).

This recipe was served at the SUNY Canton multicultural feast in 1998.

Peach Cobbler

1	cup plus 1 tablespoon sugar	2	teaspoons baking powder
		½	teaspoon baking soda
3	tablespoons cornstarch	½	teaspoon salt
6	tablespoons butter, divided	1¾	cups flour
6	(16-ounce) cans peach halves, drained—reserve ¼ cup syrup	⅓	cup shortening
		¾	cup buttermilk, approximately
2	tablespoons vanilla		

Combine one cup of the sugar with the cornstarch in a small bowl. In a large saucepan, melt 4 tablespoons of the butter with the ¼ cup peach syrup over medium heat; stir in the sugar mixture. Add the peaches, stir until they are well combined, then simmer them over medium heat for 5 minutes. Remove the pan from the heat and stir in the vanilla. Transfer the mixture to a greased 3-quart baking dish, 2¼ inches deep, and let it cool. Cover the dish and let it stand at room temperature at least 6 hours or overnight.

Combine the flour, the remaining tablespoon of sugar, baking powder, baking soda and salt in a medium bowl. Cut in the shortening until the mixture resembles coarse crumbs. With a wooden spoon, gradually stir in just enough buttermilk to moisten the flour. On a lightly floured surface, roll the dough out to ⅜-inch in thickness. Drape it over the peaches and trim it if necessary. Bake the cobbler in a preheated 375 degree oven for 25 minutes. In a small saucepan, melt the remaining 2 tablespoons of butter; brush it over the crust. Continue baking the cobbler until it is golden (approximately 5 to 8 minutes more). Serve it hot or at room temperature.

This recipe is from *The Food Lover's Guide to the Real New York.*

Banana Cake

½ cup shortening
1½ cups sugar
2 large eggs
2 cups flour
¼ teaspoon baking powder
¾ teaspoon baking soda
½ teaspoon salt

1 cup mashed bananas
¼ cup sour milk (add
 ¼ teaspoon vinegar
 to regular milk)
1 teaspoon vanilla
½ cup dates, chopped
½ cup walnuts, chopped

Cream the shortening. Beat in the sugar and eggs. Combine the flour, baking powder, baking soda and salt. Stir them into the shortening mixture with the mixer on low. Beat the batter for two minutes. Continue beating while you add the bananas, milk and vanilla, then the walnuts and dates. Bake in a greased pan in a preheated 350 degree oven for 30 to 35 minutes.

Sandra D. Schofield

It might come as quite a surprise to some, but early census records for Jefferson County indicate that African Americans began to arrive and settle in the North Country as early as the turn of the nineteenth century—about the same time that whites settled in the area. That means the county has had some black residents from its beginning. According to the Office of the County Historian, one Peter Smith, a blacksmith, moved into the town of Champion in 1801. Like his white neighbors, he was a transplant from New England, specifically from Massachusetts.

According to a definitive article about the history of blacks in Jefferson County by John Golden, "Slaves were a large part of the early black population here. Twenty-two enslaved blacks were counted in the 1810 census, half of them in the town of LeRay. That town's aristocratic French namesake, James LeRay de Chaumont, kept three slaves, making him the county's largest slave owner." In fact, Golden adds that James LeRay's children had a monument erected in memory of their black nurse, simply named Rachel, when she died a free woman in 1834. Her grave is in the old LeRaysville cemetery on Fort Drum. During the War of 1812, the population of blacks rose considerably, mostly because of military forces at Madison Barracks in Sackets Harbor.

Almost all the school children in towns along the northern border of New York have vague notions about the Underground Railroad. Usually, they know some tale about an old house in the neighborhood having been a safe haven for blacks who had escaped from slavery in the days leading up to the Civil War and who were headed for sanctuary in Canada. More often than not, the "secret rooms" in the basement or "tunnels" to the barns were root cellars for cold weather vegetable storage or dried-up cisterns for keeping a water supply. Nonetheless, the compromise Fugitive Slave Act of 1850 contributed to a significant movement of southern-born blacks into the North Country. Within the same region, the famed revolutionary John Brown purchased land near Lake Placid and planned to build a colony of freed black men there before he was hanged for his attack on Harper's Ferry. And North Country novelist Irving Bacheller later described his native St. Lawrence County in his Civil War novel *Father Abraham* as "the blackest county in the North," for its fervent abolitionist sentiments.

Census records of the 1870s show that the black population peaked in Jefferson County at over 300, and stayed pretty much that way for nearly a century. Families of skilled tradesmen like barbers or house painters lived in Watertown or, occasionally, in some of the smaller towns scattered through the region. Records show that there was a surprising lack of segregation in daily life, and quite a number of black men married European immigrant women and settled in the area. There were only a few racial incidents reported in local newspapers during that time.

The Thomas Memorial African Methodist Episcopal Zion Church on Morrison Street in Watertown, which started out in 1876 as the Young African Christian Association, was built in 1909. It was home for years to the only black congregation in the region. Then in the mid-1980s, Camp Drum was upgraded to Fort Drum and designated as home to the United States Army's newly re-activated Tenth Mountain Division. The massive buildup which followed brought noticeable changes to area schools, housing developments, and churches. It also brought large numbers of various ethnic groups to the area. A significant percentage of the officers, enlisted men and women, and civilian employees at the Fort have been African Americans.

Churches are a very important part of the black community in the North Country. In 1988 the Reverend John Jordan, a native of Edenton, North Carolina, retired from the Army and started the City of Refuge Christian Church on the border of Fort Drum in Great Bend. Since then several churches attracting and catering to African Americans have been established; most of them are charismatic and fundamentalist. They include the Rose of Sharon Apostolic Church on West Lynde Street in Watertown, the Sweet Haven Holy Church of God in Black River, and the New Hope Church of God in Christ. Some of these churches have already come and gone. The Abundant Life Church of God in Christ, the Paradise Church of God in Christ, and the Cornerstone Apostolic Church have all closed their doors recently. Many of the blacks who are practicing Muslims attend the small mosque on Route 342 in Calcium, on the road between Route 11 and Interstate 81.

As for the observance of traditional African American foodways here, Pastor Jordan recalls that shortly after he arrived at Fort Drum in 1984, he asked about neck bones and ham hocks at the PX and "they didn't know what I meant." Now he says you can find almost anything you could want, not only on base but in supermarkets and stores in the surrounding small towns. "Beans and greens of all kinds, chitlins, yams, and lots more are all over the place now, and you can even find them fresh... That should tell you something."

* * *

This history of African Americans in the North Country was written by Varick Chittenden using information gained from a conversation with the Reverend John Jordan of the City of Refuge Christian Church and from an article by John Golden entitled "Blacks Have Long Had Faith in Watertown" which appeared on page one of the Lifestyles and Leisure section of the Watertown Daily Times *for February 26, 1995.*

AMISH

An Amish teenager sells vegetables all summer long from the family buggy parked along Route 68, Lisbon, St. Lawrence County. *David Duprey Photo/Watertown Daily Times*

An Amish Saturday
Rensselaer Falls

The house, though big enough in its own right, is dwarfed by the huge barn beside it, the unweathered, unfinished wood screaming "new." In fact, the family has just hosted a barn-raising at which they cooked for 300 people. I don't hear all the details of the meal, but I do learn that 40 chickens were involved. The house, too, has an unfinished look to my "English" eyes as we drive up—no curtains dress the windows, no flowers brighten the yard. In fact there are no touches of color anywhere except the blue of the dresses belonging to the five young women in the kitchen and the plain blue wooden cupboard against the kitchen wall. Like the room, its inhabitants are unadorned. Barefoot, they wear solid blue or brown dresses fastened by pins, no buttons or zippers. Each has an apron to protect her clothing from the rigors of house-work and a cap modestly covering her hair.

It is canning day, and bushel cartons of peaches and nectarines are lined up on the floor, awaiting the jars. No adults supervise this massive project—just four young women, the oldest eighteen, the youngest about seven. As if the canning were not enough to keep them occupied, they are also watching a smaller sister and brother, minding the family's baked-goods stand out by the road, doing the lunch dishes for a family of 14 in a metal dishpan with water pumped in the back room, and mopping the floor. Their brothers are in the fields because it is harvest time. Their parents are gone for the day, visiting friends. But no one whines, "It's not faaaair. I wanted to go to the Maaaaall." For one thing, the mall is about a day and a half away by buggy. For another, the electric appliances and brightly patterned clothing one finds there are forbidden by the Ordnung. And finally, that's just how things are—you don't question the system.

Taking up the whole of the front wall of the room is a long table, topped with oilcloth, benches on either side. Normally the family's dining table, it has been pressed into service as a place to fill the canning jars. We are not talking about the puny little pints and half pints that I use to put up my chutney and raspberry jam. These are full gallons—the sort of jars you see in restaurant kitchens. How else could you come up with enough food to satisfy 14 hungry folks, and maybe a guest or two, at every meal? On one wall is the large blue cupboard that holds cookbooks, dishes, and the other necessities of food preparation and serving. Karen and I join the oldest daughter in straight chairs before this cupboard, knives in hand, metal bowls on our laps to catch the pits and any bad spots we cut out of the fruit. We develop a loathing for those little stickers that someone feels obliged to stick onto every single peach and nectarine in the box. I'm sure that, careful as we tried to be about removing them, the family will find many of those little pests floating in their dessert peaches come winter.

Across the room from us is a large woodstove. Next to it is the dry sink with a metal bowl of soapy water sitting in it. No counter space— food preparation happens on the dining table. No food processors, blenders, coffee makers, bread machines, microwaves, or toaster ovens, just a rack with some sharp knives. The walls and the floor are bare; no cushions soften the chairs and benches. Just visible through the doorway on the back wall is a smaller room with the water pump and another bowl for washing hands and two more large woodstoves for cooking. In one, bread is baking for the roadside stand; the aroma is tantalizing.

Outside, Karen's daughter and her friend play with the two smallest Amish children. They have placed the barn kittens in a box and are taking turns "selling" them to each other. The kittens look resigned; perhaps they are used to the game or maybe they have absorbed the Amish philosophy and think "that's just the way we are."

As we chop, we chat. The younger girls are shy—perhaps not used to strangers, perhaps unsure of their English since the family speaks "Dutch" when they are alone together. Their oldest sister is quiet, but friendly. She tells us about her job teaching school. Having graduated from eighth grade, she is considered sufficiently prepared to take on a one-room schoolhouse full of children. She is looking forward to the year, feeling better able to cope now that she has one year's experience. She asks me about my children. When I reply that I have none, she makes no comment, and the conversation moves on. Later, however, she asks how old I am, clearly working on the puzzle of a childless married woman, old enough to have 15 children and at least that many grandchildren, who yet seems content with her lot.

Once the fruit is in its jars, ready for canning, we begin work on 11 peach pies*. The family will eat well tonight! They insist that I shall have a pie as a "thank-you" for helping. While it bakes, we go down to the cellar to see the huge room where the family's food for winter is stored. All four walls have floor-to-ceiling shelves, with jars standing shoulder-to-shoulder on them. A free-standing range of shelves, again floor-to-ceiling, assures that the space in the center of the room is not wasted. Outside, in the basement itself, steam billows from a huge tub in which the family laundry is seething.

A knock on the door heralds the arrival of a group of people seeking quilts. In their "spare" time, the women have created piles of different-sized quilts, each using the solid Amish colors of brown, black, royal blue, red, and green in a different geometric pattern. Karen and I help hold them up, one after another. Suddenly the room is not so bare.

Because the Amish prefer not to thrust themselves into the lime-light, I have refrained from putting names on these recipes.

Peach Pie

Although peaches do not grow in the North Country, Amish fami-lies buy them by the bushel from downstate, then can them and turn them into jam for winter meals. Eager as they are to provision the household for winter, they generally manage to reserve enough to have peach pie for supper on canning day.

1	tablespoon flour	1½	cups slivered peaches
½	cup brown sugar		Cinnamon
1	cup milk or cream	1	unbaked pie crust

Mix the flour, brown sugar and milk. Place the peaches in the crust and pour the milk mixture over them. Sprinkle the cinnamon on top. Bake at 425 degrees for 10 minutes. Lower the heat to 350 degrees and bake until the custard is set (about 30 minutes).

Bean Soup

Members of the Amish community take turns hosting "church" in their homes on Sundays. After a three-hour service, everyone shares a meal prepared by the host family before heading home again. Although the meal is prepared by a different family each time, the menu does not vary within a community. Bean soup is the main dish every Sunday for the Amish of Rensselaer Falls. Along with it they serve bologna*, pickles*, and bread with apple butter* and "church" peanut butter.

2	tablespoons butter	Stale bread, broken into
1	cup cooked navy beans	small pieces
1	quart milk	Salt and pepper to taste

Brown the butter in a large saucepan. Add the beans and the milk and bring the mixture to a boil. Add enough stale bread to soak up most of the milk. Cover the pan and let the soup set for 15 minutes. When serving the soup, stir it only slightly with a dipper to bring the beans up from the bottom of the pan. Add salt and pepper to taste at the table.

Bologna

30	pounds ground meat (beef, pork, venison, or a combination)	2	tablespoons black pepper, ground
		1	tablespoon cayenne pepper
1	pound Morton's Tender Quick salt (a combination of salt, sugar and meat curing chemicals available at Agway)	2	teaspoons saltpeter dissolved in warm water
		1	tablespoon liquid smoke
		1	pound crackers, ground fine
		1	gallon warm water

Grind the meat twice with the Tender Quick, peppers and saltpeter, then let the mixture stand overnight. Add the liquid smoke, the water and the crackers. Mix everything together well and grind again. Pack it into jars and process in a pressure cooker for 1 hour at 10 pounds.

Homemade Croghan Bologna

Should the Amish recipe seem a bit overwhelming in size, this one—based on the famous sausage made by the Swiss-Germans in Croghan, New York—will give a more manageable taste of homemade sausage.

2	pounds ground chuck	2	tablespoons Morton's
1	cup water		Tender Quick salt (a
1	teaspoon onion powder (or		combination of salt, sugar
	more to taste)		and meat curing chemi-
1	teaspoon garlic powder (or		cals—available at Agway)
	more to taste)	1½-2	teaspoons liquid smoke

Mix the water, onion powder, garlic powder, salt and liquid smoke. Add the ground chuck and mix again. Allow the mixture to stand 24 hours in the refrigerator. Mix it once more, then form it into two logs. Bake the logs at 300 degrees for 1 hour and 15 minutes on a rack so that the fat can drain off.

Nancy Shea
South Colton

Sandwich Spread

6	onions	2	quarts water
6	cucumbers	1	pint prepared mustard
6	green tomatoes	5	cups sugar
6	red peppers	1	cup flour
6	green peppers	1	cup vinegar
2	tablespoons salt	1	teaspoon turmeric

Grind the first six ingredients together and let them stand for 2 hours. Add the water and boil the mixture for 15 minutes. Add the remaining ingredients and cook 5 more minutes. Put into hot jars and seal.

Cider Apple Butter

This recipe gives a sense of the scale of Amish cooking. Since families often have 10 or more children, it is necessary to put up vast quantities of food for the long North Country winters.

30	gallons cider	5	gallons corn syrup
6	bushels apples	48	pounds white sugar

Assuming that most readers of this book will not be cooking on an Amish scale, here is a slightly diminished but authentically Amish recipe which will produce about 4 pints. To be traditional, the apple butter must be made in a copper kettle and stirred with a wooden paddle.

16	medium apples (about 6 pounds)	1½	pounds sugar
2	quarts water	1	teaspoon ground cinnamon
1½	quarts apple cider	1	teaspoon ground allspice
		1	teaspoon ground cloves

Wash and cut the apples into small pieces (there should be about 4 quarts). Cover them with the water and boil until they are soft. Press them through a sieve to remove the skins and seeds. Bring the cider to a boil, then add the apple pulp and the sugar. Cook until the mixture thickens, stirring to prevent scorching. Stir in a mixture of the spices and cook until the apple butter is thick enough for spreading. (When it starts to thicken, test it by cooling a small amount on a plate, as the finished product will be thicker after it has cooled.) Pour into sterilized jars and seal.

Pennsylvania Dutch People's Cookbook
Edited by Claire Davidow and Ann Goodman

13-Day Sweet Pickles

7	pounds medium-sized green cucumbers	1	gallon vinegar
	Water to cover cucumbers	1	tablespoon celery seed
	Salt—1 cup per gallon of cucumbers	1	cinnamon stick
	Alum—½ tablespoon per gallon of cucumbers	1	tablespoon whole allspice
		6	cups white sugar

Days 1-7: Soak cucumbers in salt water.

Day 8: Drain salt water. Cover cucumbers with boiling water.

Day 9: Drain and slice the cucumbers into rings. Cover with boiling water and add the alum.

Day 10: Drain cucumbers. Cover with boiling water.

Day 11: Drain cucumbers. Bring to a boil the vinegar, celery seed, cinnamon, allspice and sugar. Pour this mixture over the cucumbers while it is hot.

Day 12: Drain the liquid from the cucumbers, bring it to the boil again and pour it back over the cucumbers.

Day 13: Drain the liquid from the cucumbers. Bring it to a boil, then put the cucumbers back into the liquid. When the mixture returns to boiling, can the pickles.

Grape Nuts

Reluctant to buy "English" prepared food, the Amish make their own breakfast cereal. A non-Amish acquaintance told me that when she eats with her Amish friends this is the quintessential breakfast.

6	cups graham flour	2	teaspoons baking soda
2	cups brown sugar		Salt to taste
4	cups buttermilk		

Mix the ingredients together to form a dough. It will be thick and hard to stir. Bake it like a cake in a greased pan [350 degrees for 30 minutes in a loaf pan]. Cool the loaf, cut it into small pieces, and pass them through a sieve until they are finely crumbled. Toast the grape nuts in the oven until they are crispy. Store the cereal in an airtight jar when it is cold.

At Christmas the Amish make large amounts of candy to share with visitors. The following two recipes are Amish Christmas treats.

Coconut Bonbons

9	tablespoons sugar	3	cups flaked coconut
6	tablespoons corn syrup	1	(12-ounce) bag semi-sweet
1	teaspoon vanilla		chocolate chips
½	cup water	½	bar paraffin
2	teaspoons margarine		

Combine the sugar, corn syrup, vanilla, water and margarine in a heavy saucepan. Bring them to a boil and cook, stirring constantly, to the soft ball stage (238 degrees on a candy thermometer). Stir in the coconut and drop spoonfuls of the mixture onto a sheet of waxed paper. When the coconut balls have cooled, melt the chips and the paraffin together, then dip the balls into the chocolate mixture, using two toothpicks to hold them while you dip. Replace them on the waxed paper until they have hardened.

Peanut Brittle

1	cup corn syrup	2	cups raw peanuts
1	cup white sugar	1	teaspoon butter
1	cup water	2	teaspoons baking soda

Place the sugar, corn syrup and water in a heavy saucepan. Bring them to a boil and cook them to the soft ball stage (238 degrees). Add the peanuts and butter. Cook until the mixture is golden brown—8 minutes or so. Remove from the heat and immediately add the soda. Working quickly, pour the mixture onto a jelly roll pan (15 x 10-inches) that has been lined with greased foil wrap and spread it out to a thin layer. When it has cooled and hardened, break it into pieces and store it in an airtight container.

Egg Noodles

When the Amish make soup they begin by making their own noodles. These are not really much work, and they taste so much fresher than the ones from the grocery that they are well worth the extra time.

6	dozen egg yolks		A little oil
1	cup water, approximately		Flour to make a stiff dough

The Amish recipe is a bit vague about amounts so here is a more usable version of the local recipe from Marcia Adams' Cooking from Quilt Country: Hearty Recipes from Amish and Mennonite Kitchens. *New York: Clarkson Potter, 1998.*

1	cup bread flour	3	tablespoons water
¾	teaspoon salt		Bread flour for rolling and
1	egg		dusting
1	tablespoon vegetable oil		

Put the flour into a bowl and make a well in the center of it. Put the salt, egg, oil, and water into this well, then stir the mixture with a fork until a ball of dough forms. Knead the dough on a lightly floured board until it is smooth (approximately 5 minutes). Add more water sparingly, only if absolutely necessary. Cover the dough with a tea towel for 45 minutes.

Cut the dough in half. Roll out each half very thin (about a 14 x 8-inch rectangle) on a piece of newspaper. Let it dry for 20 to 30 minutes, flipping it over at some time during the process to dry the other side.

Roll each piece of dough up like a jelly roll, starting from the short side. Cut the noodles to your preferred width with a very sharp knife. Unroll each slice onto the newspaper, sprinkle it with a bit more flour, and let it finish drying completely (a day or so, depending on the humidity in the air and the moisture in the flour).

Compared to other groups in the North Country, the Amish are newcomers. In the mid-1970s, lured by the large amounts of relatively inexpensive land in this area, two Amish communities moved to St. Lawrence County from Ohio—one settling near Norfolk, the other in the vicinity of Heuvelton, Rensselaer Falls and DePeyster. Today horses hitched to black buggies and tethered to the light poles are as common a sight as Ford mini-vans in the Canton Jubilee parking lot, though high taxes and distance from extended families have in the meantime caused a number of the Norfolk Amish to move away again.

The path these people traveled to upstate New York began in 16th-century Switzerland at the time of the Protestant Reformation. A group arose who believed that the church should consist of a body of adults who signified their voluntary choice of their religion by baptism and who separated themselves from the worldly society and the political state around them, committing themselves to the discipline and fellowship of their co-believers and following a peaceful, non-violent way of life. They acquired the name "Anabaptists" for their practice of rebaptizing church members once they had reached adulthood and were old enough to choose a way of life for themselves.

Persecuted by their neighbors, they suffered the loss of many of their leaders. One who survived was Menno Simons, a Dutch priest who helped unify the scattered Anabaptists so successfully that they came to be called Mennonites. In 1693 a young Swiss named Jacob Amman, fearing that the Mennonite church was losing its purity, left to found his own church. His followers, the Amish, believed that those who broke with any of the tenets of their religion should be shunned by other church members in order to protect the standards of the group and to bring the erring member back into compliance. Each Amish community is guided by a detailed list of rules called the "Ordnung," which dictates everything from how its members fasten their clothes to whether or not they place orange triangle reflectors on the backs of their buggies when they travel at night. Members of the Norfolk community live by a different Ordnung from that of the DePeyster community, and to them that creates as big a gulf as that between them and the "English," as they call their non-Amish neighbors.

Once one understands the desire of the Amish to separate themselves from the worldly society around them, it is easy to understand most of their best-known and most characteristic traits. They dress in plain clothes of solid colors without ornament of any kind, not only to distinguish themselves from the "English," but just as importantly to unify their own community and to avoid setting themselves in any way apart from the other Amish around them. They live without electricity rather than link themselves to a wider society whose standards are not theirs. They maintain their own schools so that they can teach children the things that are important to their community— reading, writing, arithmetic, and religious beliefs—without distraction from worldly subjects and classmates with different values. They prefer to take care of their own members within their community, so they neither pay into Social Security nor draw on it. Similarly, they buy neither homeowners' nor medical insurance, relying instead on their community to help replace a burned-down house or raise money to pay hospital bills.

Those outside the community are sometimes tempted to dismiss the Amish as "quaint" or "backward." But the ice storm of 1998 caused many "English" citizens of the North Country to reconsider, when their Amish neighbors generously stopped by to share their knowledge of how to hand-milk cows and chop wood. Is our society so much preferable? Like the Amish we seek personal fulfillment and a sense of meaning, in addition to food, shelter, and health, but we often do it without the help of extended families or close neighbors, the strong sense of who we are and what we believe, and the connection to the natural world that help support the Amish in their search.

ARMENIAN
AMERICANS

Several generations of the extended Bogosian family come together
for a combined American and Armenian Thanksgiving feast,
Massena, St. Lawrence County. *Mark Sloan Photo/TAUNY Archives*

Armenian Feasts

by Capril Serabian, Nevart Bogosian and Sebouh Bogosian

as told to Lynn Ekfelt

Easter is the biggest Armenian holiday. Normally, the Armenian Church would celebrate it at a different time from the Roman Catholics, but we celebrate at the same time as the Americans because that's when our families can get home. We all get together and have a big feast. We start out with appetizers—cheese boereg*, black olives, cheese, stuffed grape leaves*, and mixed pickles*. Then we have okra stew with lamb* and chicken pilaf*. We have chicken pilaf every Sunday except in the summer when we make shish kebab every weekend. By the way, there are two kinds of pilaf you can make—one with rice and one with bulghur. It's always best the next day after the flavors have mingled. There's salad and a special Easter bread*, then we have paklava or kadayif* and holiday cookies called kurabia* along with demitasse coffee.

We always dye Easter eggs, but we don't use the colored dyes from the store. Instead we dye them with onion skins. They give a nice deep brownish-red color. On the Easter dinner table there's always a bowl of colored eggs; we play a game with them. Everybody takes one, then turns to his neighbors and hits his egg against theirs. The person whose egg cracks first has to give it to the other. Finally, one person is left as winner with a big pile of everyone else's eggs in front of him. Sometimes we even go house-to-house on Easter, cracking eggs with our neighbors and friends.

In the summer we always used to go to the Bogosians' camp at Massena Point. Sebouh's father would make shish kebabs* for everyone—sometimes as many as 40 people. It gave people something special to do on weekends. He'd cook the kebabs over applewood embers, never over a flame. We'd also have jajik*—that's really refreshing on a hot day—and tahn* to drink. When my dad got home after working all day in the hot factory, he'd always sit on the step and drink a big glass of tahn to cool off.

Capril Serabian, architect, and Sebouh Begosian, retired owner of a dry-cleaning business, were both born in Massena. Nevart Begosian came to Massena from Greece as a young woman. She owned a gift shop before her retirement.

The dishes in this section were described to me in detail by Capril Serabian and Sebouh and Nevart Bogosian. Actual recipes came from their two favorite Armenian cookbooks—both listed in the bibliography, except as indicated.

Cheese Boeregs

2 eggs	¼ cup finely chopped parsley, optional
8 ounces small-curd cottage cheese, drained; or Muenster cheese, grated	Phyllo dough as needed, about 8 sheets per cup of filling
4 ounces freshly grated feta cheese	Melted butter
Salt to taste	

Place the eggs in a mixing bowl and beat them slightly. Add the cheeses and salt; blend well. Mix in the parsley. Cut the phyllo sheets into quarters lengthwise. Cover them with a dampened towel to prevent their drying out. Brush two strips with melted butter and place one on top of the other, buttered sides up. Place about a tablespoon of the cheese mixture on a bottom corner and fold over to form a triangle. Continue folding in triangles the length of the strip. Brush the seam with melted butter to seal it. Place the triangle, seam side down, on a greased baking sheet. Repeat this process with the remaining strips and filling. Brush the tops of the triangles with melted butter. Bake at 350 degrees until golden brown (approximately 15 to 20 minutes).

Derevi Sarma (Stuffed Grape Leaves)

1   cup uncooked rice
4   cups onions, chopped fine
1   cup olive oil
1   tablespoon fresh dill, finely
     chopped (or 1 tablespoon
     dried dill)
¼   cup pine nuts

Lemon juice to make tart
(about 5 tablespoons),
divided
2   cups water
60-80 fresh, tender grapevine
     leaves, depending on
     size (or a 1 pound jar of
     preserved leaves)
     Lemon wedges for
     garnish

Combine the rice, onions, olive oil, dill, pine nuts and 2 tablespoons of lemon juice in a bowl until well mixed. Adjust the seasonings if desired.

Soak fresh grapevine leaves in boiling, salted water for two minutes to soften them, then rise them under cold water. (If you are using preserved leaves, rinse them in hot water to remove the brine.) Drain the washed leaves on paper towels.

Cover the bottom of a heavy casserole with 10 of the leaves to prevent the derevi sarma from burning. For each remaining leaf, remove the stem, and spread the leaf on a plate, stem end toward you, dull side up. Place about 1 teaspoon (more for large leaves) of the rice mixture near the stem end. Fold the stem end over the stuffing, then fold over the sides to enclose the stuffing securely. Beginning at the stem end, roll the grape leaf firmly away from you toward the tip, forming a little cylinder.

Layer the stuffed leaves, seam sides down, close together in rows in the casserole. Sprinkle with the remaining lemon juice and cover with the water. Gently place an inverted plate over the top to keep the stuffed leaves in place while they cook. Bring the leaves to a boil over moderate heat, reduce the heat to low, cover and simmer until the stuffing is very tender—about 50 minutes to an hour—adding more water if necessary. After the grape leaves have cooked, keep the plate on them while they cool. This will prevent them from discoloring. Serve chilled, garnished with lemon wedges.

Nevart Bogosian
Massena

Titvash (Mixed Pickles)

1	small head cauliflower, broken into rosettes	2	large cloves garlic, peeled and halved
4	tiny cucumbers	2	one-inch pieces hot red pepper, optional
4	green tomatoes	4	fresh dill sprigs
2	sweet green or yellow peppers, quartered, seeded, and de-ribbed	4	cups water
		1	cup cider vinegar
		¼	cup salt (not iodized)

Wash the vegetables and dill. Fill two sterilized quart jars with the mixed vegetables. To each jar, add a clove of garlic, 2 dill sprigs and a piece of hot pepper if desired. In a saucepan, bring the water, vinegar and salt to a boil. Pour the boiling liquid over the vegetables in the jars to cover them completely. Seal the jars tightly and store them in a cool place. The pickles will be ready to eat in 4 weeks.

Missov Bami (Lamb and Okra Stew)

1	pound baby tender okra	2	large onions, finely chopped
3-4	tablespoons freshly squeezed lemon juice, divided	4	medium ripe tomatoes, peeled and chopped
3	tablespoons butter	2	cups hot beef broth
1	pound boneless lamb, trimmed of excess fat and cut into 1-inch cubes		Salt and freshly-ground pepper to taste

Wash the okra and remove the stem by cutting the thin, cone-shaped skin off the top, being careful not to make any opening at this end to prevent the sticky juice from running out. Put the okra into a bowl as you peel it, sprinkling it with salt and 2 tablespoons of lemon juice. Shake the bowl once or twice to mix it well.

In a heavy casserole, melt the butter over moderate heat. Add the lamb and sauté it until it is lightly browned on all sides, stirring frequently. Add the onions and sauté five minutes more, continuing to stir. Add the tomatoes, salt, pepper and broth. Cover and cook the stew over low heat for 45 minutes or until the meat is almost tender, adding more broth if necessary. Stir in the okra. Cover the pan and simmer for 30 minutes, or until the meat and okra are tender. Add the remaining lemon juice 15 minutes before the end.

Havov Pilav (Chicken Pilaf)

1	(3-pound) chicken, cut into serving pieces	2	large onions, finely chopped
¼	cup butter	1	(six-ounce) can tomato paste
⅛	teaspoon cinnamon		
⅛	teaspoon allspice	1	cup cold water
	Salt and freshly ground black pepper to taste	2	cups boiling chicken broth
		1	cup uncooked long-grain white rice

Dry the chicken with paper towels. In a large, heavy skillet melt the butter over moderate heat. Add the chicken, cinnamon, allspice, salt and pepper, and sauté, turning the pieces so that they brown evenly on all sides. Add the onions and cook until they are lightly browned. Mix the tomato paste with the water, then add them to the chicken mixture. Cover the pan and simmer until chicken is tender. Add the broth and stir in the rice. Cover the pan and simmer 20 minutes or until the rice is done.

Cheoreg (Easter Bread)

1	package active dry yeast dissolved in ¼ cup warm water (110 degrees)	1½	teaspoons ground mahlab (ground black cherry kernels—available from specialty spice stores)
1¼	cups lukewarm milk		
2	eggs, beaten	1½	teaspoons baking powder
1	cup lukewarm melted butter	6	cups all-purpose flour
¼	cup sugar	1	egg, beaten (for brushing the top)
1	teaspoon salt		Sesame seeds (optional)

Put the dissolved yeast in a large bowl. Add the milk, eggs, melted butter, sugar, salt, mahlab and baking powder; mix well. Stir in the flour, a little at a time, until a soft dough is formed. Turn it out onto a lightly floured surface and knead until it is smooth—three or four minutes. Place the dough in a lightly oiled bowl, and grease the top lightly. Cover the bowl with a clean dish towel and let the dough rise in a warm place about 2 hours or until doubled in bulk.

Punch down the dough and place it on a lightly floured surface. Divide it into two balls. Cut each ball into three slices. Roll each slice into a rope and make two braids, using three ropes in each. Place each braid on a greased cookie sheet. Cover the sheets and let the braids rise in a warm place until they are almost doubled in bulk—another hour or so. Brush the tops of the braids with beaten egg and sprinkle with sesame seeds. Bake in a preheated 350 degree oven until golden brown (approximately 20 minutes).

Tell Kadayif

Pastry
3   tablespoons sugar
1½ cups finely chopped walnuts
1½ teaspoons cinnamon
1   cup melted butter

1   pound kadayif (Long strands of very thin pastry dough, resembling shredded wheat—available from Middle Eastern and Greek specialty shops. Also available at the Potsdam Co-op)—defrosted if frozen

Syrup
1½ cups sugar
¾   cup water

1   teaspoon freshly squeezed lemon juice
1   tablespoon honey

Combine the 3 tablespoons of sugar well with the nuts and cinnamon in a small bowl. Loosen the shreds of kadayif, removing the coarse particles of dough. Sprinkle ¾ cup of the melted butter over the dough and blend gently with your hands until the strands are evenly coated. Arrange half of the kadayif in a buttered 9 x 13-inch pan and spread the nut mixture evenly over it. Cover it with the remaining dough and press it very lightly to smooth the top. Brush the top with the remaining ¼ cup of melted butter. Bake at 350 degrees for 45 minutes.

While the kadayif is baking, prepare the syrup. Combine the syrup ingredients in a small pan. Cook them over medium heat until the sugar dissolves, stirring constantly. Bring the mixture to a boil, then reduce the heat and simmer it, uncovered, for about 15 minutes or until it registers 220 degrees on a candy thermometer. Keep it warm until you are ready to put it on the kadayif.

Remove the kadayif from the oven and immediately pour the syrup evenly over it. Cover the pan and let it stand for 15 minutes. It can be served warm or cold, cut into squares and topped with whipped cream.

Kurabia

1	pound butter	1	ounce whiskey or brandy
2	cups confectioners' sugar		(optional) or use ½
3	cups flour		teaspoon vanilla or
			almond extract
			Blanched almond halves

Remove the salt and water from the butter by heating it in a double boiler over a low fire. Once the butter is melted, allow it to cool, then remove the top foam which is the salt. Use the hardened butter, leaving the water at the bottom.

Cream the butter with the sugar. Add the flour gradually until the mixture becomes pliable. Roll into round balls about 1½ inches in diameter, or form into small crescents or S-shapes. Top each with a blanched almond. Bake at 300 degrees until almonds are browned (approximately 20 minutes). Cool the cookies slightly, then sift confectioners' sugar over them to cover them completely.

Tahn (Chilled Yoghurt Drink)

On hot summer days Mr. Bogosian's father came home from work at Alcoa, plopped down on the step, and inhaled a tall glass of this refreshing drink.

1 cup unflavored yogurt	Salt to taste
½-1½ cups ice-cold water,	Ice cubes
depending on how thick	
a drink you want	

Place the yoghurt in a deep bowl and stir until it is smooth. Gradually beat in the water until it is well blended. Add the salt and mix it in well. (Or put the yoghurt, water and salt in a blender and blend until they are smooth.) Serve this drink well chilled, over ice cubes.

Shish Kebab (Barbecued Lamb)

2 pounds boneless leg of lamb—trimmed of fat and gristle and cut into 1½-inch cubes
2 large onions, quartered and separated into strips
2 medium green peppers, quartered, seeded and deribbed
2 large tomatoes, quartered

¼ cup olive oil
2 tablespoons Chianti or other dry red wine
1½ tablespoons freshly squeezed lemon juice
1 large clove garlic, finely chopped
1 teaspoon dried oregano leaves
1 bay leaf
Salt and pepper to taste

Place the lamb, onions, green peppers and tomatoes in a deep bowl. Combine the remaining ingredients and pour them over the lamb and vegetables. Turn the pieces until they are well coated with the marinade. Cover the bowl and let it stand about 6 hours in the refrigerator, turning the chunks occasionally.

Remove the lamb from the marinade and thread the cubes on long skewers, leaving a few inches bare at each end. String the vegetables on separate skewers, since the cooking time for them varies. Broil in the oven or over applewood embers (not a flame) until they have browned evenly on all sides, turning them frequently and basting with the marinade. (Broil for 15 to 20 minutes, depending on how well done you like the meat.) Since the vegetables will cook more quickly than the meat, remove them and keep them warm until the lamb is ready. To serve, push the meat and vegetables off the skewers onto individual plates. Serve with rice or bulghur pilaf.

Jajik (Cucumber and Yoghurt Salad)

8 pickling cucumbers, sliced into ¼-inch coins, or 2 regular cucumbers
1 clove garlic

¼ teaspoon salt
1 teaspoon dried mint
1 tablespoon olive oil
2 cups unflavored yoghurt

If you use regular cucumbers, chop them into small pieces and sprinkle them with salt. Squeeze them; wash out the salt, then proceed.

Mash the salt and garlic to a smooth paste. Combine with the mint, olive oil and yoghurt. Stir in the cucumbers and taste for seasoning. Serve chilled.

Nevart Bogosian
Massena

Armenia is reckoned the first Christian nation, having adopted Christianity in 301 A.D. (The Armenian Church developed independently from both the Roman Catholic and the Greek Orthodox, though it is an Eastern-rite church.) It reached its highest point as an empire from 95 to 55 B.C. At that point it was conquered by Rome; later it became part of the Ottoman Empire. Although Armenians were always at a disadvantage among their Muslim neighbors because of their religion, they found a niche as merchants and financiers, and many managed to become successful and quite wealthy.

By the close of the nineteenth century, Turkey's empire was beginning to crumble. The loss of Romania, Serbia, Bulgaria, and Montenegro raised specters of financial ruin. Sultan Abdul Hamid II took out his frustration on the religious minorities within his borders, and by 1896 more than 200,000 Armenians had been massacred. In 1908 the Sultan was deposed by a group calling themselves the "Young Turks," who promised a new secular nationalism and an end to the old theocracy. Relieved Armenians eagerly helped bring to power this group, which seemed to offer the hope of a return to peaceful co-existence.

Sadly, for the Armenians this new regime proved worse than the old one. Convinced that the only way to regain the empire's past glory was to become racially pure, the party adopted the slogan "Turkey for the Turks." They began to demonize minorities, portraying them as a threat to national security, and demanded that all businesses fire any Greek, Armenian, or Jewish workers. Finally, on April 19, 1915, an edict went out demanding the extermination of the Armenians and threatening death for any Muslim protecting a Christian.

The official stance was that the Armenians were to be "relocated" outside the Turkish borders. Between April and October of 1915, 1,200,000 people set out from thousands of villages to walk to Syria; over half of them never arrived. Many were killed on the way by the Turkish gendarmes escorting them, by Kurdish tribesmen, by the peasants in the villages they passed through, and by convicts released from prison for that express purpose by the Turkish government. Many others starved or died of thirst on the trail.

As the plans of the Young Turks became clear to the Armenians, many saw the handwriting on the wall. From 1909 on, it became common for the eldest son to emigrate to a country where he could make money, then send for the rest of the family. Many of these young men found their way to America, "the land of opportunity." They passed through Ellis Island, then found themselves in Grand Central Station, where loud-speakers advertised jobs open at the ends of the rail lines.

The Alcoa plant in Massena was one of those industries vying for the services of new immigrants. Soon there were 250 Armenians in the city. A special boarding house just for Armenian men was built on the corner of Willow Street. There were three shifts of men per day at the factory. These men took turns sleeping in the dormitory beds and cooking in the basement. Men with families often shared duplex houses with other Armenians. As time went by, some were able to leave the hard factory life and open businesses for themselves, echoing their tradition as merchants in their homeland. At one point there were eleven Armenian groceries and four dry cleaners in Massena.

Over the years the community has shrunk and those of Armenian descent have melted into the Massena community. Still, the Massena library has one of the finest collections of Armenian literature to be found in any American city of its size, and on Sundays you can walk past certain houses and smell the tantalizing aroma of chicken pilaf cooking.

FRENCH
AMERICANS

"Jacques la Tête," mascot of the Lumberjack Inn in Tupper Lake, Franklin County, represents the French American woodsmen heritage at Rotary meetings and wedding receptions, as well as for regular diners. Made by Gaile Colbert, Norwood, St. Lawrence County. *Varick Chittenden Photo, from* The Hidden Heritage/L'Héritage caché

French American Christmas Season

by Madeleine Gray

*as told to Lynn Ekfelt and to the production staff of TAUNY's
radio program "Home Cooking"*

We were the only ones of our family here in this country, so Christmas was really only our immediate family. Of course we would see our friends and neighbors at Mass and so on, but the family celebrated pretty much by itself. Meat pie, or tourtière*, was traditionally served after Midnight Mass. Any French American you speak with always associates the smell of the meat pies* coming home from church with Christmas; that was what you were going to eat when you got back from mass. The recipes are regional, pretty much. My family used pure pork and spices—that's all, pork and spices. A lot of people add mashed potato or add ground beef, but we used pure ground pork. My Grandmother used to save the fresh hams, because she felt that was the only part of the pig that was worthy of the Christmas meat pies.

For us Christmas was an important religious holiday, but New Year's was the time we really had the big party. We usually left for Québec a couple of days before New Year's, because my father had five sisters, and we were supposed to visit each one. We stayed overnight different places, awaiting the big feast on New Year's. That was held at my grandmother's house (it's an old stone farmhouse; it's still there—my uncle lives there) and we had at least eighty people. There were maybe thirty-two of us who were first cousins. Because we lived in America, Santa came to us on Christmas like he did to our American neighbors, but he came to our French Canadian cousins at New Year's. Our parents told us, "Santa is so busy it takes him a week to make the rounds."

New Year's was a big party with singing and dancing. And I remember particularly the food. My aunts had cooked for days. There was a room we called the bas-côte. It was an unheated room. It was all stone walls; it was outside the kitchen, and all the food was put out there. I remember that they had all these different things they had cooked. There was always ragoût* with the meatballs and the hocks. There was roast goose. There was chicken pie. There was a suckling pig, roasted in the wood stove, with an apple in its mouth. There was pâté de foie gras and head cheese* on crusty bread. The baker made miniature crusty loaves just for New Year's. My aunts made desserts and candies for weeks. The pastries were kept on this long table. We had sugar pies* and mokas*. It was quite a sight to behold for us children when we saw that array of food.

They always had a Yule Log*. My aunts always brought it in on a fancy platter and everyone had to admire it, then they put it in the center of the dessert table. The Yule Log was a white cake almost like a sponge cake. It was made in a thin pan, then rolled with a filling while it was warm. It had chocolate icing that my aunts used to scrape with a fork to make it look like bark and decorate it with green leaves and holly berries. They always cut a piece to make a stump sticking out as if someone had chopped a branch off of it. I remember being very intrigued with that Yule Log...Bûche de Noël.

Fifty miles was a long way then, so we stayed on a few days—until the Feast of the Kings on January 6. That day we had another big meal with lots of singing and dancing. There were fiddlers. My uncles were singers, so they sang French rounds. There were two special cakes— the ladies had a pea baked in theirs; the men had a bean. Whoever got the pieces with the pea and the bean got to be king and queen and got waited on for the evening.

Madeleine Gray is from Helena, near Massena, where she and her husband ran a general store. She was born in Massena, but her parents came from Valleyfield, Québec.

Although tourtière for the holidays is a given, the exact recipe is not. Here are two versions, quite different but equally authentic—both have been passed down for generations in the donors' families.

Tourtière (Meat Pie)

1¼	pounds ground pork	1	teaspoon ground cinnamon
¼	teaspoon savory		(or to taste)
1	teaspoon ground cloves (or	1	onion, minced
	to taste)		Salt and pepper
			Pastry for a two-crust pie

Mix all the filling ingredients and simmer them gently in a heavy pot. Cook, stirring often, until the meat loses its pink color. Do not overcook! Let the mixture cool to lukewarm, then pour it into the prepared crust. Cover it with the top crust and bake at 350 degrees until the pastry is golden (approximately 45 minutes.)

Madeleine Gray
Helena

Grandma's New Year Pork Pie (Tourtière)

2	pounds ground pork (lean shoulder or butt)	2	potatoes (approximately), mashed (or you can use
2	medium onions, chopped		the equivalent amount of
	Garlic to taste		instant) if needed
1	teaspoon ginger		Pastry for a two-crust pie
1	teaspoon sage		(10-inch)
	Salt and pepper		

Brown the meat, onion and garlic. Cover them with water (probably about a cup), then add the ginger and sage. Reduce the heat and simmer the mixture until it is cooked and most of the liquid has evaporated. Cool it overnight, then remove the fat that has solidified on the top of the dish. Stir in enough mashed potato to absorb any excess liquid. Add the salt and pepper. Place the meat mixture in your favorite pie crust and bake it at 350 degrees until the top crust is golden brown.

Beulah White sometimes also adds ¼ teaspoon of cloves and ¼ teaspoon of cinnamon to the rest of the spices.

Beulah White
Canton

Ragoût de Boulettes et de Pattes de Cochon
(Stew of Meat Balls and Pig Hocks)

4	tablespoons fat, divided in half	¼	teaspoon cloves
		¼	teaspoon nutmeg
3	pig hocks		Salt and pepper
2	pounds ground pork		Flour for rolling the meat-
1	clove garlic, minced		balls
1	onion, minced	½	cup flour, browned
½	teaspoon cinnamon	½	cup water
¼	teaspoon dry mustard		

Melt 2 tablespoons of the fat in a heavy kettle and brown the pig hocks. Cover the hocks with water and simmer two hours. To the ground pork add the garlic, onion, cinnamon, mustard, cloves, nutmeg, salt and pepper. Mix everything together well and form into meatballs. Roll the balls in flour and brown them in the remaining fat. Add the meatballs to the pig hocks and simmer another hour. (You can remove the bones from the hocks before adding the meatballs.) Mix the browned flour with the water until it forms a smooth paste. Stir the paste into the broth to thicken it.

Madeleine Gray
Helena

Tête Fromagée Sans Tête
(Head Cheese without Head)

4	pork hocks		Garlic to taste
1	onion, studded with 6 whole cloves		Salt and pepper
		2	pounds pork shoulder
1	tablespoon cinnamon	½	cup red wine

Clean the hocks and cover them with water. Add the onion/cloves, cinnamon, garlic, salt and pepper to the hocks. Add the pork shoulder and simmer until the meat detaches from the bones. Remove the meat and cut it into small pieces. Strain the broth; add the meat pieces and the red wine to it. Return it to the heat. Verify the seasonings. Rinse the molds you plan to use (gelatin molds, loaf pans, etc.) with cold water. Fill the molds with the mixture and put them in the refrigerator until the mixture has set. Serve on crusty bread.

Madeleine Gray
Helena

Bûche de Noël (Yule Log)

1	cup sugar	½	teaspoon salt
2	eggs, slightly beaten	2	tablespoons butter
1	teaspoon flavoring (almond is my favorite)	½	cup hot milk Confectioners' sugar
1	cup cake flour		Cranberry jelly
2	teaspoons baking powder		

Add the sugar to the eggs and beat them thoroughly; add the flavoring. Sift the flour with the baking powder and salt; add them to the egg mixture and mix well. Melt the butter into the milk. Add the milk mixture to the flour mixture and beat until they are smooth. Pour batter into an 11 x 16-inch greased jelly-roll pan lined with waxed paper. Bake in a moderately hot oven (375 degrees) for 10 to 15 minutes.

Immediately after removing the pan from the oven, turn out the cake onto a towel spread with confectioners' sugar. Remove the waxed paper and cut any crisp edges off the cake. Spread the cake with cranberry jelly and roll it into a log shape. The cut-off ends can be formed to simulate stumps of branches cut off the log.

Note by Madeleine Gray: The log can be frosted with any good chocolate fudge frosting. Drag fork tines through the frosting to make it look like bark. We usually mix some powdered sugar with a little milk and swirl it around on the ends for a "cut log" look. My family always made green vines and leaves from frosting, and wrote "Joyeux Noël" across the log. My own sons have further decorated the log with taffy bars rolled in their hands and formed into the shape of tiny mushrooms. You can be as artistic as you choose!

Madeleine Gray
Helena

Mémère Montpetit's "Mokas"

Cake

½	cup butter	2	cups flour
½	cup sugar	2	teaspoons baking powder
2	eggs	½	cup milk

Glaze

1	cup powdered sugar	3	tablespoons cream
½	cup butter		Coconut, toasted
1	teaspoon vanilla		Walnuts, chopped, optional

To make the cake, cream the butter with the sugar, then beat in the eggs. Sift together the flour and baking powder and add them to the sugar and butter alternately with the milk. Spread the batter in a greased 9-inch square pan and bake at 350 degrees for 25 to 30 minutes, until a toothpick inserted in the center comes out clean. Cool the cake and cut it into squares.

To make the glaze, melt the sugar, butter, vanilla and cream in a double boiler over hot water, and leave them in the boiler while you dip the cake squares in the syrup.

Immediately after dipping, roll the squares in toasted coconut mixed with chopped walnuts. Put the cakes into a cool place until the glaze has set. When they are cool, they will keep in an airtight container.

Madeleine Gray
Helena

Tarte au Sucre (Sugar Pie)

	Pastry for a two-crust pie	½	cup heavy cream
1	cup brown sugar, firmly packed		Walnut halves for garnish

Place (but do not press) the brown sugar in the uncooked pie shell. Gradually pour the cream over the sugar. Make a lattice on top with the remaining crust. Put a walnut half in each of the squares formed by the lattice. Bake the pie in a pre-heated 350 degree oven until the crust turns golden (approximately 40 minutes). Cool the pie, then refrigerate it. Serve it cold from the fridge.

Madeleine Gray
Helena

Soupe aux Pois (Pea Soup)

2 pounds whole yellow peas
10 quarts cold water
1 pound salt pork
1 large onion, minced
1 bay leaf

½ teaspoon summer savory
1 teaspoon parsley
½ cup grated carrot
Salt and pepper

Rinse the peas in cold water, then put them into a large kettle with the 10 quarts of cold water. Cut up the salt pork and add it to the kettle. Add the onion, bay, savory, parsley and carrot. Bring the soup to a boil, then simmer it over medium heat for several hours until the peas are tender. Add salt and pepper to taste. Serve it piping hot.

Madeleine Gray
Helena

Galettes de Sarrasin (Buckwheat Pancakes)

3 cups buckwheat flour
4 cups water

1 teaspoon salt
¾ teaspoon baking soda

Make a batter of the above ingredients. Let it rest a few minutes before cooking it on a thick and well-greased griddle. Serve the pancakes hot with butter.

Madelaine Gray
Helena

We have the French to thank for discovering the North Country. On August 10, 1535, explorer Jacques Cartier sailed into a great gulf leading to a wide and beautiful river which he named for the saint on whose name day he made his discovery—St. Lawrence. At first the French were less interested in settling the region as a permanent colony than were the English who were to become their adversaries. Instead, they wanted to set up a fur trade with the Native American inhabitants and to covert them to the Catholic faith. One of the first permanent settlements in our region was Fort la Présentation, built in 1749 by Abbé Picquet, a Sulpician missionary, in what is now Ogdensburg. It clearly furthered both these goals—serving as a center to instruct Indians about European agricultural methods and the Catholic religion even as it protected the French fur trading settlements on the Great Lakes from English access by water.

Another round of French settlement came at the time of the French revolution. A group calling themselves the New York Company bought up a huge tract of land along the Black River, hoping to sell lots to aristocrats eager to find a refuge from the guillotine. They planned a utopian community with a combination of public and private land ownership to be called Castorland [The French word for beaver is castor]. The present-day village of Lyons Falls lies across the river from one of the two cities planned for the new community. The planners greatly misjudged the difficulties they would face in terms of building roads and clearing their land. Fortunately for the aristocrats, but unfortunately for Castorland, Napoleon pardoned the emigrés when he assumed power in 1802 and offered to restore their lands in France. Most of the homesick emigrés rushed back immediately, leaving the community without the critical mass of inhabitants and money needed to succeed.

In 1814 James Le Ray de Chaumont, an international businessman and generous supporter of the American cause during our revolution, bought up the lands of the failed New York Company, adding them to his already-extensive holdings further north. He cut roads, built mills, and founded villages. For a brief span of time, large areas of Jefferson County were more French than American, operating under a French manorial system, with James Le Ray and his son Vincent as generous and well-loved seigneurs. They and their fellow land-owners built gracious mansions, filled them with fine furniture and dishes, and used them for lavish entertaining. The influence of these early developers remains today in the names of the towns they established—LeRayville, Chaumont (named for Le Ray's chateau in France), Theresa (for Le Ray's daughter), Cape Vincent (for Le Ray's son), Alexandria Bay (for Le Ray's other son Alexandre), and DeFeriet (for Madame DeFeriet, a close family friend with a mansion there.) The opening of the Erie Canal brought ruin to the Le Rays, for it allowed western New York with its better land and climate to compete for settlers. In 1832, the Le Ray family left the North Country, although they maintained a land agent in Carthage until 1914.

After Waterloo, Joseph Bonaparte, Napoleon's brother, used money and jewels he had acquired while acting as king of Spain to buy 26,000 acres from James Le Ray. He built himself a mansion at Natural Bridge, a summer home at Lake Bonaparte, and a mansion for his Quaker mistress, Annette Savage, at Evans Mills. There he entertained the huge expatriate community of Napoleon's former officers who had moved to Cape Vincent. They plotted endlessly to return their leader to power or at least to spirit him away to the North Country. Again, events in France depopulated the North Country, for when Louis Philippe came to the throne, these emigrés returned to their homeland.

The eastern sections of the North Country also have the French to thank for their settlement. Large numbers of the early residents of the Adirondacks were Québécois who came to work as lumberjacks. More recently a wave of immigrants came to work at Alcoa in Massena.

There is even a story linking the Mohawks at Hogansburg to French royalty. In 1789, one month before the fall of the Bastille, Louis Charles, second son of Louis XVI and Marie Antoinette, became dauphin of France when his elder brother died. During the revolution he was imprisoned separately from his family in the Temple under such horrible conditions that it was believed he went mad and died after six months. However, there is a substantial body of circumstantial evidence to indicate that another dying child was substituted for the Dauphin while he was spirited away to the North Country and raised by Thomas Williams, a Mohawk. Who would do that? Maybe the royalists hoping to restore him later to the throne. Maybe the French revolutionary government who did not want the blood of a child on their hands, but who wanted him declared dead and out of their way. Maybe his uncle who, upon the death of Louis XVI, declared the Dauphin king of France and himself the regent; the boy would clearly be a hindrance to his uncle's own plans if the Bourbons were reinstated. (Interestingly, when that happened and the uncle became King Louis XVIII, he disinterred all the royal bodies except that of the boy who died in the Temple. He had daily masses said for all the souls and reburied the bodies in state. Did he fail to do this service for his nephew, knowing that there was no need since the boy still lived?) Numerous books were written advancing this theory. According to *Le Monde* of April 21, 2000, DNA tests done on the heart of the little boy who died in the Temple prove that he was indeed the Dauphin.

GREEK
AMERICANS

Chrisoula Mesires, longtime food chairperson for the St. Vasilios Greek Orthodox Church pastry sale, prepares spinach filling for *spanakopeta*, a savory pie made with *phyllo* dough, Watertown, Jefferson County. *Allen Brook Photo/Watertown Daily Times*

Pastry Sale at St. Vasilios

by Chrisoula Mesires, Mary Mesires, and Maria Bouros

as told to the production staff of TAUNY's
radio program "Home Cooking"

Our church holds pastry sales twice a year—one two weeks before Christmas and one a week before Western Easter. (You know Eastern Orthodox Easter is a week later.) We've been doing these ever since the church was built in 1951. All the ladies of the church help; we have a morning shift and an afternoon shift on the day of the sale. The sale used to be the auxiliary's project, but now the church board's taken over running it. But the cooking, that's still the women's job! Different groups of women do their own specialties—some do the baklava; some do cookies. We start baking a month ahead for the sale and freeze things until that day.

For the sale—and at home, too—we make all the old favorites: diples*, fenekia*, koulourakia*, tsoureki*, and of course baklava. At the Christmas sale we sold 10 trays of baklava, each one with 96 pieces. We ran out in the morning and had to take orders. We made a couple of trays really fast, and people came back in the afternoon to pick it up. Everybody makes baklava at home; all Greek ladies make it, but we all have our own way of doing it. Some use almonds, some walnuts, and some do half-and-half. People used to make their own dough, but nobody around here does anymore. It's too much work; we just buy it at the store ready made. At home we cut it into diamonds—they're dressier, but for the sale we cut rectangles because there's less waste that way. We use a strip of paper as a cutting guide to make the pieces even.

Let's see, for a big pan like we make for the sale, we'd use fifteen cups of walnuts, mixed with two cups of sugar, two teaspoons nutmeg, one or two teaspoons of cloves, and two tablespoons of nutmeg. You mix it up with your hands. Then you put down nine layers of phyllo dough, brushed with butter. That's sweet butter, no salt. You have to work real fast because it dries out so quickly. Then you put in the filling, nice and even, and cover the filling with nine more layers of phyllo and butter. Then you push the edges in and bake it at 350 degrees for about 30 minutes until it's crisp and brown. Then you put the syrup on. It's the main ingredient. You have to put cold syrup on hot baklava or hot syrup on cold baklava—never hot on hot or cold on cold; that doesn't work. You make the syrup with two cups of sugar, one cup of water, and half a cup of honey. Then you put in two sticks cinnamon, some cloves, some lemon rind, and—when it's all cooked down and you take it off the heat—a jigger of whiskey.

It's a lot of work to make the baklava, so we mostly make it for special events—Christmas, Easter, name-day parties. Older people celebrate name days, but the younger generation mostly celebrate birthdays. Everyone is named after a saint, so your name day is the saint's day. It was nice—a tradition. You'd drink, have sweets, dance Greek, have a good time.

Sometimes at home we make the same thing as the baklava, but in a cigar shape. We roll the walnuts in the phyllo, then dip it in the syrup. I made 500 pieces once when my son got married. My neighbor said, "Let me know when you make it," because she wanted to come over and help. When she saw how much work it was, she said, "I'll eat it, but I won't make it."

We three make the Easter bread for the sale, too. We make it there, at the church. We go down at 7 am and mix up the dough, then at 11:30 we weigh it and braid it. At 3 pm we go back and bake it. It freezes really well, so we can make it a month in advance. I never count the flour for the bread; I've been making it so long I just know how it should be. It's got special spices in it. You can use a spice from Turkey. It has a nice flavor and is very expensive—$16 a pound. It's got a tongue-twisting name, mahlab; you get it in Syracuse. It's ground up cherry pits and you can smell it. Or sometimes you can put in mastic. It's spruce flavor, like from the pine tree; it tastes like that spruce gum.

It's too bad we don't have many young women in our church to take over the sale after us. The young people go to college, then move away; there just aren't any jobs for them in Watertown. There's nothing for them here.

According to Marilyn Rouvelas in her book A Guide to Greek Traditions and Customs in America, *in Classical times sophisticated Athenians raised food and dining to an art form on a level with drama and sculpture. Greek cooking was so famous even in those early days that wealthy Romans often imported Greek chefs. Naturally, Greece's location and its political history have resulted in substantial Middle Eastern influence. Its foodways have been enriched by this borrowing, but it has always managed to maintain its own cuisine as well. In fact, Ms. Rouvelas says that the custom of chefs wearing white hats has its roots in the long period of Greek subjugation by the Ottoman Empire. In those days Greek chefs fled to Orthodox monasteries to preserve their culinary traditions. There they wore tall white hats to distinguish themselves from the priests who wore tall black ones.*

The recipes in this section are for foods prepared in the Watertown Greek community. Actual wording of the recipes, given to me by Samuel Thomas, is from The Complete Greek Cookbook: The Best from 3000 Years of Greek Cooking *by Theresa Karas Yianilos. NY: Avenol Books, 1970.*

Maroulosalata Anamikti
(Greek Lettuce Salad)

1	head firm iceberg lettuce, finely cut	1	cucumber, peeled and sliced thin
¼	onion or 4 scallions, finely chopped	2	stalks celery, finely chopped
¼	green bell pepper, slivered		Oil and lemon dressing
¼	cup parsley, finely cut with scissors		[see page 151]
6	radishes, sliced		Greek olives, anchovies, cubed feta cheese for
2	tomatoes, cubed		garnish

In a Greek salad, the lettuce is cut with a knife, not torn. It should be served immediately after being tossed with the dressing.

Salatica Ladolemono
(Greek-Style Vegetables)

For Greeks salads are the heart of the meal. Adding olive oil, lemon juice or vinegar, and a little crushed oregano will turn any boiled vegetables into a salad, the Greeks' most common way of eating vegetables.

Use any combination of the following fresh, canned, or frozen vegetables:

Artichoke hearts	Green leafy vegetables,
Asparagus, whole or chopped	e.g. Swiss chard, mustard
Beans, boiled	greens, kale, etc.
Green beans, sliced	Green peppers, slivered
Beets, whole or sliced	Leeks, sliced
Broccoli flowerets	Okra, whole
Brussels sprouts, whole	Spinach, chopped
Cabbage, chopped	Tomatoes, cut in wedges
Cauliflower flowerets	Zucchini, sliced
Eggplant pieces	

In addition to:

	Salt and pepper to taste	1	teaspoon oregano
¼	cup chopped onions or	1	teaspoon spearmint flakes
	scallions		Oil and lemon or yoghurt
			dressing [see page 151]

If using fresh vegetables, boil them in salted water until they are soft, then drain off the liquid. If using frozen, follow the directions on the package, adding four minutes to the recommended cooking time. Vegetables in a Greek salad are always soft.

To prepare eggplant and green peppers, bake them in a shallow dish at 375 degrees for 30 minutes. Plunge them into cold water to loosen the skins, then peel them carefully.

Sprinkle the vegetables with scallions, oregano, mint, and your choice of dressing. Serve warm, room temperature, or slightly chilled.

Kounoupidi (Greek Cauliflower)

In her introduction to this recipe, Theresa Yianilos says that boiled cauliflower originated in Cyprus thousands of years before it was introduced to England in 1586. The English called the new vegetable Cyprus cabbage or colewort.

1	head of cauliflower or 2 packages frozen	One of the following sauces [see pages 151 and 152]:
2	cups water	Oil and lemon dressing
¼	teaspoon salt	Cheese sauce
		Egg and Lemon sauce

Make six 2-inch-deep cuts into the stem of a head of cauliflower. Break it apart into flowerets. Bring the water to a boil; add the salt and the flowerets. Cover the pot and boil the cauliflower rapidly on high heat for 15 minutes (8 minutes if the cauliflower is frozen). Drain the flowerets and serve with one of the suggested sauces.

Melitzanes Vizantiou (Eggplant Byzantine)

1	large eggplant, sliced into ½-inch thick slices	1	cup water	
	Salt	1	teaspoon oregano	
½	cup olive oil	1	onion, finely chopped	
1	cup tomato purée or tomato sauce	¼	teaspoon salt	
1	cup yoghurt or cream cheese		Pepper to taste	
		½	cup grated Parmesan or kefaloteri cheese	

Salt the slices of eggplant generously, set them aside for 15 minutes, then rinse them well in cold water. Place the slices on an oiled broiler pan and brush the tops with olive oil. Broil for 5 minutes on each side.

Make a sauce by blending the tomato sauce, yoghurt, water, oregano, onion, salt, and pepper in a blender for ½ minute. Place one layer of eggplant in a greased casserole. Spread half the sauce over it. Arrange a second layer of eggplant on top, covered with the remainder of the sauce. Top with the cheese, salt, and pepper. Bake at 350 degrees for 45 minutes.

Tiganites Melitzanes meh Saltses
(Fried Eggplant with Greek Sauces)

1	eggplant, sliced into ¼-inch thick slices	1	cup oil for frying
	Salt		One of the following sauces [see pages 151 and 152]:
1	cup flour		
¼	cup grated Parmesan or kefaloteri cheese		Garlic dressing
			Tomato sauce
2	eggs, beaten		Yoghurt dressing

Sprinkle the slices of eggplant generously with salt and let them stand 15 minutes, then rinse them in cold water and pat them dry. Combine the flour and cheese. Dip the eggplant slices in the flour mixture, coating both sides, then dip them in the beaten eggs. Fry the slices in hot oil until they are light brown on both sides (approximately 10 minutes). Serve them hot with any of the listed sauces.

Psiti Kota meh Lemoni kai Rigani
(Lemon Chicken Oregano)

1	roasting chicken, whole or disjointed	2	lemons, juice only
		3	cups boiling water
¼	pound butter	2	tablespoons flour or cornstarch
¼	cup oil		
2	teaspoons salt	½	cup cold water
⅛	teaspoon pepper		Mashed potatoes or cooked rice
1	tablespoon oregano		

Wash the chicken under cold running water. Heat the butter and oil together until they are hot. Pour half of the mixture into a shallow baking pan, spreading it to cover the bottom. Lay the chicken pieces in the pan and sprinkle them with the salt, pepper and oregano. Mix the remaining butter mixture with the lemon juice and baste the chicken. Bake at 375 degrees for 1½ hours, basting 3 or 4 times during the baking. When the chicken is cooked, remove it to a platter and keep it warm.

Add the boiling water to the drippings in the pan, scraping the bottom with a spatula. Dilute the flour or cornstarch in the cold water; stir it into the boiling water in the pan. Bake at 475 degrees for 5 minutes. Serve this gravy over mashed potatoes or rice along with the chicken.

Moussaka (Baked Eggplant)

1	large eggplant	¼	pound butter or margarine
½	cup oil		

Filling

1	pound ground lamb (or beef)	½	cup parsley, chopped
		½	cup tomato sauce
2	onions, chopped	½	cup red wine
1	clove garlic, pressed	1	cup water

White Sauce

2	tablespoons cornstarch	½	teaspoon salt
½	cup cold water	4	eggs, slightly beaten
2	cups milk		

Topping

1	cup grated Parmesan or kefaloteri	¼	teaspoon cinnamon

Wash the eggplant and cut it into ½-inch thick slices. Sprinkle the slices with salt and let them stand in a bowl for 10 minutes, then rinse them with cold water and dry them with a towel. Place the slices close together, side by side, on an oiled cookie sheet. Melt the oil and butter together and brush the tops lightly with some of the mixture. Bake the slices in a preheated oven at 350 degrees for 10 minutes.

While the eggplant bakes, prepare the filling. Heat a tablespoon of the butter/oil mixture in a frying pan and cook the meat, onions, garlic, parsley, tomato sauce, wine and water in it for 7 minutes.

Oil the bottom and sides of a square or rectangular cake pan. Place one layer of eggplant on the bottom of the pan. Cover it evenly with the meat filling. Layer the remaining eggplant on top. Brush with some of the butter/oil mixture.

Mix the cornstarch into the cold water. Heat the milk and salt almost to boiling. Add the cornstarch, stirring as it thickens. Remove the pan from the heat. Add some sauce to the beaten eggs, then add the eggs to the sauce, mixing them in well. Pour the sauce over the top of the eggplant. Sprinkle with the cheese, cinnamon and any remaining butter/oil. Bake at 325 degrees for 45 minutes. Cut the moussaka into squares and serve immediately.

Psito Psari (Baked Fish Mykonos)

	Whole fish, approximately	¼	teaspoon tarragon
	2 to 3 pounds	¼	teaspoon rosemary
½	cup olive oil	¼	teaspoon thyme
2	lemons, juice only, or ½	¼	teaspoon parsley
	cup white wine		Black olives, feta cheese,
1	teaspoon salt		raw vegetables for
⅛	teaspoon pepper		garnish

Rinse the fish and lay it full length in a shallow pan. Combine the remaining ingredients and ladle the resulting mixture over the fish. Let it stand in the refrigerator for 30 minutes. Turn the fish over and marinate the other side for another 30 minutes. Spoon off some of the marinade to use as a basting sauce.

Bake the fish at 375 degrees, allowing 10 minutes per pound. Baste the fish frequently with the sauce as it bakes. Serve it whole, garnished with black olives, feta cheese or raw vegetables.

Plaki (Baked Fish Salonika)

2	pounds boneless whitefish,	½	cup parsley, chopped
	filet of halibut, bass, or	1	teaspoon oregano
	cod, sliced	⅛	teaspoon cinnamon
¼	cup olive oil, divided	1	teaspoon salt
4	onions, thinly sliced		Pepper to taste
1	clove garlic, pressed	½	cup red port or
2	cups tomatoes, or 1 cup		mavrodaphne wine
	tomato purée diluted with		
	2 cups water		

Rinse the fish with cold water. Oil a baking pan with half the oil. Place the slices of fish on the pan.

Heat the remaining oil in a frying pan and fry the onions and garlic over medium heat for 5 minutes. Add the remaining ingredients and cover the pan. Cook for 10 minutes. Pour the resulting sauce over the fish. Bake at 375 degrees for 45 minutes.

Spanakopita (Spinach Pie)

2	pounds fresh spinach	5	eggs
1	cup chopped onion	1	teaspoon basil
2	sticks plus 3 tablespoons butter, divided	½	teaspoon oregano Salt and pepper to taste
2	tablespoons flour	1	(1-pound) package frozen phyllo dough, defrosted
2	cups crumbled feta cheese		
2	cups (1 pound) cottage cheese		

Wash the spinach well (do not drain it) and remove the stems. Adding no water, cook it until it is wilted (approximately 5 minutes), then chop it very coarsely. Cook the onions in the 3 tablespoons of butter. When they are soft, combine them with the spinach, flour, cheeses, eggs, basil, oregano, salt and pepper.

Melt the 2 sticks of butter. With a pastry brush, spread some of the butter on the bottom of a 9x13-inch pan. Place a leaf of phyllo in the pan, allowing the edges to climb the sides if need be. Brush it with butter. Continue adding leaves of phyllo, brushing each with butter, until you have a stack of 8 leaves. Spread the stack with half the spinach mixture. Add another stack of 8 leaves, brushed with butter, and cover them with the remaining spinach. Put the remaining phyllo leaves, buttering as you go, on top of the stack and turn under any edges to make them tidy. Bake the pie uncovered at 375 degrees until it is golden (approximately 45 minutes).

Nancy Alessi
Russell

Nancy found this recipe in Mollie Katzen's The Moosewood Cookbook. *Berkeley, CA: Ten Speed Press, 1977.*

Arni meh Prassa Mahala
(Lamb and Leeks Mahala)

2	tablespoons oil	1	bunch leeks, washed and
2	pounds lamb, cut in 2-inch		cut in pieces
	pieces	2	teaspoons salt
1	clove garlic, peeled and		Pepper to taste
	halved	3	cups water

Heat the oil and brown the lamb on high heat for 10 minutes, stirring constantly. Add the remaining ingredients, cover, and reduce the heat to simmer for 2 hours.

Diples (Greek Crullers)

Diples

3	eggs	2½	cups flour
2	tablespoons orange juice	½	teaspoon baking powder
¼	cup oil	1	quart oil for frying

Topping

2	cups honey		Cinnamon
1	cup water	1	cup powdered sugar,
½	cup ground nuts		optional

Beat the eggs with an electric mixer until they are thick, adding the juice and the ¼ cup oil as you beat. Sift the flour with the baking powder and add them to the eggs. Knead the resulting dough until it is elastic, then let it rest about 1 hour.

Divide the dough into four balls. Roll out one ball at a time on a lightly floured board until it is as thin as possible. Using a pastry wheel, cut 3 x 1-inch strips. Heat the quart of oil to 375 degrees. Shape each strip into a figure 8 or a rosette and drop it into the hot oil which has been heated to 375 degrees. Do not crowd the crullers in the pan. Using a slotted spoon, turn them so that they can fry on both sides, then transfer them to a tray lined with paper towels.

When all the crullers have been fried, arrange them on a large tray. Dilute the honey with the water and dribble a spoonful over each cruller. Sprinkle them with nuts and cinnamon, or sift powdered sugar over them. Serve them the same day, as they do not keep well.

Fenekia (Venetian Honey Cookies)

These cookies were brought to Greece by Venetian bakers between the 14th and 17th centuries, when Venice ruled some of the Greek Islands.

Cookies

1¼	cups butter or oil	2	teaspoons baking powder
1	egg yolk	⅛	teaspoon salt
¼	cup orange juice	½	teaspoon ground cloves
¼	teaspoon soda	1	teaspoon cinnamon
1	ounce whiskey	½	teaspoon grated orange
½	cup sugar		peel
3½	cups flour		Ground nuts for filling, optional

Syrup

2	cups honey	½	cup ground walnuts or
1	cup boiling water		almonds

To make the cookies, melt the butter and allow it to cool slightly. Put the egg yolk, juice, soda, whiskey and sugar into a bowl; mix them together. Add the butter or oil and continue mixing until the mixture is as thick as mayonnaise.

In a bowl, sift the flour with the baking powder and spices. Add the orange peel. Stir the flour mixture into the eggs and finish by kneading the resulting dough until it is smooth and stiff. Place a tablespoon of dough in your hand and squeeze it slightly to form an oblong egg shape. If desired, you can put a small amount of ground nuts in the center of the cookie before pressing it.

Place the cookies on an ungreased cookie sheet and press the top slightly with a fork, making a crisscross design. Bake the cookies in a preheated 350 degree oven for 20 minutes. Cool them on a rack.

To make the syrup, bring the honey and water to a boil and allow them to simmer. Dip the cookies for a few seconds in the syrup and place them on a cookie sheet to absorb the syrup. Sprinkle with nuts and allow them to cool. These taste better after a day, and they keep well.

Tsoureki (Sunday Bread)

This sweet and spicy bread is baked for Sundays and holidays. For New Year's Day it is called vasilopitta and baked with coins wrapped in foil inside it. The person who finds the coins will have luck in the coming year. At Christmas it is decorated with a cross and called christopsomo or "Christ's bread." On Easter, it is called lambropsomo and topped with a dyed red egg and sesame seeds.

2	tablespoons dry yeast	1	ounce ouzo, optional
¼	cup warm water	½	cup water
½	teaspoon cinnamon	7	cups flour
½	teaspoon anise seeds	½	cup sugar
½	teaspoon orange peel	½	teaspoon salt
1	bay leaf	½	cup hot milk
¼	teaspoon mahlab—ground cherry pits available in spice shops, optional	¼	pound butter or 6 tablespoons oil
		3	eggs

Topping

Egg yolk	¼	cup sesame seeds

Dissolve the yeast in the warm water and set it aside. Put the cinnamon, anise, orange peel, bay leaf, mahlab, ouzo and the ½ cup water into a saucepan and bring them to a boil. Set them aside to steep and cool. Put the flour, sugar, and salt into a large bowl. Heat the milk, then remove it from the fire; add the butter or oil, and allow it to cool slightly.

Make a hole in the middle of the flour and mix in the eggs, yeast, milk and flavored water (first removing the bay leaf). Use a spoon to push the flour from the sides into the center. Knead the dough on a lightly floured board until it is smooth (approximately 20 minutes). Place the dough in an oiled bowl and allow it to rise until it has doubled in bulk.

Punch the dough down, then knead it for five minutes. Shape the dough into one round loaf or two rectangular loaves and place them in greased baking pans. Glaze the tops with egg yolk and sprinkle with sesame seeds. Allow the loaves to rise once again for approximately 2 hours. Bake in a preheated 350 degree oven for 1 hour.

Sweet Koulourakia

These rolls look and taste like cookies. They are baked as wreaths, figure eights, or coiled snakes—a design dating from the Minoans, ancient residents of Crete, who worshipped the snake for its healing power.

1	cup butter	1	teaspoon vanilla
1	cup sugar	5	cups flour
3	eggs (save one white for topping)	3	teaspoons baking powder
		¼	cup sesame seeds
¼	cup milk		

Allow the butter to soften at room temperature, then beat it until it is light and fluffy. Add the sugar, eggs, milk and vanilla, beating continuously. Sift the flour, baking powder, and salt into the mixture and combine them. Knead until they are well blended.

To shape each cookie, break off a small piece of dough, roll it between your palms to make a rope 4 inches long, then braid or coil it. Place the cookies 2 inches apart on an oiled baking sheet and glaze the tops with beaten egg white. Sprinkle with sesame seeds. Bake in a preheated oven at 350 degrees for 25 minutes.

SAUCES USED IN THESE RECIPES

Ladolemono (Oil and Lemon Dressing)

½   cup olive oil
1   lemon, juice only, or 2
     tablespoons vinegar
¼   teaspoon salt
     White pepper to taste

¼   teaspoon oregano
2   tablespoons Parmesan,
     blue, or Greek kefaloteri
     cheese, optional

Mix the ingredients with a few whisks of a fork just before serving.

Yaourti Mayoneza (Yoghurt Salad Dressing)

1   cup yoghurt
1   teaspoon vinegar
1   clove garlic
½   teaspoon dry mustard
½   teaspoon oregano

½   teaspoon salt
½   teaspoon sugar
     Pepper to taste
2   ounces blue cheese,
     optional

Blend the ingredients together and let the dressing stand one hour before serving. Keep it refrigerated.

Skordalia (Garlic Dressing)

¼   cup water
5   cloves garlic
½   teaspoon salt
1   cup mashed potatoes or 4
     slices fresh bread

½   cup walnuts, pine nuts or
     almonds, optional
2   tablespoons vinegar and
     ½ cup olive oil, or ½ cup
     mayonnaise and
     1 teaspoon vinegar

Put the ingredients into a blender in the order listed; blend until smooth.

Saltsa Avgholemono (Egg and Lemon Sauce)

3	eggs	2	lemons, juice only
		1	cup hot broth

Beat the eggs until they are thick and light yellow, at least 5 minutes with an electric beater or 10 to 15 minutes by hand. Add the juice slowly, beating constantly. Mix one cup of hot broth into the beaten eggs, stirring it in quickly so that the heat will not curdle the eggs. Pour the sauce over hot food in a serving dish.

Saltsa Domata (Tomato Sauce)

2	tablespoons oil	1	teaspoon sugar
1	onion, chopped	2	teaspoons salt
1	clove garlic, minced	⅛	teaspoon pepper
1	can tomatoes or tomato purée	½	teaspoon sweet basil
		½	teaspoon oregano
1	(2-ounce) can tomato paste	½	teaspoon cinnamon
4	cups water	½	teaspoon parsley
½	cup wine or 1 tablespoon vinegar	½	teaspoon spearmint
		1	bay leaf

Heat the oil in a frying pan. Fry the onion and garlic for three minutes. Add the remaining ingredients. Bring the mixture to a boil, reduce the heat to low, and simmer 45 minutes, stirring occasionally.

Krema meh Teree (Cheese Sauce)

2	tablespoons cornstarch	½	cup grated cheese— kefaloteri, Parmesan, or cheddar
½	cup cold water		
2	cups milk		
1	tablespoon butter	1	egg, well beaten
1½	teaspoons salt		

Dilute the cornstarch in the cold water and set it aside. Bring the milk, butter and salt just to the boiling point over medium heat, but do not let them boil. Add the diluted cornstarch, stirring as the sauce thickens. Add the cheese and stir until it is melted and blended in. Remove the pan from the heat. Add some sauce to the beaten egg, then add the egg to the sauce, mixing it in well.

The first large group of Greek immigrants to America were indentured laborers who arrived in 1768 and settled south of St. Augustine, Florida, in a community named New Smyrna. After enduring many hardships and losing many of their members, they were granted their freedom in 1777. At that point they moved to St. Augustine; the St. Photios Shrine there marks the house where they worshipped and serves as a memorial to these first Greek Americans.

The largest wave of Greek immigrants arrived in America between 1890 and 1917. Unfortunately written records of these people are slim; all we know of their experiences comes from oral tradition, stories passed down from one generation to the next. Like other immigrant groups, they made their way to American cities seeking a better life than the one they'd left at home. In New England they became blue-collar workers in textile and shoe factories; in the Midwest and West they worked in mines and helped build railroads. Around 1910 a number of the Greeks living in New York City became aware of the booming North Country economy with its many business opportunities. Many families moved north, settling in Watertown and Carthage, Gouverneur, Canton, Potsdam, and Massena. They found jobs in various segments of the food industry—in restaurants, wholesale food companies, food markets, and confectionery shops—and working as custodians, laborers, seamstresses, and employees at Camp Drum.

Meanwhile life was becoming very uncomfortable for family and friends at home. The Greco-Turkish conflict of 1919 to 1923 ended in a forced resettlement of populations: 1.5 million Greeks in Asia Minor were resettled to Greece; 800,000 Turks were sent from Greece to Turkey; and 80,000 Bulgarians were returned from Greece to Bulgaria. Many of the refugees from Asia Minor arrived in Athens hoping to find safety and stability; sadly, they were greeted instead by great economic and political unrest. Many North Country Greek Americans sponsored immigrating relatives during this period of upheaval, creating a second wave of Greek immigration to our area. These new Americans often went to work for their sponsoring family and friends, who owned restaurants, theaters, confectionery shops, food markets, shoe repair shops, or apartment buildings around the North Country.

The Greek Orthodox Church has played a major role in maintaining the religious and cultural traditions of North Country Greek Americans.

In earlier days, they traveled to Syracuse to attend the Greek Orthodox church there. Many times during the year, the priest from that church would visit Watertown, conducting liturgies in the homes of parishioners and at the Episcopal church. Then, in 1951, St. Vasilios Church in Watertown was consecrated. It is still the only Eastern Orthodox church in the North Country. Its members come from as far away as Massena and Lake Placid, and they include Syrians, Russians, Albanians, and Serbs, although most, naturally, are Greek Americans. In addition to its primary religious functions, the church provides Greek language programs and organizations for both youths and adults aimed at fostering pride in their Greek heritage.

Like other immigrants to the North Country, the Greeks worked to provide a better life for succeeding generations. They saw education as the key to success and encouraged their children to study hard; the majority of second-generation Greek Americans earned college degrees and settled into professional careers. Often this resulted in their relocating to other parts of the country. At one time, St. Vasilios Church had nearly 150 family memberships; today it has 75. Although the remaining Greek American community is small, it is close-knit and strongly committed to maintaining its religious and cultural traditions.

* * *

Adapted from a history of the North Country Greeks written by Samuel Thomas and edited by Eugenie Calender of Watertown.

HOMESTEADERS

Members of the Birdsfoot community, Canton, St. Lawrence County, prepare new ground for spring planting of their large communal garden, early 1980s. *Photo courtesy of Doug Jones*

Wedding at Birdsfoot

by Peter Van de Water

I wore a coat and tie to Steve's marriage celebration. Becky said I shouldn't, that I'd be conspicuous, but I told her I would feel comfortable enough, and besides, it was okay to be different. Steve was to be married, but this wasn't a wedding like any wedding I knew. My weddings were in solemn churches, with demure brides in white satin and taffeta bridesmaids, and groomsmen looking like Antarctic penguins lined up to pose for some fur-hooded photographer.

We got to Birdsfoot, an organic farming community, a few minutes before the marriage celebration was about to start. The guests were working their way up the garden paths to an open hayfield. We followed. At the hilltop the path led under an arch of cedar poles; on the ground cedar chips slowly released their welcoming fragrance. Steve, barefoot, stood athwart a farm wagon, throwing bales of hay to the wedding guests who were arranging them end to end in a giant circle. Bright banners of cloth like Tibetan prayer flags fluttered from poles ringing the circle of bales. Druids probably married in such surroundings, I thought.

The marriage hour passed. No one seemed to care. People stood in small groups, whispering, waiting for instructions. A few latecomers hurried up the path. A robin called from a hedgerow at the hayfield's edge. Finally, we guests were told to sit in a circle on the bales of hay. Patreesha, gentle mistress of ceremonies, said we should be quiet and think thoughts of peace and love. Steve and his bride took opposing places in the circle. The rippling breeze blew the cloth banners almost straight out, and the sun warmed us when it wasn't under scudding clouds. I peeked around. Women, mostly young and middle-aged, wore bright, embroidered shirts of cotton or silk. Some were barefoot, most wore billowing skirts; momentarily, I was unsettled by the sight of black hair curling on feminine legs. Bright vests, broad hats, raiment from foreign travels distinguished the men. Steve wore a fez-like felt hat, multi-colored embroidered shirt, and black silk pants like those worn by Vietnamese peasants. He had been barefoot, but now the pants were tucked into white fur boots which could have come straight from

156

a "Dr. Zhivago" set. Steve's father, the only other one in a coat and tie, looked uncomfortable. I dipped my head in a sympathetic nod, wedged myself closer to Becky on our bale, and relaxed a little.

Suddenly Dulli, Steve's bride, a pretty, wholesome-looking young German woman, leaped to her feet. "Steff, I luff you. I vant to marry you," she bellowed into the breeze. The ceremony had begun. Steve and Dulli, now in the middle of the circle of bales, exchanged vows they had written, and around the circle each of us in turn spoke our thoughts to them. Wanting to be wise and witty in my oral offering, I failed miserably, and spoke instead some vacuous platitudes about health and happiness. The bride and groom read from each other's love letters, remnants of a long-distance courtship. A local minister pronounced them married; it seemed apparent her involvement was needed only to satisfy the legal strictures of the State of New York.

A great round of hugging followed the ceremony. It didn't seem to matter that men hugged men and women hugged women. Some of Steve and Dulli's closest friends were crying tears of joy; it felt good to observe such happiness for the newlyweds, and it was obvious that the residents of Birdsfoot community, past and present, shared a deep affection for each other.

After the marriage ceremony everybody was invited to a potluck dinner reception at the Community Center in Crary Mills, an old Grange Hall with a tin ceiling and, upstairs, a stage for the band and wooden floors for dancing. I feared a marathon and three hours is about my limit for weddings and receptions, so deliberately Becky and I got there a little late. I was plenty hungry, but there wasn't much left. The remnants of salads, tofu in dozens of glutinous forms, breads, and fruits littered the banquet tables, but there was an untouched platter of sliced beef and ham, obviously shunned by the vegetarian crowd. Hoping nobody would notice, I piled my plate high. Upstairs there was contra dancing, and Becky and Lee, my grandson, were stomping happily. I was a reluctant dancer, but once dragged into the circle found to my relief that contra dancing was little different from the square dances of my youth. Skill level didn't seem to matter, anyway. Old and young, graceful and gauche, pranced and pirouetted—circles of swirling color—as the ancient floor heaved gently in time with the music.

On the way home Becky and I pondered our day. We felt honored to be invited to Steve's marriage celebration. We knew we had been included in a world unknown to our usual professional colleagues. Did our new friends represent a nostalgic but vain attempt to return to a bucolic past? Would the sweep of progress bury their outdated lifestyles and crush their misguided idealism? Or were they, instead, a link with our forgotten forebears, a Biblical "remnant" clinging to the best of the past, preserving it for the modern world until the rest of us were ready?

* * *

Adapted with permission from an essay in North Country: Essays on Life and Landscape in Northern New York, *edited by Natalia Rachel Singer and Neal Burdick, soon to be published by North Country Books. Peter Van de Water, retired from a position as Vice President for Student Affairs at St. Lawrence University, raises and sells organically grown apples and blueberries outside the village of Canton. He has taken an active role in directing the Canton revitalization effort.*

Minestrone Genoa

Nancy Alessi grows everything for this soup in her garden except the beans.

6	cups basic vegetable stock	3	cups cooked cannellini or
2	cups chopped onions		white kidney beans (2
1	cup chopped celery		15-ounce cans rinsed
1	cup chopped carrots		and drained)
2	cups cubed and peeled	1	cup pesto
	potatoes		Salt and ground black
2	cups chopped cabbage		pepper to taste
1	cup cut green beans, in		
	2-inch pieces		

Bring the stock to a boil in a soup pot. Add the onions, celery and carrots. Lower the heat and simmer about 10 minutes. Add the potatoes, cabbage and green beans; simmer for 10 to 12 minutes more, until the potatoes are tender. Stir in the white beans and the pesto and heat thoroughly. Add salt and pepper to taste.

Nancy Alessi
Russell

Nancy found this recipe in Moosewood Restaurant Low-Fat Favorites, *1996.*

Carrot Soup

Jill and Scott adapted this recipe from one used at Canton's Willow Island Restaurant. They like it because all the ingredients, save the seasonings, come out of their garden and it is very easy to make. Since they grow enough carrots, potatoes, garlic and onions to last until the next year's harvest, they eat this soup regularly year-round. Their favorite time to make it, though, is in the fall after a hard frost, because the parsley tastes best then. Cold treatment greatly improves the flavor of parsley.

3	medium carrots	¼	cup olive oil
1	large potato, cut into large chunks for cooking		Tamari and ground black pepper to taste
2	whole cloves garlic		Fresh parsley, chopped
¼	cup chopped onion		

Put the carrots, potato, garlic and onion in a pot and cover them with just enough water to boil them in. Add just enough tamari for a bit of flavoring (about 1 tablespoon). Cook until the carrots and potato are soft. Add the olive oil at this point, and blend in a blender or food processor until the whole mixture is smooth. (If you drizzle in the olive oil slowly as you are blending and use a bit more than the ingredient list shows, the results are nearly creamy in consistency.) Then add additional tamari and black pepper to taste. Serve the soup topped with liberal amounts of chopped parsley.

Scott Miller & Jill Breit
Norwood

Beets in Tangy Sauce

	Beets	1	part non-dairy whipped topping or whipped cream
1	part sour cream or yoghurt		
1	part mayonnaise (can be light)		Horseradish to taste

Cook the beets, then peel and dice them. Blend the sour cream, mayonnaise, whipped topping and horseradish. Mix the beets with the sauce. Serve warm.

Judy DeGraaff
Canton

Cream of Basil Soup

¼	cup butter	3	tablespoons butter
1½	cups finely diced onions	3	tablespoons flour
1	cup finely diced leeks	¼	cup cream
¾	cup chopped fresh basil	½	teaspoon dry mustard
⅓	cup dry white wine		Nutmeg, salt, pepper to
3	cups chicken stock		taste

In a medium-sized heavy pot heat the ¼ cup butter over medium-high heat. Add the onions, leeks and basil, then cook them until the onions and leeks are limp. Stir in the wine and bring the mixture to a boil. Keep boiling until the mixture is reduced by half, then stir in the stock. Return the mixture to boiling, reduce the heat to medium and simmer for 5 minutes. Melt the 3 tablespoons of butter and stir in the flour to make a smooth paste. Slowly whisk in one cup of the soup until the mixture is smooth. Add this mixture to the soup pot, whisking constantly. Simmer until the soup is slightly thickened.

Stir in the cream. Season to taste with the mustard, nutmeg, salt and pepper. Serve the soup hot.

For this soup, you can use any type of basil you grow in your garden. The red gives it a particularly strong flavor, but it is equally good with the green.

Marilyn and John Ross
Canton

Baked Romano Beans

Jill and Scott admit that this is not a low-fat dish, but they love it. And whenever they serve it, their guests want the recipe.

One standard colander-full of Romano beans, cut in half and ends trimmed off
½ stick butter
2-3 generous tablespoons Dijon mustard

1 cup Parmesan cheese, coarsely grated (start with a block & grate it yourself)

Steam the beans lightly. Melt the butter. Stir in the mustard. Toss this mixture with the beans, then pour them into a greased casserole dish, topping them with the Parmesan cheese. Bake at 350 degrees until the cheese is thoroughly melted. Serve as a side dish.

Scott Miller and Jill Breit
Norwood

Milk Beans

Eric and Jean raise the beans, onions and tomatoes in their garden for this Tanzanian recipe.

1 cup chopped onions
1 cup fresh or canned chopped tomatoes
1 tablespoon oil
2 cups cooked pinto, kidney or other beans with a bit of liquid

⅔ cups milk, for gravy-like consistency
1 teaspoon salt
Pepper to taste
1 teaspoon curry powder or 1½ teaspoons chili powder

In a large saucepan, sauté the onions and tomatoes for 2 to 3 minutes in the oil. Add the beans, milk, salt, pepper and curry or chili powder. Bring the mixture to a boil. Reduce the heat under the pot and simmer the beans for 15 to 20 minutes to blend the flavors. Serve over rice.

This can also be made with dried beans: Soak and cook one cup of dried beans in four cups of water. Drain the beans and proceed as above.

Jean Bergen-Williams
Canton

Carbonada Criolla

¼	cup vegetable oil	1	pound sweet potatoes, peeled and cubed
1	large onion, chopped		
1	garlic clove (or 2 or 3—to taste), crushed	2	cups squash, peeled and cubed
2	pounds stew beef, cubed	1	large green pepper, cut in strips
1	(1-pound) can tomatoes (or use fresh)	1	cup corn
½	teaspoon oregano	1	cup cubed frozen or canned peaches
1	bay leaf		
1	cup bouillon	1	apple, cubed

Sauté the onions and garlic in the oil. Add the meat and brown it, then add the tomatoes, oregano and bay leaf and cook one minute. Add the bouillon and bring the mixture to a boil. Lower the heat and cook, covered, for about one hour. Add the sweet potatoes and squash and cook until they are tender—about 25 minutes. Add the green pepper, corn, peaches and apple. Cook until they are tender—about 5 minutes more.

Serves 6.

Jane Eaton
Canton

Dilly Beans

2	pounds green or wax beans	2½	cups water
		1	teaspoon cayenne pepper
4	cloves garlic	2½	cups vinegar
4	heads dill	¼	cup salt

Divide the beans, garlic and dill among four pint jars. Heat the water, cayenne, vinegar and salt together and pour them over the beans. Process the jars for 10 minutes in boiling water.

Birdsfoot Community
Canton

Tummybuster Summer Squash Casserole

1	medium onion, chopped
3	cloves garlic, minced
	Olive oil
4-6	cups chopped tomatoes and juice
2	medium zucchini (about 10 inches), sliced
2	medium yellow squash, sliced
1	cup spinach or chopped kale or other green vegetable

1	teaspoon honey
1	teaspoon oregano
1	teaspoon basil
1	teaspoon parsley
1	can cannellini beans
4	cups brown rice, cooked according to package directions
	Romano or Parmesan cheese, freshly grated

In a large frying pan sauté the onion and garlic in olive oil. Add the tomatoes, zucchini, squash, spinach, honey and herbs. Cook until the mixture is soft (approximately 30 minutes.) Add the beans. Serve the vegetables over the rice, topped with grated cheese.

Since summer squash is not particularly nutritious by itself, Ginger Storey-Welch tries to fix this with another vegetable that is compact nutritionally, such as kale or broccoli.

Ginger Storey-Welch
Colton

Sesame Dressing for Chard, Spinach or Kale

1	tablespoon soy sauce
2	tablespoons sesame oil
1	tablespoon toasted sesame seeds (or more to taste)
1	clove garlic, minced
1	tablespoon honey or sugar

1	tablespoon vinegar
	Dash pepper
1	pound greens, steamed then squeezed to remove the water

Mix all the ingredients except the greens. Mix in the greens, then serve the dish at room temperature.

If you don't have sesame oil handy, Doug Jones suggests using vegetable oil and adding more toasted sesame seeds.

Birdsfoot Community
Canton

Zucchini Relish

Kathleen Babbitt grows all the vegetable ingredients for this relish in her garden.

10	cups finely chopped zucchini (if small, leave in the seeds; if over 8 inches remove seeds)	2	tablespoons cornstarch
		4	cups white sugar
		1	teaspoon ground nutmeg
		1	teaspoon turmeric
4	large onions, peeled and quartered	2	teaspoons celery seed
		½	teaspoon ground black pepper
4	green bell peppers, seeded and quartered	2½	cups white vinegar
4	red bell peppers, seeded and quartered	6	(1-pint) canning jars
		6	canning lids
½	cup salt	6	metal screw bands for jars

Wash and peel the zucchini, removing the stems and blossom ends. Put the vegetables through the food grinder, using the grinder's coarse knife attachment. (With a food processor, use the shredding disc—the steel blade can make these ingredients lose too much texture.) Put the ground vegetables in a crockery or stainless steel bowl and stir in the salt. Hold the vegetables down in the resulting brine with a weighted plate. Let them stand overnight.

The next day, drain the vegetables. Rinse them with cold running water and drain them into a cheesecloth-lined colander, twisting the cheesecloth to remove extra moisture. Mix the cornstarch with the sugar, nutmeg, turmeric, celery seed and black pepper. Add this mixture to the vinegar, blending well. Over medium heat, bring the resulting mixture to a boil, stirring well to prevent lumping. When the sugar is melted and the syrup is clear, add the vegetables. Simmer for 30 minutes, stirring often.

While the relish is simmering, wash the jars in very hot water. Put the hot jars into the canner and fill the canner half full of hot water. Bring that water to boiling. Put the lids and rings in a small saucepan, cover them with water, and bring them to a boil. (This softens the sealing compound on the lids.)

When the relish is ready, use canning tongs to remove the jars from the water. Pour the relish into the jars, leaving ½ inch of headroom. Remove any air bubbles by sliding a rubber spatula between the glass and the food. Readjust the head space to ½ inch. Wipe the jar rim, removing any stickiness. It is very important that the jar rim be absolutely clean; the jar will not seal if there are any food particles or syrup on the rim.) Center the lid

Zucchini Relish *(continued)*

on the jar, using tongs to move the lid from the saucepan to the jar. Apply a screw band just until fingertip tight. Place the jar in the canner. Repeat until all the relish has been put into jars. Process the jars for 15 minutes after the water has returned to a boil, then remove them from the bath.

Cool the jars for 24 hours. Check the jar seals. (Sealed lids curve downwards.) Remove the screw bands and store them separately. Wipe the jars, then store them in a dark place.

Kathleen Babbitt
Canton

Kathleen adapted the recipe from **Putting Food By** *by Ruth Hertzberg, Beatrice Vaughan, and Janet Greene. 3rd edition.*

Baked Parsnips

Parsnips   Vegetable oil

Depending on the size of the parsnips, slice them lengthwise into halves, quarters, etc., so that the slices are about 1 inch thick. Place them on a cookie sheet and wipe them with vegetable oil. Bake them at 350 degrees until they get brown (approximately 45 minutes.)

They can also be cut crosswise into coins and stir-fried until they are brown.

Parsnips don't really taste good until they've been subjected to cold to develop their sweetness. Doug Jones suggests that you not pick them until late in the fall or that you even allow them to overwinter in your garden. If you must pick them earlier, then keep them a while in the refrigerator before using them.

Doug Jones
Canton

Hutsput

Bob DeGraaff grows everything himself for this traditional Dutch dish. His family has always eaten it instead of plain mashed potatoes at Thanksgiving.

6	large potatoes	¼	cup milk, approximately
6	large carrots		Salt to taste
2	medium onions		

Cut up the potatoes. Transfer them to a pot and just cover them with water. Cook them until they are soft. Drain, then whip them. Follow the same procedure for the carrots, but do not whip them. Dice the onions and cook them in a small amount of water until they are soft.

In a large bowl combine the whipped potatoes with the cooked carrots and onions. Whip them all together using enough milk to achieve the desired consistency. (You may prefer to leave some carrot chunks.) Salt to taste.

Transfer the mixture to a greased baking dish. Sprinkle the top with paprika and bake it, covered, in a slow oven (275 degrees) for about 2 hours. Uncover the pan for the last 30 minutes.

Robert DeGraaff
Canton

Pesto

7	medium cloves garlic	⅓	cup sunflower seeds, toasted
½-1	cup Romano or Parmesan cheese, cubed	4	cups basil, tightly packed
⅓	cup plus 2 tablespoons olive oil, divided	⅛-¼	lemon, juice only, optional

Grind the garlic, cheese and ⅓ cup of the olive oil together in a food processor. Grind in the seeds. Grind in two cups of the basil, then the other 2 cups, combined with the 2 remaining tablespoons of olive oil (and the lemon juice, if desired). Makes one pint.

Doug Jones says that Birdsfoot is trying to become less dependent on the power grid. If you, too, want to get away from motorized technology, he says that you can make this recipe in a meat grinder. If you do, then grate the cheese separately and add it after the other ingredients have gone through the meat grinder.

Birdsfoot Community
Canton

Rhubarb Pudding

3	cups diced rhubarb	1	egg
5	tablespoons butter, divided	½	cup milk
⅔ plus ½ cup sugar, divided			Heavy cream or vanilla ice
1½	cups all-purpose flour		cream
¼	teaspoon salt		
3	teaspoons baking powder		

Pour enough boiling water over the rhubarb to cover it; set it aside for 10 minutes, then drain it. Spread 2 tablespoons of the butter in the bottom of a shallow 1½-quart baking dish or a pie plate. Sprinkle the dish with the ⅔ cup of sugar. Place a pie bird or a vented dome of aluminum foil in the center. Place the rhubarb all around.

Stir together the flour, salt, the ½ cup sugar, and the baking powder. Melt the remaining 3 tablespoons of butter. Beat the egg with the milk and the melted butter. Add the wet mixture to the dry and stir until they are blended into a fairly thick dough. Spread the dough over the rhubarb. Bake at 400 degrees for 25-30 minutes. Serve hot with cream or ice cream.

Martha says, "The cobbler is fabulous for breakfast, too. I sometimes use more fruit and sugar for an even juicier end result. I also freeze diced rhubarb for winter puddings. And I've eaten it with 2% milk."

The recipe makes six servings, but two people have been known to eat the whole thing.

Martha Foley Smith
Canton

This recipe came from **Secrets of Better Cooking**, *published by* **Readers' Digest**, *a book Martha's father gave her when she graduated from college.*

Sometimes it seems as if everyone in the North Country has a garden. Maybe it's because the growing season here is so short that fresh vegetables are particularly precious to us. Most of us think of our gardens as recreation and of the food produced in them as a welcome supplement to what is available at the supermarket. But for some among us growing food is more than a hobby or a business; it is part of a vision of how humans should be relating to each other and to the planet we share.

In the 1960s and 1970s St. Lawrence County began to attract young, bright, often college-educated people who were not interested in mainstream materialistic culture. Local residents, fearing drug-inspired orgies, called them "hippies" or "drop-outs" and eyed them with suspicion. But still they came, drawn to this area by the abundance of inexpensive land and the natural beauty of the region. Many set up communes—Big Dog, Birdsfoot, Beaver Creek—seeking the same sort of utopia that their spiritual ancestors had hoped to create at Oneida or Brook Farm. Others built their own homes, with the help of like-minded friends. By consensus, they set up a schedule of work days: clear brush for John and Valerie this Saturday, cut wood for Todd and Nancy next weekend, build a fence for Doug and Ginger next month. As the years passed by, most of the efforts at true communal living failed, but the members of those groups often remained in the area, quietly joining the larger community of single-family homesteaders. Over time their industry, helpfulness, and gentleness have allayed the fears of their North Country neighbors and, although they continue their alternative lifestyle today, the homesteaders have by now been accepted as valued members of the community at large.

Whether living communally or in their own homes, the homesteaders live a simple, non-acquisitive life in which people are valued for who they are, not what they own. Many home-school their children, concerned about the values promulgated in the public educational system.

Self-sufficiency is the goal they aim for, but with varying degrees of zeal. Most homesteaders have woodstoves. On the other hand, most own some sort of car. Some do without electricity altogether; others generate it on their own property with windmills or solar cells; still others are attached to the main grid. Many have jobs in the town to help pay for the necessities they can not provide with their own hands. The Potsdam Co-op was organized to serve these people who were interested in organic foods and a healthful diet—in 1973, before such ideas became trendy.

One is tempted to draw parallels between the homesteaders and another group who moved to the North Country at the same time, the Amish. Both societies share a deep love and concern for nature; both eschew materialism; both believe in non-violence; both place a very high value on community; and both mistrust big government and big business. But there are some major differences, too. The Amish purposely set themselves apart from non-believing neighbors; the homesteaders, though often alienated from national politics, take an active role in their local communities when issues arise that affect quality of life. They were in the front ranks of the anti-incinerator campaign, the effort to stop Horizon Corporation from building thousands of vacation homes in the Adirondacks, the attempt to stop the 765kv power line, and the coalition to stop the low-level flights of B-52s over our area. Although they believe in simple living, the homesteaders do not join the Amish in their avoidance of adornment. They enjoy wearing colorful clothing and jewelry, and they decorate their homes with flowers, beautiful pottery, and attractive artwork—as long as these items are simple, natural, and preferably hand-made. The Amish go to great lengths not to stand out from others in their own community; homesteaders welcome and admire individuality. Finally, the Amish lead a life which they believe to be prescribed for them by their God; homesteaders for the most part are as wary of organized religion as they are of other institutions, though they place great value on the spiritual side of their lives.

Although most of the early attempts at communal living have failed over the years, one has survived and, after a rocky period in the 1980s, is thriving. Birdsfoot Community, founded in 1972 just outside Canton, is well known in the area for its high-quality organic vegetables; summer salads in much of Canton are built on a base of Birdsfoot spinach. In the near future, one of the members will be opening an alternative elementary school on the property. Other members work in the community at large as educators, physical therapists, and house-cleaners. This quote from the brochure they send out to those interested in joining their community is a good summary of Birdsfoot values and of those of the homesteaders as a group:

"Besides our farming, food and education focus, our visions for Birdsfoot also include cottage industries, an alternative school, healing work, income sharing, and improving our ability to take care of more of our needs and consume fewer resources and commercial products.

We are committed to consensus decision-making, peaceful resolution of conflicts, caring for each other, and equality of rights, responsibilities, and ownership. We welcome diversity and have a variety of interests both on and off the land: music, poetry, dance, spinning and weaving, self-sufficiency, income sharing, political involvement, Process Work, Physical Therapy, personal growth, non-violence, environmental activism, alternative education, and raising kids. We enjoy making and eating wonderful, nutritious meals using the food we grow; our dinners are a time that we all come together each day."

HUNGARIAN
AMERICANS

Hungarian American cooks dish out cabbage rolls at the annual Hungarian dinner at the Church of the Visitation, Norfolk, St. Lawrence County. *Mark Sloan Photo/TAUNY Archives*

Hungarian Holiday Memories

by Beverly Sabad and Magda Breg

as told to Lynn Ekfelt

Once the first generation kids got to school, they stopped the old customs; they wanted to fit in and it wasn't fashionable to celebrate the old country way. So this is how we remember it, not the way we do it now. Easter was always the biggest holiday for the Hungarians. During Lent, of course, you fasted, so Easter dinner was a special meal. On the day before Easter you made up a big basket with all the food you'd be eating the next few days: a big baked ham, lamb with stuffing, colored eggs, special Easter meatloaf*, bread, butter molded into the shape of a lamb, even the horseradish to go with the meat. Then on Easter you took the basket to the church to be blessed by the priest. After church the family sat down to enjoy the feast. We all shared the first hard-boiled egg; we passed it around so everyone could have a bite. Easter Sunday dinner was a family affair—just for the immediate family.

Easter Monday was different; that was when the boys would come to call. The girls would make special eggs to give them. You'd wrap an egg in cheesecloth with a little piece of fern or a dried flower; the cheesecloth had to be tight around the egg to hold the flower in place. Then you'd put it into a pot with onion skins for a while. Ten minutes was enough to color it but you could leave it longer if you wanted a deeper color. You could tell how popular a girl was by how many eggs she had to give away on Easter Monday. The boys would bring bottles of perfume and sprinkle us and wish us Happy Easter. Then we'd give them an egg and invite them in for some pastry.

The first day of Easter was for church and the immediate family; the second morning the boys came, then the third day everyone visited. Married families came home to see relatives, and neighbors stopped by for drinks and pastries.

The other big holiday was Christmas. We'd all go caroling around town. Whenever we'd stop at a house, the owners would come out and give the kids pennies and treats like nuts and fruits and cookies. The men in the group would get wine and kifli*. By the time they'd sung at lots of houses, the men got pretty jolly!

Together with her husband Shine, Beverly Sabad formerly owned and operated Sabad's, a Hungarian restaurant in Norfolk. In the late 1980s Magda Breg moved from Rumania to Norfolk, where she took a job as a chef at Sabad's.

Habart Zöldbab-Leves
(Creamed String Bean Soup)

Beverly Sabad remembers helping her mother-in-law snap the ends off the beans for this soup. The older Mrs. Sabad made so much at one time that she used a washtub. Whenever she made a batch, all the neighbors would come to the house bringing bread, and there would be a giant soup and bread feast.

1	pound string beans— preferably fresh, but could use frozen	3-4	tablespoons flour
		½	pint sour cream
		2-3	cups milk
	Salt	¼	cup vinegar
2	quarts water		

Cook the beans in salted water. Mix the flour with a small amount of water until it makes a smooth paste. Add the sour cream and milk; mix well. When the beans are cooked, pour the cream mixture over the beans. Add the vinegar. Let the soup come to a boil, then serve it hot.

Beverly Sabad
Norfolk

This recipe appears in Hungarian Recipes, *compiled by the Dorcas Guild of the Magyar United Church of Christ.*

Pörkölt (Hungarian Goulash)

Gulyás is a rough translation of "cowboy." This stew was made by Hungarian herdsmen, traveling with their steers or sheep to find suitable pastures on the very dry plains of Hungary. According to Eva Kende in Eva's Hungarian Kitchen, *where this recipe appears, it was the Austrians who started to call the dish after its cowboy creators instead of simply calling it pörkölt or paprikás as the Hungarians did.*

1	large onion, minced	1	pound beef chuck, cut into
1-2	diced green peppers,		small cubes
	optional	½	teaspoon salt
2	tablespoons vegetable oil	⅛	teaspoon cayenne,
2	teaspoons paprika		optional

Sauté the onions (and the peppers if desired) in the oil until the onions become transparent. Remove them from the heat and mix in the paprika well. Add the meat and salt. Stir until the meat is thoroughly coated with the onion-paprika mixture and simmer, covered, until the meat is tender. If necessary, add a little water or stock to keep the meat from burning. (Ordinarily, the meat juices are sufficient liquid.) The slower the cooking the better the flavor, so this dish works well in a crockpot.

In Hungary, this stew is often turned into a soup (gulyás leves). To make the soup, cube three medium potatoes and add them to the stew along with one teaspoon caraway seed and four cups of water or stock. Cook until the potatoes can be pierced easily with a fork, then add the following dumplings and cook for another 10 minutes before serving hot.

Csipetke (Dumplings)

1	egg	¼	teaspoon salt
½	cup flour		

Work all the ingredients together, kneading until the mixture is smooth. This dough should be hard and stiff; add a little more flour if the dough is sticky. Roll out the dough by hand to make a flat circle the size of a small plate. Pinch small pieces from the circle into the boiling soup until all the dough is used up.

Beverly Sabad
Norfolk

Vagdalt Hús (Easter Meatloaf)

1	pound ground meat (not too lean)	⅛	teaspoon pepper
1	egg	¼-1	teaspoon garlic powder (to taste)
1	medium onion, minced	⅓	cup bread crumbs
½	teaspoon salt	3	hard-boiled eggs, peeled

Mix together all the ingredients except the hard-boiled eggs. Grease a one- quart ovenproof glass loaf pan. Place half of the meat mixture into the pan, pressing gently. Line up the eggs end-to-end in the center. Cover the eggs with the remaining mixture. Smooth the sides and top of the loaf with wet hands so that no seam remains. Bake the meatloaf uncovered at 325 degrees for one hour, basting occasionally.

Beverly Sabad
Norfolk

This recipe appears in Eva's Hungarian Kitchen.

Káposztas Kocka (Cabbage Noodles)

2	medium heads cabbage	2	pounds dry noodles, boiled and drained
1	pound butter (do not use shortening)	½	teaspoon black pepper
1	teaspoon salt		

Grate the cabbage on a medium-fine grater. In a large pot (do not use a Teflon-lined pot; it browns the cabbage too much) melt the butter, then add the cabbage and salt. Cook this mixture together slowly for about 2 hours. Add the hot boiled noodles and the pepper; mix them together well with the cabbage. Serve the dish hot.

Magda Breg
Norfolk

Csirkepaprikás (Chicken Paprikás)

Chicken

1	onion, chopped	4-5	pounds chicken, cut up
4	tablespoons shortening	1½	cups water
1	tablespoon paprika	½	pint sour cream
1	teaspoon salt	½	pint sweet cream, optional
¼	teaspoon black pepper		

Dumplings

3	eggs, beaten	1	teaspoon salt
3	cups flour	½	cup water

To prepare the chicken, brown the onion in the shortening. Add the paprika, salt, pepper and chicken, then brown the chicken for 10 minutes. Add the water. Cover the pot and let the chicken simmer slowly until it is tender. Remove the chicken. Add the sour cream to the drippings in the pan and mix well.

To prepare the dumplings, mix all the ingredients together and beat the mixture with a spoon. Drop the batter by teaspoonfuls into boiling salted water. Cook about 10 minutes, then drain and rinse with cold water. Drain the dumplings well before adding them to the paprikás.

Add the dumplings to the sour cream and pan drippings. Arrange the chicken on top. Heat the dish through, then serve it. For more gravy, add the sweet cream to the sour cream, along with flour to thicken the mixture.

Instead of the dumplings, you can also make this dish with home-made noodles:

Tarhonya (Noodles)

2	cups sifted flour	4	tablespoons butter
2	eggs	3	cups chicken soup or stock
½	teaspoon salt		Salt and pepper to taste

Mix the flour, eggs and salt together. Add water if necessary to make a stiff dough. Knead the dough into a ball and grate it on the medium side of a grater. Spread it out to dry overnight.

Csirkepaprikás *(continued)*

When you are ready to assemble the paprikás, melt the butter in a frying pan. Add the dried noodles and brown them for 5 to 10 minutes, stirring frequently to prevent them from burning. Add the soup, ½ cup at a time. Cook the noodles, covered, until the liquid is absorbed. Season them to taste, then add them to the paprikás.

Beverly Sabad
Norfolk

This recipe appears in the Dorcas Guild's Hungarian Recipes.

Töltöttkáposzta (Stuffed Cabbage)

1	large head cabbage	2	teaspoons salt
1	large onion, minced	½	teaspoon black pepper
3	tablespoons shortening	¾	pound rice
¾	pound ground beef	1	small can sauerkraut
¾	pound ground pork	1	(#2) can tomato juice
1	tablespoon paprika	½	pint sour cream

Core the cabbage and place it in enough boiling salted water to cover it. With a fork in one hand and a knife in the other, keep cutting off the leaves as they become wilted. Drain the leaves. Trim the thick center vein of each cabbage leaf. Brown the onion in the shortening. Combine the onion, beef, pork, paprika, salt, pepper and rice; mix them well. Place a tablespoon of filling along the edge of each cabbage leaf and roll it up, turning in the edges as you roll. Place the rolls in a pot and put in enough water to come ⅔ of the way up the rolls. Arrange the sauerkraut on top of the rolls, then add the tomato juice. Cover the pot and cook the rolls slowly for about 1½ hours or until the rice is tender. Spread the sour cream on top of the rolls and cook 5 minutes more.

Beverly Sabad
Norfolk

This recipe appears in the Dorcas Guild's Hungarian Recipes.

Turós Palacsinta
(Crêpes with Cottage Cheese)

Filling

1	pound dry cottage cheese	¼-½	cup sugar
1	egg, well beaten	3	drops vanilla extract

Crêpes

2	cups sifted flour	4	eggs, beaten
1	teaspoon salt	2	cups milk
2	teaspoons sugar		Butter

To make the filling, mix all the ingredients well, adding the sugar to taste.

To make the crêpes, mix the flour, salt and sugar. Combine the milk and beaten eggs thoroughly, then add them gradually to the flour mixture, beating until they form a smooth, thin batter. Spoon three tablespoons of the batter onto a hot buttered skillet. The layer will be very thin. Brown the crêpe lightly on both sides. Continue making crêpes until all the batter is used up, keeping the finished ones warm. Put a layer of the filling along one side of each crêpe, then roll them up. Place them in a buttered baking dish and sprinkle the tops with powdered sugar. Heat them thoroughly at 325 degrees (approximately 25 minutes). Serve them topped with sour cream and strawberry preserves.

Beverly Sabad
Norfolk

This recipe appears in the Dorcas Guild's Hungarian Recipes.

Kifli (Crescent Cookies)

Dough

1½	pounds butter	½	can sweetened condensed milk
½	pound vegetable shortening	1	teaspoon salt
9	cups flour	2	lemons—peel of both; juice of one
1	package dry yeast		
¼	cup warm water	2	teaspoons almond extract
6-7	eggs, beaten		

Filling

2	egg whites, beaten	½	can sweetened condensed milk
1	cup sugar		
2	pounds walnuts, ground	½	teaspoon vanilla
1	stick butter, melted		

To make the dough, cut the butter and shortening into the flour as for pie dough until the mixture is coarsely crumbly. Dissolve the yeast in the warm water. Add the eggs, milk, yeast, salt, lemon peel, lemon juice and almond extract to the flour mixture and work them into the dough with your hands until it is no longer sticky. Place the bowl in the refrigerator overnight.

To make the filling, beat the egg whites. When they are stiff, gradually beat in the sugar. Fold in the nuts, butter, milk, and vanilla.

To assemble the kifli, roll out about ⅙ of the dough at a time, leaving the rest in the refrigerator until you are ready to use it. Cover the counter with powdered sugar, then roll the dough out thin (about ⅛ inch thick) in a circle. Cut the circle into pie-shaped wedges. Place some filling along the rounded side of each wedge, then roll the wedges toward the point. Curve the rolls into a crescent shape and bake at 350 degrees until brown (approximately 15 minutes.)

Magda Breg
Norfolk

Torte (Striped Cake)

Cake I—chocolate

8	eggs, separated	2	teaspoons baking powder
2	cups sugar	2	cups sifted flour
8	tablespoons warm water	2	tablespoons cocoa powder

Cake II—white

4	eggs, separated	1	teaspoon baking powder
1	cup sugar	1	cup sifted flour
4	tablespoons warm water		

Filling

1	cup milk	2	tablespoons cocoa powder
1	cup sugar	½	pound butter
8	ounces unsweetened chocolate		

To make the cakes, beat the egg yolks with the sugar and warm water. Mix in the baking powder, flour, and cocoa powder (for Cake I only). Beat the egg whites and fold them into the yolk mixture. Bake at 350 degrees for 25 to 30 minutes in greased 9 x 13-inch pans lined with waxed paper. Cool the cakes, then cut Cake I horizontally through the middle into two layers.

To make the filling, cook the milk, sugar, chocolate, and cocoa powder together to pudding consistency. Allow the mixture to cool, then beat in the butter.

Place a chocolate layer on the serving plate and ice the top. Place the white layer next and ice the top of that. Top the cake with the other chocolate layer, then ice the top and sides with the remaining filling.

Magda Breg
Norfolk

Animal Cracker Dessert

1 (1-pound) bag animal crackers	1 pound sweet butter
2 cups water	1 teaspoon rum, vanilla, or almond flavoring
4 tablespoons cocoa powder	Coconut (optional)
2 cups sugar	

Crush the animal crackers coarsely (each cracker should be in four or five pieces.) Bring to a boil the water, cocoa powder, and sugar. Add the butter and flavoring. Once the butter has melted in, let the mixture cool, but don't let it get completely cold. Pour it over the crushed crackers, then pour the resulting mixture into a 9 x 9-inch pan and cover it with aluminum foil. Place the pan in the freezer. Let the dessert sit at room temperature for five minutes before cutting it into small pieces to serve. You can sprinkle it with coconut before serving if desired.

Magda Breg
Norfolk

According to the census records for 1900, the first Hungarian in St. Lawrence County was John Jacobs, who immigrated in 1887. The political and economic situation in Hungary at the time was not good, unless you happened to belong to the aristocracy. Most Hungarians were farmers, very poor, and without a vote since there was no universal suffrage. Most did not own their land. Desperate to better their lot, many men looked to the United States as a land of plenty. Generally they planned to come here, work for a while, make some money, then return to their homeland and families. By 1910 there were approximately 150 Hungarian immigrants in Norfolk and over 300 in Massena.

Most Hungarians came to Norfolk to work in the paper mills, of which there were several in the immediate area. Most of these men lived on West Main Street, going to work every day by means of a foot bridge over the Raquette River. Single, or having left their families at home awaiting their return, most lived in boarding houses owned by other Hungarian immigrants. Since most of the men came from one town, Turterebes, they found familiar faces in these boarding houses—friends and relatives willing to help them learn English and find work. Many of the Hungarians who moved to Massena worked at Alcoa, which opened in 1903. Like their compatriots in Norfolk, they often lived together in boarding houses run by those who had arrived earlier.

Once they were on American soil, many of the men found their goals changing. Instead of focusing on making money to take back to Hungary, they began to think of ways to bring their families here. The community grew as wives and children joined the working men.

At the end of World War I in 1919, Hungarian emigration was given added impetus by the break-up of the country. As part of the treaty that ended the war, the dual monarchy of Austria-Hungary was split apart, and pieces of Hungary were given to Czechoslovakia, Yugoslavia, Rumania, and the Soviet Union. Turterebes became a Rumanian village as a result of this shift, and young men suddenly found themselves receiving draft notices to serve in the military of a country to which they felt no loyalty. A second wave of immigration to the United States took place as these men set out to join relatives who had already begun a new life here. Beverly Sabad remembers the huge gardens by all the houses—vegetables for the table and flowers to turn the houses into homes.

Shortly after this second wave of immigrants arrived in the North Country, the Depression settled in and the community began to disperse. Families moved to Detroit, Buffalo, or Cleveland in hopes of finding work. As the years went on and the paper mills closed, more families left the area. Children married and moved away; older people died. But driving down the street in Norfolk, one still sees a number of Hungarian names on the mailboxes, and though the stores no longer stock specialty items for Hungarian cooks, the American Legion holds a cabbage roll dinner as its annual fund-raiser.

* * *

Adapted from an article by Marcia Eggleston entitled "History of the Hungarian People in St. Lawrence County," which appeared in The Quarterly *[St. Lawrence County Historical Association], October 1988, pp. 14-18.*

ITALIAN
AMERICANS

Women of St. Anthony's Church in Watertown, Jefferson County, gather each July in the commercial kitchen of Alteri's Bakery to bake dozens of trays of Italian cookies to sell at the pastry table of the Feast of Our Lady of Mt. Carmel. *Varick Chittenden Photo/TAUNY Archives*

St. Joseph's Day (March 19)

by Jennie Spaziani and Rosalind Morgia

as told to Lynn Ekfelt and to the production staff of
TAUNY's radio program "Home Cooking"

My mother, Mrs. Rose Root, was born in a small mountainous village in Calabria named Guardia Piemontese. When she came to this country at the turn of the century, one of the many customs she brought with her was the celebration of St. Joseph's Day on March 19. She first observed this feast in 1903 in thanksgiving for a favor she had asked on my brother's behalf. She continued the observance for over 50 years, after which I, Jennie Spaziani, carried on the tradition until my daughter, Rosalind Morgia, took it over for the last 11 years. Though it's an Italian religious affair, not everybody observes it the way we do. Some of them will go to church and that's the end of it. But where my mother came from in Italy, that was their main holiday—they observed it just as much as Christmas.

During the preceding week, we make all the preparations—whatever we have to do. The morning of the feast you start working in the kitchen. You can't do it alone, so Mother was always here when she was alive. Two of my sisters, and my daughters as they grew up—they'd help us. Then, you have your priest come and bless all the food, bless your altar, bless your whole house. The time varies; sometimes the guests are here at 12:30 or 1:00 for the dinner.

The participants in the dinner are invited by the family to represent the saints being honored—one guest for each saint. The number can vary from year to year, but there are always three to represent the Holy Family, with a child to represent the Infant. Only one person per family is allowed and no members of your immediate family who live in the house with you. Otherwise you can have different saints different years if you want; my mother did that. Sometimes she'd have maybe two or three. I always had the same six—they were my favorite saints. I'd always have St. Jude. Sometimes if I was down and out, I'd say, "Oh, St. Jude, please—." St. Jude is for the impossible. And St. Theresa—well, she's for almost anything. St. Anthony is for lost articles.

Sometimes you lose something and you say, "St. Anthony, please let me find—." It happened to me and I did find my answer. St. Lucy is for your eyes. And then St. Leonard and St. Rocco. He was one of my mother's patron saints; he helped people with sores. Rosalind does it differently. She has eight or 10 elderly or sick people sit at table representing various saints; one year there were lots of pregnancies in the family so she had all the "fat ladies" sit.

As they come in, you greet them and they all sit down and wait till they are called to the table. Then when they're ready to sit down, you kneel down, kiss their feet and all that; then you sit them all at their places in rotation. They have to taste every food you put in front of them, whether they like it or not. If they don't like it they can just pick at it. First you serve them a little anisette to start. Then you pass around the cookies, the tarales*. Then you start with your salad—just lettuce and oil and vinegar. After the salad they have their spinach. And from the spinach, you give them their macaroni, just plain macaroni, and a meatless meatball which is made of just ricotta cheese and eggs*, and fried fish. (There's never any meat because it's during Lent.) Then they have the pasta a ceci*. When they're done with that they have their fruit. We have different kinds of fruit and nuts and all on one big plate. Then, there's always someone making a nice cake, a sponge cake or whatever, and they have the cake and coffee.

When they're through, they get up and say prayers and I sing a special song to St. Joseph in Italian. It says: we have to pray to St. Joseph who's like a grand signore. In his hand he has the lily, the flower; in his arm he has our Lord. Please give us a favor every hour. We have to thank St. Joseph who is a great savior and chaste spouse.

Then after we say our prayers, we all get up and kiss the feet again and that's the end of the meal. The saints all get a loaf of bread to take home; it's braided in a ring to symbolize Christian unity. And they get a little of everything they ate to take with them. Then, it's open house for everyone; anybody wants to come, they can taste whatever food we have. The whole community knows about it, you don't have to call them up or send them a special invitation. If they can't make it that day, then they'll try to find out if you still have your altar up for a while and come later.

On the altar you have to have something to represent St. Joseph or the Holy Family. After that you can put whatever you want. Some people put a lot of pictures of different saints, rosary beads, lots of little statues, flowers of all kinds. People who come as guests bring flowers or candles; they feel they want to do something for St. Joseph. Some of them will say, "Here's some money; I would like a Mass said for St. Joseph." So, we give it to the priest and tell him to have Masses.

It takes weeks of work and preparation, but it is done, with a great deal of devotion and fervor, to honor St. Joseph.

Tarales

Cookies

6	eggs	2	teaspoons vanilla or lemon extract
2	cups sugar		
½	pound margarine or shortening, melted	6	cups flour
		6	teaspoons baking powder
1	cup milk		

Frosting

1	pound confectioners' sugar	¼	cup milk
2	tablespoons shortening		Vanilla or lemon extract

To make the cookies, beat the eggs with the sugar. Add the melted shortening, milk and whichever extract you have picked. Combine the flour with the baking powder and add them to the egg mixture. Roll the dough into any shape or size you prefer. Bake at 325 degrees for 10 to 12 minutes.

To make the frosting, beat all the ingredients together until they are smooth. Spread the frosting on the cooled cookies.

Jennie Spaziani
Watertown

Pasta a ceci (Macaroni and Chick Peas)

2	tablespoons oil			Salt, black pepper, and
1	clove garlic, minced (or			basil to taste
	more to taste)		1	pound ditalini macaroni
2	cans chick peas, undrained		2	eggs
3	chick pea cans of water		1	tablespoon Romano cheese
				Parsley to taste

Put the oil and garlic in a saucepan and cook until the garlic is lightly browned. Add the chick peas, water and all, plus three more cans of water. Add the salt, pepper and basil and let the mixture simmer for 20 minutes. Cook the macaroni al dente and drain it. Add it to the chick peas and cook them together for five minutes. Put the eggs in a small bowl with the cheese and parsley, and beat them well. Add the egg mixture to the macaroni/chick peas and simmer them all together for 5 minutes.

Jenni Spaziani
Watertown

Ricotta Balls

2	cups bread crumbs		½	cup Romano cheese,
2	tablespoons salt			grated
1	tablespoon black pepper		6	eggs
2	tablespoons parsley		½	cup milk
8	ounces ricotta cheese			Vegetable oil for deep
				frying

In a mixing bowl, thoroughly combine the crumbs, salt, pepper and parsley. Add the ricotta and Romano cheeses to the bowl and mix them in well. Beat the eggs with the milk and add them to the cheese mixture. If the resulting mixture seems too stiff, add another egg. Roll into 1½-inch balls and deep fry them in hot oil until they are golden brown.

Jennie Spaziani
Watertown

Mincemeats

Filling

3	(9-ounce) packages condensed mincemeat	1¼	cups water
1	(15-ounce) box seedless raisins		Vegetable oil for frying
			Confectioners' sugar

Crust

3¼	cups sifted flour	¾	cup cold water
1	tablespoon salt		Confectioners' sugar for sprinkling
½	pound lard		

To make the filling, break up the mincemeat in a heavy pan. Add the raisins and water. Cook slowly over low heat until the mincemeat has absorbed the water, then simmer it for about 10 to 15 minutes, stirring frequently to prevent it from sticking to the pan. Allow the mixture to cool.

To make the crust, mix the flour and salt. Cut in the lard until the mixture is crumbly. Sprinkle the cold water over the flour/lard mixture, then toss them together lightly. Roll the dough out thin and cut it into circles with a large, round cookie cutter.

Place approximately one tablespoon of the mincemeat in the center of a dough circle. Bring the edges together so that a semi-circle is formed. Pinch the edges together, using a fork to press them and seal them tightly. In a skillet or a heavy pan, heat the oil to 370 degrees, then fry the pies— first on one side, then the other, until they are golden. When the pies have cooled, sprinkle them with confectioners' sugar.

Rosalind Morgia
Watertown

The following three recipes are also holiday fare, but not for St. Joseph's Day. All three are favorite Christmas Eve dishes.

Baccala (Codfish in Sauce)

1	package salted codfish	1	large can tomatoes
1	small onion, minced		Salt, pepper, basil to taste
2	tablespoons oil		

Soak the codfish in water for two days, changing the water at least twice a day. In a saucepan, brown the onion lightly in the oil. Crush the tomatoes and add them to the pan with the seasonings to your taste. Simmer for 20 minutes or more, adding water if the sauce seems too thick. Add the pieces of cod and cook until the fish is tender (approximately ½ hour more).

Rosalind Morgia
Watertown

Pizza alla Napoletana (Neopolitan Pizza)

Dough

1	envelope yeast	1	tablespoon salt
1	cup warm water	4	tablespoons olive oil
2½	cups flour		

Topping

2	pounds (4 to 5 whole) fresh tomatoes, peeled and chopped—may substitute canned	1	small oval of sliced Mozzarella
		1	small can anchovies
			Black pepper
			Olive oil

To make the dough, stir the yeast into the warm water. Combine the flour and salt, then mix all the ingredients together. Shape the resulting dough into a ball and let it rise to more than double its volume. Pat it out by hand to a disk about ¼ inch thick. Place it on a large, well-oiled baking sheet. Spread the surface liberally with chopped tomatoes, mozzarella, strips of anchovies, black pepper, and several spurts of olive oil. Bake it at 450 degrees until the crust is golden and the filling is bubbly (approximately 10 to 15 minutes). Serve immediately.

Makes one large or two medium pizzas.

Rosalind Morgia
Watertown

Linguine with White Clam Sauce

1 pound pasta	1 teaspoon basil
2 cloves fresh garlic or	½ teaspoon parsley
1 teaspoon garlic powder	½ cup grated Romano or
1 cup olive oil	Parmesan cheese
2 (8-ounce) cans minced clams	Salt and pepper to taste

Cook the pasta in boiling salted water. In a saucepan, brown the garlic in the oil over low heat. Slowly add the minced clams, basil and parsley. While the pasta is cooking, let the clam mixture come to a slow boil and simmer for 10 minutes. Drain the pasta well, cover it with the clam sauce, and stir. Sprinkle the cheese over the sauce and serve the plates immediately.

Rosalind Morgia
Watertown

Ricotta Gnocchi

1 pound ricotta cheese	Sauce of your choice—pesto,
1 large egg	marinara, meat sauce
2 cups flour, approximately	Parmesan or Romano
	cheese for topping

Combine the egg and cheese. Add ½ cup of the flour, then keep adding flour gradually as you begin kneading the dough gently, working it like a pie dough, shaping it and pushing it forward. Continue to add flour until the dough does not feel wet. Be sure to keep the surface on which you are working well floured. The gnocchi dough is kneaded enough when it begins to feel elastic and somewhat firm. This usually takes about 5 minutes.

Form the dough into a rope of ½ to ¾ inches in diameter. Roll it flat on the floured board, using both hands. If the dough crumbles and/or splits too much, add a bit more flour and knead a little longer. (The finished rope need not be absolutely uniform.) Cut the rope into ¾-inch segments, pushing a dimple into each segment with your thumb. This thins the center, making the cooking process more even and allowing the sauce to cling better. When all the gnocchi are formed, toss them into a lightly floured bowl and set them aside for no longer than an hour.

Boil the gnocchi in salted water as you would any pasta. Gnocchi are done when they float to the surface. Add the drained, cooked gnocchi to Ragu meat sauce or any good tomato or pesto sauce for a delicious entrée. A good finishing touch is a dash of grated Parmesan or Romano cheese.

Marie Regan
Potsdam

Meatballs di Plati

Meatballs

2	pounds ground pork	2	eggs
1	cup grated Parmesan or Romano cheese	1	tablespoon minced garlic
1	cup grated Italian bread crumbs	1	cup water
1	tablespoon chopped fresh parsley or 1 teaspoon dry parsley		Salt and black pepper to taste

Sauce

2	(2-pound-13-ounce) jars green pepper and mushroom sauce	2	cups water
		½	cup fresh basil, chopped

To make the meatballs, mix the ingredients well in a large bowl; add another ¼ cup water as needed to make the consistency better for rolling the meatballs. Roll the mixture into balls about the size of a silver dollar, placing them on a platter or tray. When all the mixture has been made into balls, place all the balls gently into a simmering tomato sauce. Cook over low heat, occasionally stirring gently, for 45 minutes.

To make a quick, easy, delicious sauce for cooking the meatballs, combine the bottled sauce with the water and basil. This recipe makes 75 to 80 meatballs even if you reserve ⅔ cup of the mix to make the soup on page 192.

Marie Regan
Potsdam

Chicken Soup with Meatballs and Escarole

1	can white chicken meat, shredded	⅔	cup acine de pepe macaroni
3	(49½-ounce) cans chicken broth	2	large or 3 small eggs
⅔	cup pork meatball mix (see previous recipe)	1⅓	cup grated Parmesan or Romano cheese
1	head escarole or endive, washed and chopped		Salt and pepper to taste

Heat the chicken meat in the broth. Meanwhile, roll the meat mixture into dime-sized balls. (You should get about 40 meatballs from this amount of mix.) Add the meatballs to the chicken broth and simmer them together for 20 minutes. Add the escarole or endive; cook for 3 or 4 minutes. Add the acine de pepe. Turn up the heat, stirring the soup occasionally, and cook it until the pasta is tender (approximately 5 minutes).

Mix the eggs with the Parmesan or Romano to form a stiff mixture. Place heaping tablespoons of the cheese/egg mixture into the boiling soup. Cover the kettle and cook the soup for 3 or 4 minutes until dumpling-like egg drops are formed.

If some soup remains the next day, more chicken stock may be added to the remainder.

This recipe will serve twelve easily.

Marie Regan
Potsdam

Lack of detailed census records makes it difficult to pinpoint exactly when the first Italians arrived in Watertown, but it was probably in the 1880s. The stream increased over the years, with the biggest push coming in the early 1900s. Like immigrants from many other countries, they came in hopes of finding a more secure life than the one they had had at home. Once one member of a large and close-knit Italian family came to the United States, the rest usually followed and settled nearby. In this way the Watertown Italian community expanded until by 1916 it was well established on the city's west side.

The majority were from southern Italy; very few were from north of Rome. Many were from an area known as Guardia Piemontese, between Naples and Reggio Calabria; the name means "a colony for the Piedmont people." It had been settled by Protestant Waldensians from Turin who were then forcibly converted to Catholicism during the Bourbon era.

Although we generally think of Ellis Island as the way-station through which our ancestors entered this country, the Italians who eventually ended up in Watertown passed through almost every conceivable port: Boston, New Orleans, Philadelphia, Baltimore, and even Tampico, Mexico.

The obvious next question is "Why Watertown?" How did illiterate laborers fresh off the boat from southern Italy—sometimes after a brief detour through the tenements of New York City—end up in a small, cold city in northern New York? The answer lies in the system of agents common to industries at the time. Immigrants needed interpreters, people to lend them money to get started, scribes to help them communicate with families at home, notaries public, and people to help them find lodgings and make travel arrangements for the wives and children who were planning to follow them to the land of opportunity. Upstate railroads, paper mills and foundries knew this and sent agents to the port cities who provided assistance, then signed up grateful workers.

Large numbers of Watertown's Italians began their working lives in America as laborers on the Rome, Watertown & Ogdensburg Railroad (later the N.Y. Central). They were track workers or mechanics, or they worked in the car shops, switchyards, or roundhouses. Others worked for the New York Air Brake Company. Many lived in boarding houses, saving every cent they could until they could afford to bring wives and children to join them. When that happy day arrived, the wives, in turn, took in other boarders to help make ends meet. The boarders were never strangers; they were friends and relatives from home in Italy. The women not only fed these men but also did their washing and ironing, made their beds, and tidied their rooms—all for very little money because the boarders had very little to spare.

Although most of the immigrants were railroad workers, at least at first, others put skills from home to work in the new country. There were a number of successful Italian truck gardeners and tailors. During the peak years of the Italian community, almost every corner had a small grocery, in many of which the shopkeeper made his own sausage by his secret family recipe. Whatever they did for a living, the Italians acquired a reputation as hard workers.

As the first- and second-generation immigrants give way to their children and grandchildren, Watertown's Italian community is slowly becoming a less distinct and separate entity. However Americanized they may seem during the rest of the year, though, at the three-day Bravo Italiano Festa, Italian Americans take time to celebrate their heritage with equal parts of good music and good food.

* * *

Adapted from Frank Augustine's book La Bella America: From the Old Country to the North Country. *Watertown NY:* Watertown Daily Times, *1989.*

JEWS

Children from several families participate in the ceremonies of a community Passover seder in Potsdam each spring. *Mark Sloan Photo/ TAUNY Archives*

Passover Seder at Barbara Heinemann's

with further information from Judith Glasser

The week before Easter, Barbara calls to invite Nils and me to share their Passover seder. That night he and I debate whether or not to go, a bit fearful of intruding on a religious ceremony that is not part of our tradition. What if we commit some terrible faux pas and ruin the evening for everyone? Hesitantly we express our concern to Barbara who assures us that one of the purposes of the seder ceremony is to explain the history of the Jews to children and outsiders. Fears allayed, we accept eagerly, knowing from delightful experience Barbara's cooking expertise.

Once our coats, scarves, mittens and boots are stowed away (Spring festival indeed!) she hands us each a haggadah, a book containing the Bible stories and songs which we will be using during the evening. She explains that this is just one of many different versions of this "guidebook." All are alike in the basic form and content, but vary according to the interests of the participants. Feminist? Environmentalist? Interested in world peace? There's a haggadah designed especially for you.

Browsing through the book, we learn that Passover is actually a combination of two holidays, an ancient festival celebrating the first grain harvest and the more recent one marking the deliverance of the Jews from Egyptian bondage. The most vital aspect of Passover is the absolute ban on all sorts of leavening. No beer is allowed, no yeast or baking powder, and no grains which might ferment in the presence of water, for example wheat, barley, rye, or oats. Since the harvest festival involved placing the new grain in the storage bins, it made sense to remove first any old, fermenting grain which might contaminate the new crop. This practical prohibition became symbolic as well when the unleavened bread came to represent the haste with which the Jews departed from Egypt—so quickly that they could not wait for their bread to rise.

Moving to the dining room, we sit down and discover that Barbara has set an extra place at the table. No, she explains, not a momentary memory lapse, but a reminder of those Jews who are unable to celebrate a Seder because they live in countries with oppressive governments. In front of Gary Levin, who will be leading the Seder, sits a napkin-covered plate holding three Matzohs (unleavened wheat bread resembling big, flat crackers; Matzoh is made by a special process which ensures that the flour will remain completely dry throughout so it can not possibly ferment) and another holding an odd assortment of bits of food: a bone, a pile of horseradish, a hard-boiled egg, some parsley, and a brown mixture resembling chutney. At each of our places there's a little dish of salt water.

Gary begins by filling our wine glasses and explaining that we will be drinking four glasses of wine throughout the dinner, representing the four promises of redemption in the account of the Jews' deliverance from Egyptian bondage in Exodus: I will bring you out; I will deliver you; I will redeem you; I will take you to be my people. As we read and sing our way through the Haggadah, the meanings of the mysterious objects on the table become clear—all stand for some part of the Exodus story: the parsley which we dip in our dish of salt water for the tears the Jews shed while they were in Egypt; the bone for the lamb which they sacrificed and whose blood they used to mark their doors so the Angel of Death would pass over their houses; the egg for rebirth and the hopefulness of spring (though one must wonder along with Judith Glasser's husband just how hopeful a hard-boiled egg really is); the horseradish for the bitterness of slavery; and the Charoset, which proves to be a mixture of grated apples, nuts, cinnamon, and wine, for the mortar and bricks the Jews made while working for the Egyptian Pharoh.

By now the smells from the kitchen are driving our stomachs, empty except for pinches of the symbolic foods, wild with expectation. The chicken soup with matzoh balls*, gefilte fish*, vegetable stew (called tzimmes)*, pot roast*, and sponge cake* prove well worth the wait. Barbara's family is from Spain (Sephardic Jews) and Carol and Gary's from Eastern Europe (Ashkenazi Jews); the dinner-table discussion involves interesting comparisons of customs and traditions in the two cultures.

After the last crumb of sponge cake has disappeared, Gary passes around the afikoman, a chunk of the middle Matzoh which has been saved under the napkin, and we all break off and eat a small piece. The Seder can't end until the afikoman is eaten. He tells us that had there been any children in our group, they might have stolen this during the course of the meal, and he would have had to redeem it from them for a small prize so he could end the ceremony. If it meant a piece of that cake to take home, I'd consider stealing it myself!

Cholent (Meat Stew)

This hearty stew is traditionally served for lunch on the Sabbath, when cooking is not allowed. It was originally meant to simmer on the back of the wood or coal stove overnight. A crock pot works best in these gas- and electric stove times.

1½ cup beans (My mother used large limas or marrowfats, but any combination of red and white beans will do.)
1 pound stew meat
6 medium potatoes, quartered

2 medium onions, quartered
2 cloves garlic, finely chopped
½ cup barley
1 bay leaf
Salt and pepper to taste

Soak the beans overnight. Drain them and place them in a crockpot with the remaining ingredients. Pour in water to about 1 inch over the top of the food in the pot, cover it, and turn the crock pot to high. After about 2½ hours turn it down to low and forget it. It will be ready at dinnertime that night if you start it in the morning. It takes about 18 hours if you do not put it on high at first. If you leave it overnight, check to be sure your crockpot does not lose water. If it does, replace the water so that the stew will not dry out.

Judith Glasser
Potsdam

Chicken Soup with Matzoh Balls

Chicken Soup

4	pounds chicken (necks, backs, bones, "back quarters"—the meat will be tasteless when you are done so use the cheapest kind you can find)	2	large stalks celery
		½	teaspoon thyme
		½	teaspoon basil
		¼	teaspoon peppercorns (about 6 to 8)
1	large onion	1	bay leaf
1	large carrot	3	cloves garlic
		4	quarts cold water, approximately

Matzoh Balls

These amounts will serve two people. They can be multiplied indefinitely without harm to the final product. To make a lower-fat version, replace one tablespoon of the chicken fat with one tablespoon of soup stock or water and increase the amount of matzoh meal to ¼ cup.

1	large egg	½	teaspoon salt, divided
2	tablespoons chicken fat or oil		A few grinds pepper
3	tablespoons matzoh meal	1	tablespoon chopped parsley

To make the soup, place all ingredients in a large pot, using about 4 quarts of cold water. (If you can't fit in that much, you need a larger pot!) Place the pot on low heat and leave it alone for about four hours. It should not ever boil hard. If the vegetables are soft and the meat tasteless, the broth will be great. If not, cook it longer.

Drain the broth into a large bowl and chill it. Discard all the solids. When the soup is cold, the fat will be congealed in a hard disk on the top and can be lifted off without loss of any broth. (The broth will be jelled.)

To make the matzoh balls, beat the egg briefly, then add the fat and beat again. Add the matzoh meal mixed with ¼ teaspoon salt, the pepper and the parsley. Allow the batter to stand a few hours; it will stiffen. Form the batter into 1-inch balls and drop them into boiling water containing the remaining ¼ teaspoon of salt. Cook, covered, for 20 minutes.

Meanwhile heat the jellied chicken broth. Drain the cooked balls and put them into the hot chicken broth. (Do not cook the balls in the broth, though they can be reheated there.)

Judith Glasser
Potsdam

Gefilte Fish (Stuffed Fish)

The name of this dish comes from the old custom of using this fish-vegetable mixture as a stuffing in the fish skin. Now it is always served as skinless portions.

2   pounds boneless lean fish (traditionally whitefish, carp, etc., but the best locally available store-bought alternative is about half haddock or cod and half sole or flounder—or you can use pike you have caught yourself)

3   large onions

2   eggs, beaten

¼   cup matzoh cake meal (you can use regular matzoh meal and powder it in the blender to the consistency of flour)

Salt and pepper to taste (about 1 teaspoon salt and ½ teaspoon pepper)

1   bay leaf

2   carrots

Several stalks celery

Put the fish through the fine blade of a meat grinder. Then regrind it with two of the onions. Gently mix in the beaten eggs and matzoh meal, being careful not to squash the air out of it. Season the mixture to taste.

Bring water to boil in a large pot or Dutch oven. Simmer the water with the remaining onion, the celery, the bay leaf and the carrots for about 30 minutes, until the onion is soft. Remove and discard the vegetables, reserving the carrots.

Form oval balls from the fish mixture, using about ½ cup in each and being careful not to pack them so they squash down. Place the balls gently with a spoon into the simmering broth. When the broth returns to a simmer, cover the pot and cook the fish gently for an hour. Chill the fish in the broth, but remove it for serving. Serve the balls cold with a few slices of the reserved carrot as a garnish, and horseradish on the side. Be sure to save the delicious broth for soup.

Some people jelly the broth by boiling it down to half the original volume and adding gelatin. They dice up the resulting aspic and serve it with the fish.

Judith Glasser
Potsdam

200

Cranberry Pot Roast

1	(3-pound) beef brisket	1	(16-ounce) can whole
2	stalks celery, sliced		berry cranberry sauce
1	medium onion, diced	1	(16-ounce) can marinara
1	medium green pepper, diced		sauce or tomato sauce
½	cup water	1	clove garlic, diced

In a 3-quart Dutch oven or saucepan, brown the meat for 5 minutes on each side. Browning the meat longer adds extra flavor. Remove it from the saucepan, replacing it with the prepared celery, onion and green pepper, and the water. Simmer the vegetables over low heat until they are soft. Add the cranberry and marinara sauces to the vegetables and heat until the mixture is bubbly. Add the garlic.

Return the meat to the pot and simmer it over a low flame for 1 ½ to 2 hours. Remove the meat, allow it to cool, then slice it. Return the slices to the pot to warm them. Serve them with the sauce.

Yields 6 to 8 servings.

Jan Lavine
Potsdam

Potato Latkes (Pancakes) or Kugel (Pudding)

1	onion	1	tablespoon oil (for the kugel)
2	eggs		Applesauce (to accompany
	Salt and pepper to taste		the latkes)
2	pounds potatoes, peeled and cut into chunks		

Quarter the onion and put it into a blender with the eggs; grind it on medium until the big chunks are gone. Add about ½ teaspoon salt and a pinch of pepper. Add the potatoes and blend until all the chunks are gone.

For kugel, mix in the oil, then turn the mixture into a well-greased baking pan and bake at 350 degrees until it is firm in the center (about 30 minutes.)

For latkes, heavily grease a frying pan and ladle out the batter onto the hot pan—about 2 tablespoons per pancake. Fry the cakes until browned; turn them and brown them on the other side. Serve the latkes with applesauce.

This recipe serves four.

Judith Glasser
Potsdam

Stuffed Cabbage

10	large cabbage leaves	1	egg, slightly beaten
1	pound lean ground beef	1	pound sauerkraut
1	medium onion, chopped fine	2	cups canned tomatoes
¾	cup cooked rice	1	slice onion
1¼	teaspoons salt, divided	½	cup seedless raisins
¼	teaspoon white pepper	¼-½	cup dark brown sugar, to taste

Select leaves from the outside of a large head of cabbage. Place them in boiling water for 5 minutes, then drain them. Mix together the beef, chopped onion, rice, ¾ teaspoon salt, pepper and egg. Put about ¼ cup of this mixture in each cabbage leaf at the stem end, then roll it up so that the filling is completely covered. Place the sauerkraut in a heavy 4-quart saucepan, cover it with the meat-filled cabbage rolls, then add the tomatoes, onion and raisins. Cover the pan tightly, bring it to a boil, then simmer for two hours (or pressure cook for 30 minutes at 15 pounds, reducing pressure quickly after the time is up.) Taste the gravy and add brown sugar and the remaining salt to taste.

Serves 5.

Claire Schulman
Potsdam

Claire Schulman found this recipe years ago in Mildred G. Bellin's The Original Jewish Cookbook *and has been using it ever since.*

Sweet Potato and Carrot Tzimmes

This recipe is good with turkey at Thanksgiving. The prunes make it deliciously sweet.

1 pound carrots	¼ teaspoon cinnamon
6 sweet potatoes	2 tablespoons margarine
½ cup pitted prunes, optional	1 (20-ounce) can pineapple
1 cup orange juice	chunks, drained, optional
½ cup honey	1 (11-ounce) can mandarin
½ teaspoon salt	oranges, drained

Peel the carrots and cut them into 1-inch slices. Peel and slice the sweet potatoes into ½-inch slices. In a 3-quart saucepan, cover the carrots and sweet potatoes with boiling, salted water, and cook until the vegetables are tender but firm. Drain the carrots and sweet potatoes and combine them gently in a 3-quart casserole with the prunes. Preheat the oven to 350 degrees.

Mix the orange juice, honey, salt and cinnamon. Pour this mixture evenly over the casserole. Dot the top with margarine. Bake, covered, for 30 minutes. Uncover the casserole, stir the contents gently, add the mandarin oranges and the pineapple if desired, then bake another 10 minutes. The tzimmes can now be transferred to a crock pot to keep warm in order to open up oven space.

Jan Lavine
Potsdam

Matzoh Cheese Kugel for Passover

4	matzohs	¼	cup orange juice
5	eggs, divided	2	tablespoons lemon juice
1	pound cottage cheese	¾	cup sugar
	Cinnamon to taste		Melted butter or oleo
2	cups milk or sour cream		

Soak the matzohs in water until slightly softened, then remove them carefully from the water and place them on a paper towel. Beat one of the eggs and add it to the cheese with a little cinnamon and sugar, mixing well. Beat the remaining four eggs well with the milk or sour cream, orange juice, lemon juice, and sugar. Melt butter or oleo in a 9 x 9-inch pan, swirling it to cover the entire pan. Place one matzoh in the bottom of the pan. Spread with ⅓ of the cheese mixture, then repeat, ending with a matzoh on top. Pour the egg-milk mixture over the top. Allow the pan to stand while the oven is pre-heated to 375 degrees. Bake one hour.

Reva Kerker prefers to use sour cream in this recipe instead of the milk.

Reva Kerker
Potsdam

This recipe originally appeared in a cookbook put out by a Hadassah from Syracuse.

Passover Brownies

This recipe is also good for anyone with an allergy to wheat.

4	eggs, beaten	4	tablespoons powdered cocoa
1½	cups sugar	1	cup potato starch
1	cup oil		Chopped nuts, optional

Cream the eggs and sugar. Add the oil, then mix in the cocoa, potato starch and nuts (if desired). Pour the batter into a 10½ x 15-inch foil pan. Bake at 325 degrees for 40 to 45 minutes.

Potato starch can be found in the kosher section of the grocery store year round.

Jan Lavine
Potsdam

Passover Sponge Torte

7 eggs, separated	1 cup pecans, grated
1 cup sugar	(measure the whole nuts,
1 tablespoon orange juice	then grate them with a nut
1 teaspoon vanilla	grater; do not use a
½ cup matzoh cake meal (very	blender or food processor
finely powdered matzoh	as those will produce
meal; it can be made by	paste instead of shavings.
grinding matzoh meal in a	You will have more than
blender to the consistency	one cup of grated nuts.)
of flour)	

Beat the egg whites until they are stiff. Beat the egg yolks until they are light in color, then beat in the sugar gradually until the mixture is very thick. Beat in the vanilla and orange juice. Fold the whites and yolks together, then gradually fold in the matzoh meal and, finally, the nuts.

Turn the mixture into an ungreased two-piece angel food cake pan (the kind with a removable bottom) and bake at 325 degrees for 1 hour. Invert the baked pan onto a rack and cover the bottom and sides with a clean wet dish towel until the cake cools. The cake may be decorated with powdered sugar; it should not be frosted.

Judith Glasser
Potsdam

Ingberlach (Ginger Candy)

1 cup sugar	2 tablespoons powdered ginger
¾ cup honey	½ cup ground or finely
2 eggs, well beaten	chopped almonds (do not
1 cup matzoh meal	use almond paste)

Bring the sugar and honey to a boil in a deep saucepan. Cook until the mixture turns a reddish golden color (about 10 minutes). Remove the pan from the fire. Combine the other ingredients and add them to the sugar-honey mixture. Cook them over low heat until they are thick, stirring constantly (about 10 minutes). Turn the mixture out onto a wet board and pat it out to ½ inch in thickness—first with a spoon then, after the mixture has cooled a bit, with the palm of your hand dipped in cold water. Sprinkle it with sugar and a little ginger. Cut it into squares or diamonds with a greased knife while it is still warm. (If it is too soft to cut, you can roll it into balls and coat the balls with chopped almonds.)

Judith Glasser
Potsdam

Noodle Kugel

1	stick butter	1	cup white raisins (or dark ones if white are unavailable) OR 1 (20-ounce) can crushed pineapple with the juice
4-6	eggs (depending on size of eggs)		
½	cup sugar		
10	ounces sour cream		
20	ounces ricotta cheese	1	(16-ounce) package extra wide egg noodles
1½	teaspoons vanilla		
½	teaspoon cinnamon	1	cup graham cracker crumbs
6	ounces half-and-half		

Preheat the oven to 375 degrees. Put the butter in a 13 x 9 x 2-inch glass baking dish and set it in the oven to melt. Combine the eggs, sugar, sour cream, ricotta cheese, vanilla, cinnamon, half-and-half and raisins or pineapple with juice in a large mixing bowl and mix them thoroughly with a wire whip.

In a large pot, cook the noodles in boiling water until just al dente (still a bit hard). Drain the noodles and run cold water over them to stop them from cooking further. Add the noodles to the bowl of liquid ingredients.

Pour the melted butter into the cheese mixture and stir well. Pour the mixture into the baking dish in which you melted the butter, and sprinkle the graham cracker crumbs on top.

Cover the dish with aluminum foil and bake at 375 degrees for about 45 minutes, or until lightly set. Remove the foil and bake for an additional 15 minutes to brown the crumbs.

Serve either warm or at room temperature.

The raisins or pineapple may be omitted entirely or replaced with apples.

Cynthia Bynon
Potsdam

Holiday Challah (Bread)

Because of the yeast and flour, this would not be an appropriate recipe for Passover, but it is wonderful on other holidays.

3	packages instant yeast	8	cups all-purpose flour, divided
½	cup honey		
1½	cups lukewarm water	1	teaspoon salt
⅔	cup white raisins	4	tablespoons canola or salad oil
2	cups very hot water		
5	large eggs, divided		

In a very large bowl combine the yeast, honey and the lukewarm water. Let the mixture sit for five minutes to activate the yeast. Meanwhile, in a smaller bowl beat four of the eggs and set aside. In another small bowl, place the raisins in the hot water to swell them. Set these aside as well.

After the yeast mixture has sat for five minutes, add the beaten eggs, three cups of the flour, the salt and the oil. Stir until this mixture becomes stretchy. Begin to add the remaining flour cup by cup, mixing with a wooden spoon until the dough is too stiff to stir. At that point, turn it out of the bowl onto a floured board and knead in the rest of the flour. (In other words, don't break your wooden spoon.) Kneading the dough is the MOST IMPORTANT step in making bread. Vigorously knead the dough until it is soft and smooth—at least ten minutes. Drain the raisins and add them as you knead the dough.

Wash the mixing bowl and spray it with non-stick cooking spray. Place the dough in the bowl, smooth side down, then turn it over to coat it with the oil. Place a clean towel on top of the bowl and let the dough rise until it is three times the original size (about three hours.)

[Note: Cynthia Bynon often allows it to rise even more than this.]

Remove the dough from the bowl and knead it down again, making sure to get all the air bubbles out. Divide the dough into two equal pieces and shape each piece into a round loaf.

Allow the dough to rise again until it has doubled in bulk. Beat the remaining egg and brush it on top of the loaves. Bake the two loaves in a preheated 325 degree oven until they are dark golden brown and tapping on them gives a hollow sound (approximately one hour.)

This method gives round loaves for Rosh Hashana. For regular Challah, as it is eaten on every Shabbat, leave out the raisins. Divide each half of the risen dough into thirds. Roll each third into a snake shape and braid the three of them together into a long loaf. Brush the loaves with egg and bake as above.

Cynthia Bynon
Potsdam

Kasha Varnishkas

According to Jan Lavine, this is a classic Eastern European dish which would never be served during Passover because it contains grain. When she first started making it, her husband turned up his nose, but then one Sunday while it was cooking and he was particularly hungry, he nibbled a bit. He found it so delicious that he now eats two and three servings at a time.

2	tablespoons oil	2	cups boiling water or soup stock
1	onion, diced		
1	cup diced mushrooms, optional—but best if included	1	teaspoon salt
		¼	teaspoon pepper
1	cup whole kasha	1½	cups bowtie noodles, cooked and drained
1	egg, beaten	2	tablespoons margarine

Heat the oil in a 2-quart saucepan over medium heat. Sauté the onion and mushrooms until they are golden brown (about 5 minutes.) Add the kasha. Stir in the beaten egg. Sauté the resulting mixture for 2 minutes on high heat, stirring with a fork or wooden spoon until the grains are separate.

At the same time, in a 1-quart saucepan, bring the water or stock to a boil. Pour the boiling liquid over the kasha, add the salt and pepper, cover, and simmer for 10 to 15 minutes, until the kasha has absorbed all the liquid and is dry and fluffy.

In a serving bowl, combine the drained noodles with the kasha while both are still warm. Melt in the margarine and mix until everything is well combined. Serve warm.

Jan Lavine
Potsdam

Blintzes

Pancakes

4	eggs	1	cup water
1	cup flour	½	teaspoon salt, optional
1	cup milk		

Filling

1	pound cream cheese (not fat-free)	1	pound ricotta (not fat-free)
		2	eggs

Beat the eggs and stir in the flour. Add the milk a little at a time until the mixture is smooth. Finally add the water (and the salt if you wish to use it). Let the batter stand in the refrigerator at least ½ hour.

Meanwhile beat together the filling ingredients until they are smooth.

Take a crêpe pan or any small (up to 6-inch) frying pan and wipe the sides with a little butter until they just glisten. Heat the pan over medium heat, then when the pan is hot, pour in a tablespoon or so of batter, tipping the pan so as to coat the whole bottom. The amount of batter you need will depend on the size of the pan. Cook the pancake until it is well set. Turn it out onto waxed paper and continue making pancakes until the batter is used up.

After the cakes have cooled, put about 2 to 3 tablespoons of filling along one edge. Roll that edge over once toward the center to cover the filling. Fold the sides into the center, then continue rolling until the blintz is completely closed and cigar shaped. When you are ready to serve them, brown them in butter until the cheese inside puffs up and the pancake is lightly browned. Serve them with sour cream and strawberry or blueberry preserves, or with cinnamon sugar.

These freeze very well and can be cooked from the frozen state.

Judith Glasser
Potsdam

The great majority of North Country Jews arrived from the Russian Pale in the early part of the 20th century. The Pale, an area which had at earlier times been variously part of Lithuania and Poland, was a section of Russia to which the Czar had decreed that all Jews be restricted. There they lived as country peasants, unlike the Jews in Germany and Poland, who lived and worked primarily in cities. Most were poor and in constant fear of pogroms, vicious attacks by their Russian neighbors which had begun in the late 1800s and had escalated in intensity as the years went on. Still, many Jewish families were reluctant to pick up stakes and move to some unknown area where, after all, life might be no better than it was at home.

For many, the final straw was the Russo-Japanese War of 1904-5. The Russians, losing the war, indiscriminately conscripted Jews, some as young as 12 or 13, demanding that they serve for unlimited periods regardless of whether they had previously fulfilled their required military duty. Desperate to prevent their men from dying as front-line cannon fodder, huge numbers of Russian Jews decided to make the leap into the unknown and emigrate to the United States.

Often one member of a family would move to one of the North Country towns—Massena, Gouverneur, Watertown, Lake Placid, Tupper Lake, or Ogdensburg—then he would bring over relatives and neighbors from home, thus creating Jewish communities in those towns which grew until each eventually had enough people to build a synagogue.

Almost invariably Jewish men began their working lives in America as peddlers, traveling on foot from farm to farm selling safety pins, socks, thread, and gloves. They were welcomed by the North Country farmers, for they served as living newspapers, carrying gossip and information from farm to farm in a time before mass communication. Usually the next step was to acquire a horse and wagon. This purchase enabled them to begin to act as brokers, buying apples, rags, and junk from the farmers, which they then carted to Massena, Watertown, or Ogdensburg for resale. Eventually most earned enough to enable them to give up the traveling life and settle down in one of the cities as a shopkeeper. Many of the furniture and clothing businesses in North Country cities were started by Jewish immigrants who had begun their lives here as itinerant peddlers.

There was a second wave of Jewish settlement in the North Country when World War II refugees arrived in Potsdam. The community there grew even more quickly after the war as the colleges in Potsdam and Canton expanded, hiring Jewish faculty and attracting Jewish students. Today, Potsdam is one of the most active of the various area congregations.

* * *

Adapted from Joan Dobbie, Louis Greenblatt, and Blanche Levine's book Before Us: Stories of Early Jewish Families in St. Lawrence County. *Potsdam, NY: Congregation Beth-el, 1981.*

KOREAN
AMERICANS

Representing one of the newest food traditions to be introduced in the North
Country, Korean American cook Suk Hui Hi of Watertown, Jefferson County,
shows a variety of her specialties in one of several new Korean restaurants
near Fort Drum. *Peter R. Barber Photo/Watertown Daily Times*

Saturday Afternoon at Shin Tupper's House

Pierrepont

Inside Shin's back door, brightly colored fabric slippers stand in a row awaiting guests. I kick off my shoes and slip gratefully into comfortable scuffs printed with a fuschia design. Having lived in Austria, I find the concept of house shoes familiar, and I wonder briefly why Americans—especially here in the muddy North Country—have never adopted this very practical custom. Even Yankee Puritans not attracted by the luxury of unfettered toes ought to be won over by the prospect of considerable savings on rug-cleaning expenses.

The food spread out on the kitchen table is as pretty as it is abundant— reddish kimch'i*, mahogany baked mackerel, bright green leaves of curly lettuce*, pure white rice, creamy fried tofu with green onion decorations*, black seaweed, and little round picnic rice* mosaics containing all those colors. A Korean meal always includes three basics—soup, rice, and kimch'i—along with two or three side dishes and some meat or fish; so the table is loaded. It looks like one of those pictures in a Martha Stewart book that make you roll your eye and say, "Get real! I could do this, too, if I had twenty chefs helping me." But Shin tells me she cooks this way every night.

We pile our plates high then move into the living room with the rest of her Methodist women's group. Their church in Black River, eight miles from Watertown, is celebrating its second birthday this week. Founded with only three local members, the congregation has now grown to twenty people from towns all around the North Country.

The meal tastes as good as it looks. Intently we devote ourselves to eating, second helpings immediately replacing firsts. Replete, I finally glance around the living room and admire a family portrait over the couch. Shin explains that it was taken when she traveled to Korea last year with her husband and son for her mother's sixtieth birthday. It seems almost like a photo of a garden, for the women are all in the colorful traditional dress called hanpok. Each dress is in two parts: on top a short blouse tied with ribbons, on the bottom a long, very full skirt fastened high under the armpits. Shin's sister-in-law wears one which has both blouse and skirt of buttercup yellow; Shin's is in two tones of lavender, and her mother's is red and white. Korean women on swings have been compared to birds or butterflies, but I think they most resemble gently ringing bells.

Traditionally the sixtieth birthday is a major rite of passage for Koreans. In former days, when life expectancies were shorter, only the lucky few were alive to celebrate turning 60. Anyone surviving to that happy day was assumed to be fully retired, and from that time on enjoyed a life of well-deserved rest, waited on by loving relatives. Family, friends, and neighbors all gathered on the big day to offer congratulations and gifts; the festivities went on for half a week or so. In some cases a sixtieth birthday party wiped out a person's life savings, but no one felt the money had been badly spent.

Today, better health care has made the sixtieth birthday more attainable, and sixty-year-olds less ready to retire to rocking chairs. In fact the big celebration is slowly migrating to the seventieth year. Even so, many people like Shin's mother still have a nice party to celebrate turning sixty. Attending young people bow to them and offer blessings; the honoree gives each some words of wisdom and a gift of money. Min Kyung Jung remembers getting a dollar as a child at such parties, but now inflation has swollen the going rate to $10. It's easy to see how a large family could wipe out a savings account! Shin shows me her photo album with pictures of her mother's party. In front of the head table are cylindrical stacks of cookies and candies. Each is shaped like a small pickle barrel; the colors of the food form geometric patterns on the sides of the stacks—pink diamonds with green edges, red zig-zag stripes on a white background. Shin explains that sometimes these decorations are actually edible, but that often they are rented for the day from the restaurant.

Equal in importance to the sixtieth birthday is the first. Again, this celebration has its roots in a time when infant mortality was high and it was something of an achievement to get through your first year. Families would prepare a feast for relatives and friends, setting it out on a table with a pieces of yarn, money, and stationery. It was a game to see which the baby would reach for. The yarn promised longevity, the money riches, and the stationery (more recently replaced by a pencil) portended scholarship. Even though no one totally believed in these omens, it was still fun to interpret later events in light of the baby's early choice.

Shin and her son celebrated his first birthday in Korea with her family. I ask her which item he reached for. She smiles and replies "the pencil." On the wall is a photograph of him, smiling infectiously in his ceremonial tulpok—a robe not unlike the women's hanpoks—and little peaked black cap. On each finger he sports a 20-karat gold ring and around his wrist is a gold bracelet—gifts from the family. Shin has saved them all so that when he is older he can have them made into jewelry for himself or his future wife.

The afternoon is over, and some of the guests have the long ride to Watertown ahead of them. Reluctantly I surrender my comfortable slippers at the door, gratefully accept a plate of leftovers for Nils, and head home wishing I had a hanpok. It would be such a lovely way to camouflage the results of those extra helpings.

Shin Tupper came to this country in 1988. She works for Dining Services at St. Lawrence University. Min Kyung Jung is the minister of the Black River Korean Methodist Church. He has been in the United States for only two years.

The recipes in this section are ones I ate at the potluck at the home of Shin and Kevin Tupper in Pierrepont. The wording of the recipes is from Lee Wade's Korean Cookery, *edited by Joan Rutt and Sandra Mattielli (Elizabeth, NJ: Hollym International Corp., 1996.)*

Miyŏkkuk (Seaweed Soup)

Seaweed is rich in iodine, calcium, and vitamins. For this reason, Koreans have always served this soup to new mothers to strengthen them and cleanse the system after childbirth. It is traditionally served on birthdays as well.

½	pound brown seaweed (miyŏk in Korean)	1	teaspoon sesame salt
¼	pound lean beef, thinly sliced	3	tablespoons soy sauce
		2	teaspoons sesame oil
3	cloves garlic, finely chopped	½	teaspoon black pepper

Wash and soak the seaweed in water for one hour, then drain it and cut it into 2-inch pieces. Put the beef into a pan with the garlic, sesame salt, soy sauce, sesame oil and pepper; cook until the meat is brown. Add the seaweed and 6 cups of water and simmer until the seaweed is tender (approximately 30 minutes). Check the seasoning, bring the soup back to the boil, then serve it.

To make sesame salt, heat sesame seeds gently in a heavy pan until they turn brown and swell. Pulverize the seeds in a mortar with one teaspoonful of salt per cup of sesame seed.

Takkogiguk (Chicken Soup)

A Korean meal always includes soup of some sort, accompanied by rice and a variety of kimch'i. Usually there are two or three side dishes as well—meat or baked fish—but the meal is not complete without the soup/rice/kimch'i triumvirate. In their book Discover Korea, *Lee O-young and Lim Jong-han say that Koreans are so fond of soup and juicy food that they even use the word "juice" to describe tips, bonuses, and charitable donations.*

1	small whole chicken	1	large green onion or leek, chopped
6	cups water		
3	potatoes, diced	3	cloves garlic, finely chopped
1	carrot, diced		
1	tablespoon soy sauce	¼	teaspoon black pepper

Cook the chicken in the water for one hour. Add the remaining ingredients and cook for ½ hour more. Remove the chicken from the pan and take out the bones, putting the flesh back into the soup in bite-sized pieces. Check the seasoning, reheat, and serve.

Tubu Puch'im (Fried Bean Curd)

1	cake bean curd (tofu)	1	teaspoon red pepper threads
3	tablespoons cooking oil	⅛	teaspoon black pepper
3	tablespoons soy sauce	2	tablespoons sesame salt
5	small green onions or chives, cut in 1-inch lengths		(see recipe for Seaweed Soup on page 215 for how to make this)

Cut the bean curd into slices ¼ to ⅓ inch thick. Fry them in the oil over low heat until they are light brown on both sides. Sprinkle the remaining ingredients on top and cook two minutes more on each side.

Kimpap (Picnic Rice in Seaweed)

2	cups uncooked rice	1	undercooked carrot
2¼	cups cold water	4	eggs, separated
½	pound lean beef	½	cup cooked spinach
2	tablespoons soy sauce	1	teaspoon red pepper
1	onion, finely chopped		threads
1	teaspoon sesame oil	20	full-sized sheets of laver
1	yellow pickled radish		(kim in Korean)

Cook the rice in the water. It should not be moist after cooking. Cut the beef into thin strips and fry it with the soy sauce, onion and sesame oil. Cut the pickled radish and carrot into thin strips. Fry the beaten egg yolks and whites separately in very thin layers on a lightly oiled pan, then cut them into thin strips.

To assemble the rolls, cover a sheet of laver with a thin layer of rice, leaving a 1-inch-wide strip uncovered along the edge furthest away from you. Two inches in from the near edge, and parallel to it, lay the strips of beef, radish, carrot, egg white, egg yolk, pieces of spinach and red pepper threads. Beginning with the near edge, roll the laver up like a jelly-roll. The vegetables and meat will be in the center. Seal the roll by moistening the uncovered far edge of the laver and pressing the roll down on it. Repeat this process with the other sheets of laver. With a sharp knife dipped in cold water, cut the rolls into 1-inch slices.

Paech'u Kimch'i (Napa Cabbage Kimch'i)

Kimch'i (fermented vegetables) is eaten at every Korean meal. It doubtless originated as a way to preserve summer vegetables so that they would last through the long, cold winters in Korea. Over the centuries, the variety has expanded until it is almost endless; cabbage, turnips, cucumbers, scallions, eggplants, radishes, Korean lettuce and mustard greens—all can become kimch'i. The kimch'i varies by region and by family, but that is only the beginning. There are also special varieties for each season and holiday. Preparation of winter kimch'i to last the family until fresh cabbages are again available is a big annual family event, even something of a festival, at which friends and relatives join together to make kimch'i for each household in turn.

2	Napa cabbages	1	head garlic, finely chopped
10	cups water		
1¼	cups salt, divided	¼	cup small green thread onions or chives, cut in 1-inch lengths
1	medium white radish		
½	cup red pepper powder		
⅓	cup salted baby shrimp	¼	cup very thin green onion, cut in 1-inch lengths
1	cup minari stems, cut in 1-inch pieces		
		⅓	pound fresh oysters
2	teaspoons fresh ginger, finely chopped		Red pepper thread

Cut each cabbage in half lengthwise. Make a brine with the water and one cup of the salt; soak the cabbage sections in it. When the cabbages are well salted, rinse them thoroughly in cold water and drain them. Cut one third of the radish into thin strips. Mix the red pepper powder well with the salted shrimp juice. Add the mixture to the radish strips and mix well until the reddish color is set. Then add the remaining ingredients. Season with salt. Pack the mixture between the leaves of the wilted cabbage. Cut the remaining part of the radish into large pieces and mix it with the remaining seasoned mixture. Place the stuffed cabbages and radish pieces in a large crock.

Allow the kimch'i to ferment for 2 days at 70 degrees. (It will take longer in a cooler room and less time in very hot weather when room temperature is higher). It is ripe when the liquid no longer tastes like brine. It will keep in a refrigerator for up to a week, but the jar must be very tightly covered.

Shin Tupper sometimes uses purchased anchovy paste or oil in place of the shrimp and oysters.

Bulgogi (Broiled Beef)

1	pound well-marbled beef tenderloin or sirloin	⅛	teaspoon black pepper
2	tablespoons soy sauce	4	medium green onions, coarsely chopped
1	tablespoon sugar	3	cloves garlic, finely chopped
1	tablespoon sesame oil		
1	tablespoon sesame salt (see recipe for Seaweed Soup on page 215 for how to make this)	1	teaspoon fresh ginger, finely chopped
		2	tablespoons water, rice wine or white wine

Cut the beef into thin slices about 3 inches square and ⅛ inch thick. This can be done at the butcher's shop. Marinate the beef in the remaining ingredients for up to 1½ hours. Traditionally, this meat is broiled at the table over charcoal. It can be broiled in the oven, pan-broiled or cooked on an outside grill as well. Since it is so thin, it will cook quickly, so be careful not to overcook it.

Shin Tupper often marinates her beef overnight in mashed kiwi fruit, Ruby Red grapefruit juice, or Coke to tenderize it.

Chapch'ae
(Noodles with Meat and Vegetables)

½	pound lean beef	10	medium green onions, cut
¼	pound pork		into 1-inch lengths
3	tablespoons soy sauce	5	wild leeks
1	tablespoon sugar	2	onions, chopped
1	tablespoon sesame salt	3	p'yogo mushrooms
	(see Seaweed Soup		(shiitake)
	recipe on page 215 for	5	nŭt'ari mushrooms (com-
	how to make this)		mon button mushrooms)
½	teaspoon black pepper	10	mogi mushrooms (ear
2	tablespoons sesame oil		mushrooms)
⅓	pound Chinese noodles	10	sŏgi mushrooms (stone
	(tangmyŏn)		mushrooms)
2	large carrots, cut into	1	cup cooked spinach
	matchsticks		

Cut the beef and pork into fine strips and fry them with the soy sauce, sugar, sesame salt, black pepper and sesame oil until they are tender and well cooked.

Cook the noodles in boiling water until they are soft; rinse them in cold water.

Fry the carrots, green onions, leeks, and onions together in a lightly greased pan for 10 minutes until they are soft, but not brown.

Soak the p'yogo, mogi, and nŭt'ari mushrooms in warm water for 10 minutes, then cut them into strips and fry them as you did the vegetables. Immerse the sŏgi mushrooms in boiling water for 2 minutes, then cut them into strips.

Combine all the ingredients including the spinach. The dish may be heated before serving or it may be served cold.

It is not necessary to use all four different kinds of mushrooms, although a variety is nice. Oriental specialty shops in Watertown, Ottawa and Montreal have many dried mushrooms if you want to try some that are not available in your local grocery.

Pindaettok (Mung Bean Pancake)

Basic recipe

4	cups dried mung beans, crushed to split the skins	Salt to taste
		Water

Optional additions

1   pound shredded pork, fried until well done

½   cup minari stems, cut in 1-inch lengths and scalded

2   leeks, chopped

1   head garlic, finely chopped

1   tablespoon sesame salt (see Seaweed Soup recipe on page 215 for how to make this)

1   teaspoon fresh ginger root, finely chopped

½   cup paech'u kimch'i, chopped

Soy sauce

Soak the beans in water overnight or for ten or twelve hours. Cover the beans with fresh water and rub them between your hands to remove the skins which will float to the top of the water. Repeat this process until all the skins have been removed. Drain the beans well, then grind them in a mortar or blender. Add enough water to make a thick paste. Season the batter with a little salt, but do not make it too salty since the pancake will be served with soy sauce for dipping. Drop the batter by tablespoonfuls onto a heated, greased pan or griddle and cook it as you would pancakes, browning the cakes lightly on both sides.

The pancakes can simply be made as described above, but it is usual to add some meat or vegetables to the batter as well. The quantities depend on what is available and on whether the pindaettok is to be a main dish or a side dish. The suggested meat and vegetable quantities above are suitable for a fairly substantial main dish. Mix any or all of them well with the batter before frying it.

Sangch'ussam (Lettuce Bundles)

Soy bean paste has a special status in Korean homes. The diversity of sauces and pastes in a home indicates that a family is thriving. Because these pastes are so important in the culture, a host of customs and traditions have grown up about making them. Often an astrologer is consulted to choose the perfect day for the project, and the act of preparing the paste is surrounded by taboos. The fermenting paste is stored in jars on a dais, which itself takes on the aspect of a shrine. Women often go to the dais to pray when someone in the family is sick or in crisis. Although these traditional pastes and sauces are mass-produced in factories today, many families still prefer to make their own, keeping the tradition alive.

	Leaf or romaine lettuce, separated into leaves	2	tablespoons red pepper paste
	Cooked rice	1	tablespoon soy bean paste
1	medium green onion, chopped	1	tablespoon sesame seed
		½	teaspoon sesame oil

Wash the lettuce well, adding a drop of sesame oil to the water. Mix the onion, red pepper paste, bean paste, sesame seed and sesame oil to make a sauce. To serve, wrap a spoonful of rice and a dab of sauce in a lettuce leaf, then roll it up and eat the bundle.

Yakshik (Sweet Spiced Rice)

4	cups glutinous rice	½	cup dark brown sugar
2	cups chestnuts	¼	cup pine nuts
20	dried jujubes (Korean dates)	2	tablespoons soy sauce
¼	cup sesame oil	½	teaspoon cinnamon

Wash the rice, cover it with warm water, allow it to stand for two hours, then drain it, and steam it for 30 minutes. Boil the chestnuts for 10 minutes, then peel them. Soak the jujubes in warm water for 30 minutes and pit them. Mix the rice, chestnuts, jujubes, sesame oil, brown sugar, pine nuts, soy sauce and cinnamon. Make sure the fruit and nuts are well distributed. Pack the mixture firmly in a bowl and cover it tightly with aluminum foil.

Put the bowl into a pan containing enough boiling water to come halfway up the side of the bowl, then steam the mixture for 5 hours, adding more water as it boils away. Lift the edge of the foil to check the color of the rice underneath. The dessert is done when the rice has turned dark brown. (Sometimes Korean cooks add caramel to the mixture before steaming it to make it turn darker.) To serve, remove the foil and cut the dessert into cubes or rectangular pieces.

Yakkwa (Fried Honey-cakes)

2	cups flour	½	teaspoon powdered cinnamon
¼	cup sesame oil		
2	tablespoons honey	½	cup finely chopped fresh citron or 1 tablespoon finely chopped ginger
2	tablespoons sugar		
3	tablespoons rice wine		
	Vegetable oil for frying	½	cup finely chopped pine nuts
2	cups honey		

Mix the flour, sesame oil, honey, sugar and wine; knead the dough until it is smooth. Roll the dough to ¼ inch thick, then cut it with a round cutter 1½ inches in diameter. Prick each circle of dough with a fork. Heat the frying oil to 300 degrees and deep-fry the cakes until they are light brown and float to the surface. Remove them from the oil and drain them. Mix the honey with the cinnamon and citron. Soak the hot cakes in this mixture for 30 minutes, then remove them from the syrup and roll them in pine nuts.

Compared to many of the other nationalities represented among North Country residents, Koreans are newcomers. Most are first-generation immigrants who arrived here within the last fifty years. Some came as doctors, helping to alleviate the shortage of physicians in this rural area. Others came as graduate students or faculty at Clarkson University. By far the largest number arrived here as spouses of military personnel at Fort Drum. There are now 400 Koreans in Watertown alone, and at least three Korean churches—Baptist, Presbyterian, and Methodist.

Because so many North Country Koreans are wives of soldiers, their experience differs from that of previous immigrant groups. In most other cases, the men came first, then brought their wives and children to join them. Often the groups came from a single village or region in their home country, so they knew each other well. Usually they married within their community here for one or two generations before beginning to intermarry with other Americans. In contrast, the Korean community here is largely female, and even though they are first-generation immigrants, they are already married to non-Koreans.

It might seem that this situation would lead to a quick assimilation of Koreans into American culture, but the pull in the other direction is very strong. The Korean churches help their members to retain their culture and language. North Country Koreans travel up to two hours to attend church in Watertown on Sundays and to socialize at church activities during the week. Also, in Korean culture family is paramount. There is great pressure to be loyal to aging parents, to be respectful of them and to care for them. Clearly this is a challenge for North Country Koreans, literally halfway around the globe from their families. Some have solved the problem as did many immigrants in the past—by bringing their parents here. Those who have been unable to do that have settled instead for spending considerable time traveling back and forth to Korea. Even those who were able to bring their families here to join them make frequent trips to visit extended family and friends, keeping close ties with their homeland and traditions.

LEBANESE AMERICANS

Members of the Aseel, Salamy, Akiki, Bellamy, Mikall, and Maroun families of Tupper Lake, Franklin County, raise their glasses in a toast to Rose (Moubarak) and Gabriel Salamy's wedding anniversary, ca. 1955. *Photo courtesy of Ellen N. Maroun.*

Lebanese Graduation Parties

by Ellen (Aseel) Maroun with Nora (Maroun) Akiki

The Lebanese are proud of their hospitality. It is an honor both to offer and to receive hospitality. People are often judged by how well they treat their guests. Any special occasion is a welcomed excuse to bring extended family and friends together. Though sad times, funerals are an example of an event that provided an occasion for people to keep in touch with each other. In days long past, friends and family would come from very long distances, despite the difficulties of travel, to support and mourn with the grieving family. Because of those long distances, some might stay for days. There was great respect shown to these visitors. At meals, especially, during the several days of the wake, the women would cook and visit in the kitchen, consoling and catching up on each other's lives, while the men did the same as they ate their dinner. When the men and the guests from out of town who were returning to their home communities were finished with their meals, the women would then sit to eat and continue their visiting.

One of the big and joyous celebrations in our community was the high school graduation. Many of the immigrants who came to this area were very poor and had only an elementary education at best. They came here to provide a better life for themselves and their families. And when their children graduated from high school, it symbolized a proud achievement of a goal they had worked hard for. Graduation also represented a major transition in the life of the graduate. Families are extremely important to the Lebanese, and these young people were not going off to adulthood alone! Not that graduation was the final goal; the immigrants were committed to sending their children on to higher education. Government tuition assistance was unheard-of. Regardless of the immigrants' occupations and income levels, it was assumed that it was their honor and responsibility to offer their children the opportunity of a higher education.

When my son graduated from high school, we had a combined graduation party with his two cousins, who were also graduating in that same year. Over a hundred people came to the party, and what a wonderful celebration it was! While my daughter's graduation party was somewhat different, it was still an occasion at which one of my non-Lebanese friends exclaimed, "Wow, if this is a graduation, what do you do for a wedding?!" The graduate would not go off and leave the adults to celebrate without the guest of honor; they would stay for the entire party. Everyone would come—parents, grandparents, teenagers, and very young children—all the generations together. Even the youngest children were included and enjoyed. No one thought of them as a bother nor, Heaven forbid, would they ever be left behind with a babysitter!

Toasts to the graduate would be bountiful. Lebanese toasts are considered to be solemn, and always include mention of God. For instance one might say to a graduate: "May God (Allah) protect and guide you." Further toasts would include congratulating and blessing the parents as well. The order of toasting is prescribed also. Honored guests such as godparents or uncles and respected elders would toast the graduate and the parents first. Others, most often the men, would then come forward to toast. Those left behind in Lebanon were not forgotten, as toasts would also be offered in their honor.

Eventually, someone would always bring out the dhrubbuki. This Lebanese drum is shaped like a goblet, open on the bottom, with a skin stretched over the top. The dancing usually begins with all standing around in a circle clapping their hands and singing to give the melody. Again, the honored elders begin. Sometimes one of the women will begin dancing alone with a scarf in hand. One of the men will join her, and he will hold a handkerchief. Each will pass the scarf and handkerchief on to someone else and the dancing continues in this way. When a man and woman dance together, they do not touch. The dances are compelling and beautiful, like poetry. Young and old, the women are admired for their grace, and the men for their robustness and athleticism. After a while the men, women, and children would join hands and begin to dance the dehbkie, a Lebanese folkdance, to the rhythm of the drum, with the most skilled dancer leading the others through the sequence of special steps as the circle continued to move around and around.

Of course there's an abundance of food at the graduation party. Not a sit-down meal, but truly a buffet of plenty. Even if the food isn't served until late into the evening, everyone knows it is wise not to eat dinner before going to a graduation party. You can be sure that the women have been cooking for days preparing lots of "mazzah," small appetizer-type foods such as hommos bi tahina*, baba ganouj*, lift makbus*, fatayer*, and zeitoun*. Still the dishes come—kibbee (both raw* and cooked*), yabrak malfouf bi hamith*, yabrak anab*, taboulleh*, and much more. Sweet delicacies are always sure to include baklawa* or sambouska*. At the end of the meal we say "Sahtayn," an Arabic word meaning "Two healths to you." No one goes away hungry!

Like other immigrant communities, the Lebanese community has been diluted over the generations as children have married non-Lebanese and moved away. In their effort to fit into the mainstream culture, many children of the original immigrants turned from the customs and traditions. Today, in their middle and older years, they are wisely reflecting on what a great loss that represents and are trying to keep alive the spirit and traditions of their parents.

Both Ellen (Aseel) Maroun and Nora (Maroun) Akiki are lifelong residents of Tupper Lake. Nora, a retired school teacher enjoys frequent trips to Lebanon with her husband Kozhaya. Ellen is currently employed as a strategic planner at St. Joseph's Rehabilitation Center in Saranac Lake.

The foods in this section were described to me in detail by Ellen Maroun. Actual recipes are from the cookbook she uses: The Lebanese Kitchen: a Celebration of Lebanese Cuisine, *compiled by the Ladies Society of St. Elijah's Orthodox Church. Carp, Ontario: Gai-Garet Design and Publication, 1990.*

Yabrak Anab (Stuffed Grape Leaves)

100	medium grape leaves, stems removed	½	teaspoon allspice
2	pounds coarsely ground lamb or beef	2	lemons, juice only, divided
		1	clove garlic
1	cup rice, washed and drained		Lamb or beef bones, optional
			Water
3	teaspoons salt, divided	¼	cup butter
¼	teaspoon pepper		

Pour hot water over the grape leaves to soften them. Drain them well and squeeze out the excess water. Combine the meat, rice, one teaspoon of the salt, the pepper, and the allspice with the juice of one lemon. Place the leaves, vein side up, on a flat surface. Place 1 tablespoon of the meat and rice mixture at the stem end of each leaf and spread it across. Fold the end of the leaf over the filling, then fold both sides inward, and roll the leaf into a small cigar shape. Continue rolling leaves in this fashion until all the meat mixture has been used. (The leaves may be frozen at this point.)

Line the bottom of a deep pot with any remaining or broken leaves, adding bones, if desired. Pack the stuffed leaves tightly in layers, alternating the direction of each row, and covering the last row with extra leaves. Add the remaining two teaspoons of salt, the butter and the garlic. Add enough water to cover the rolls completely. Place an inverted dish on top of the rolled leaves to hold them in place. Cover the pot and bring the water to a boil. Reduce the heat to low and cook the leaves for 30 to 35 minutes. Carefully drain off any remaining liquid. Add the remaining lemon juice and let the pot rest, covered, for five minutes.

Hommos bi Tahina (Chick Pea Dip)

1	(19-ounce) can chick peas	1	teaspoon paprika
1	clove garlic, mashed	1	tablespoon olive oil,
4	tablespoons sesame seed		optional
	paste (tahina)	1	tablespoon parsley,
¼	cup freshly squeezed		chopped
	lemon juice	2	tablespoons pine nuts,
½	teaspoon salt		lightly browned, optional
¼	cup water		

Drain and rinse the chick peas, then place them in a blender or food processor. Add the mashed garlic, sesame seed paste, lemon juice, salt and water. Blend well until the texture of the mixture is smooth. Serve the hommos on a platter, garnished with paprika, oil, parsley and/or pine nuts, and surrounded with pita wedges for dipping. Hommos is also good as a dip for vegetables.

Baba Ganouj (Eggplant Appetizer)

1	large eggplant	2	tablespoons cold water
1	teaspoon salt	1	lemon, juice only
1	clove garlic		Olive oil
4	tablespoons sesame seed		Parsley
	paste (tahina)		

Remove the stem from the top of the eggplant. Pierce the eggplant with a fork in several places, then bake it at 350 degrees until it is very soft (approximately one hour). Cut it in half, remove the pulp, and discard the skin. Purée or mash the eggplant pulp, then let it cool.

Mash the garlic with the salt. Add the sesame paste, then gradually add the water and lemon juice. Mix everything together well and fold the garlic mixture into the mashed eggplant.

To serve, sprinkle the baba ganouj with olive oil and garnish it with finely chopped parsley.

Kibbee bi Saniyeh (Baked Kibbee)

Meat Filling

1½	pounds lamb or beef	1½	teaspoons salt
½	cup pine nuts	½	teaspoon pepper
2	tablespoons butter	½	teaspoon allspice
1	medium onion, finely chopped		

Kibbee

2	cups fine cracked wheat (#1 burghul)	1	teaspoon pepper
		½	teaspoon cinnamon
3	pounds very lean lamb or beef	1	teaspoon allspice
		¼	cup ice water
1	large onion, ground fine	½	cup olive oil
2	teaspoons salt		

To make the meat filling, coarsely grind the lamb or beef. Lightly brown the pine nuts in the butter. Remove them from the pan and set them aside. In the same pan sauté the meat, onion and seasonings together until the meat is browned. Add the pine nuts and stir them in. This mixture can be prepared ahead; it freezes well.

To make the kibbee, wash the cracked wheat several times in cold water In a large bowl. Soak it in warm water for 15 minutes, then drain it well, squeezing out all the moisture. Remove the fat from the meat and cut it into cubes. Grind it twice through the fine blade of a meat grinder until it is finely chopped (or process it in small amounts in a food processor for 30 seconds each).

Mix the meat and the wheat, kneading well. Grind or process the mixture once more. Add the onion, salt, pepper, cinnamon and allspice to the meat and knead it by hand, dipping your hands into ice water as you work, until the mixture is soft and smooth. Generously grease a 10 x 14-inch pan. Taking a small amount at a time, pat half the meat mixture smoothly but firmly over the bottom of the pan and smooth it very well with water-moistened hands. (The layer should be ¾ inch thick.) Place the meat filling evenly over the bottom layer, pressing down firmly. Pat out the remaining half of the kibbee mixture a little at a time in the palm of your hand, and place it over the meat filling so that it is completely covered. (This should leave about ½ inch free at the top of the pan.) Pat the mixture smooth with water-moistened hands.

Score the meat into diamond shapes, using a sharp knife dipped in cold water. Loosen the edges from the sides of the tray with the knife. Pour the oil over the top and bake it in a preheated 350 degree oven for about 45 minutes. Place it under the broiler for a few minutes until it is golden brown.

It helps to make the mixture ahead and refrigerate it overnight; it will then be easier to work with.

Kibbee Nayeh (Raw Kibbee)

This is often considered the national dish of Lebanon, according to the Ladies Society of St. Elijah's Church.

3	pounds very lean lamb or beef, trimmed well	1	tablespoon salt
2	medium onions	1	teaspoon pepper
1	cup fine cracked wheat (#1 burghul)	1	teaspoon cinnamon
		1	teaspoon allspice

Remove all the fat from the meat and cut it into cubes. Using a meat grinder or food processor, grind the meat twice until it is very fine. Grind the onions fine also. (If you are using a food processor, process in small amounts for 30 seconds each.)

Wash the cracked wheat several times in cold water. Soak it in warm water for 15 minutes, then drain it very well, squeezing out all the moisture. Mix the wheat with the ground meat, onions and spices and grind it once again.

Mix everything well by hand, dipping your hands in ice water as you work, to give the mixture a soft consistency. Place the meat on a serving platter and shape it into an oval. Smooth it over with cold water. To decorate it, make impressions in the oval with the tines of a fork or the top of a spoon. Serve it with melted butter or olive oil drizzled on top, and onion wedges, meat filling (see recipe for baked kibbee on page 231), and Lebanese bread on the side.

Yabrak Malfouf bi Hamith
(Lemon Cabbage Rolls)

Cabbage

1	large head cabbage	1	teaspoon salt
6	garlic cloves, sliced	2	tablespoons dried mint,
	Water to cover the rolls		crushed
2	lemons, juice only		Lemon wedges for garnish

Filling

1	pound lean lamb or beef	½	teaspoon pepper
1	cup long grain rice	1½	teaspoons salt
½	teaspoon cinnamon	2	tablespoons melted butter
½	teaspoon allspice		

Core the center of the cabbage and place the whole head in boiling water. Cook the cabbage, removing each leaf when it is tender. Drain the cabbage leaves; cut the large ones in half and remove the center veins.

To make the filling, grind the meat coarsely. Wash and drain the rice. Combine all the filling ingredients.

Place one tablespoon of filling on one end of each cabbage leaf. Fold the end of the leaf over the filling, then fold both sides inward, and roll the leaf tightly into a cigar shape. Line the bottom of a large saucepan with broken or extra leaves. Place the rolls side by side evenly in layers, adding a few garlic slices between each layer. Alternate the direction of the cabbage rolls for each layer. Cover the rolls with boiling water. Add the lemon juice and sprinkle the rolls with salt. Place an inverted plate over the cabbage rolls to keep them firm and intact while they cook. Cover the pan and bring the water to a boil. Reduce the heat to low and simmer for approximately 30 minutes. Sprinkle the rolls with crushed mint. Serve them garnished with lemon wedges.

Lift Makbous (Pickled Turnips)

4	pounds baby white turnips	3	cups water
½	cup salt	1½	cups white vinegar
2	uncooked beets, peeled and sliced		

Wash and peel the turnips; cut them into wedges. Sprinkle them with the salt and let them stand for a few hours. Drain off the excess water. Place the turnips with a few pieces of beet in clean jars.

Boil the water and vinegar together. Let the mixture cool, then pour it over the turnips, leaving 1 inch at the top of the jars. Seal the jars with lids, and allow one week before serving the pickles.

Fatayer bi Sabanekh (Spinach Pies)

1	recipe Lebanese bread dough (see page 235)	1	large onion, finely chopped
2	large bunches of spinach (about 1 pound)	½	cup lemon juice
		¼	cup vegetable oil
1½	teaspoons salt, divided	½	teaspoon pepper
		2	tablespoons soft butter

Prepare the bread dough, as instructed in the bread recipe, and let it rise until it has doubled in bulk.

While the dough is rising, wash and drain the spinach well. Chop it coarsely and sprinkle it with 1 teaspoon of salt. Let it stand until it is wilted (approximately 10 to 15 minutes). Squeeze the spinach well to remove any excess water. In a large bowl, mix the spinach with the onion, lemon juice, oil, pepper and the remaining salt. Set it aside.

Using a rolling pin, roll out half the bread dough to ⅛ inch in thickness on a lightly floured surface. With a 3-inch cookie cutter, cut out individual circles, saving the dough left from the cutting to roll and reuse.

Place one heaping tablespoon of filling in the center of each circle, squeezing out as much juice as possible from the filling first. Bring up three edges of the dough to form a triangle. If the dough does not stick well in some places, put flour on your finger tips to help the seal. Place the triangles on a lightly greased cookie sheet. Bake them in a preheated 450 degree oven until golden brown (approximately 10 to 15 minutes). Brush the tops with the soft butter.

Khubis Talameh (Lebanese Bread)

1   package active dry yeast   2   teaspoons salt
2   cups warm water, divided   ½   cup plus 1 tablespoon
1   teaspoon sugar   vegetable oil, divided
5   cups all-purpose flour

Mix the yeast with the sugar in ½ cup warm water. Let it rest until the mixture bubbles (approximately 10 minutes).

Mix the flour and salt together in a large bowl, then push them to one side. Pour the remaining 1½ cups warm water, the ½ cup of oil and the yeast mixture into the empty side of the bowl. Knead the flour into the water until it is well blended and the dough is smooth, adding more water or flour if necessary.

Brush the sides of the bowl with the tablespoon of oil and roll the dough in oil so that the entire surface is covered; this prevents sticking and cracking. Cover the bowl with plastic wrap and a towel and let it rest in a warm place until the dough has doubled in size (approximately 1 to 1½ hours). [One way to do this is to turn your oven on to the lowest setting, put in the bowl, then turn off the oven.]

Divide the dough into grapefruit-sized balls. Roll them lightly in flour, cover them with plastic wrap and a tea towel and let them rest on a table for 30 minutes. Pat each ball with floured fingertips into an 8-inch disc, ½ inch thick. Place the discs on cookie sheets and bake them in a preheated 375 degree oven until lightly browned (approximately 10 to 15 minutes). If the tops do not brown, place them under a broiler for a minute or so, watching them closely. Brush the tops with cool water to keep them soft.

To make pocket bread, do not pat the rounds out. Instead, roll the dough with a rolling pin to ¼ inch in thickness and proceed with the cooking.

Taboulleh (Parsley-Wheat Salad)

½   cup fine cracked wheat
    (#1 burghul)
½   cup fresh lemon juice or to
    taste
½   cup olive oil or vegetable oil
2   teaspoons salt
½   teaspoon pepper

5-6 cups parsley, well washed
     and finely chopped
     (about 5 large bunches)
1   cup fresh mint, finely
     chopped, or 2 table-
     spoons dried mint, crushed
8   green onions, chopped
4   large tomatoes, finely
     chopped

Rinse the cracked wheat and soak it in cold water for 20 minutes. Drain it well, squeezing out the excess moisture with your hands. Place it in a large bowl. Add the lemon juice, oil, salt and pepper. (To enhance the flavor of the salad, do this well in advance of serving it.) Combine the parsley, mint, onions and tomatoes; add them to the cracked wheat mixture. Toss everything together just before serving.

Lettuce leaves or tender grape leaves often replace forks as scoops to eat this salad.

Zeitoun (Marinated Olives)

2   pounds black or green
    olives, cracked
½   cup lemon juice
1   teaspoon oregano

1   teaspoon savory
1   large clove garlic, sliced
    Olive or vegetable oil

Wash and soak the olives in cold water for twelve hours, changing the water frequently. Drain and rinse the olives, then pack them tightly into a glass jar. Add the lemon juice, oregano, savory and garlic. Pour enough oil into the jar to cover the olives. Seal the jar with a lid and store it in a cool place.

You can replace the lemon juice and oil with a mixture of ¾ cup water, ¼ cup vinegar and ¼ cup oil for a different taste.

Sambusak (Walnut Crescents)

Syrup
4 cups sugar
2 cups water
1 tablespoon lemon juice

1 tablespoon orange
  blossom water

Filling
4½ cups walnuts, finely ground
½ cup sugar

2 teaspoons lemon juice
2 tablespoons orange
  blossom water

Crescents
7 cups flour
1 teaspoon black cherry
  kernels (mahlab), finely
  ground—available from
  specialty spice shops
½ teaspoon baking powder

½ cup sugar
1 cup melted unsalted butter
1 cup oil
2 eggs, beaten
1½ cups water

To make the syrup, mix the sugar and water in a heavy saucepan and bring them to a boil. Add the lemon juice, reduce the heat to medium, and continue to boil the syrup for 15 minutes. Remove the pan from the heat; add the orange blossom water. Stir the mixture, then let it stand until it is cold. It will keep up to six months, refrigerated.

To make the filling, combine all the ingredients, mixing them together well. Set them aside.

To make the crescents, combine the flour, mahlab, baking powder and sugar in a large bowl. Add the butter, oil, eggs and water; knead the resulting mixture well. Pinch off a large ball of dough the size of a grapefruit. On a floured surface, roll it out with a rolling pin to about ⅛ inch in thickness. Cut out rounds with a floured 3-inch cookie cutter. Place one teaspoon of the filling in the center of a dough circle and fold one edge over, making a half moon. Press the edges together. Place the half moons on a cookie sheet and bake them in a preheated 350 degree oven until they are lightly browned (approximately 25 minutes). Remove them from the cookie sheet and place the hot crescents in the cold syrup for five minutes. Remove them from the syrup and allow them to cool before serving them.

Baklawa

1½ pounds walnuts or pista-chios, finely chopped	2 pounds phyllo dough
½ cup sugar	1 pound unsalted butter, melted
1 teaspoon lemon juice	1 recipe syrup (see recipe for Walnut Crescents on page 237)
2 tablespoons orange blossom water	

Combine the nuts, sugar, lemon juice and orange blossom water in a small bowl and set them aside.

Brush the bottom of a jelly-roll pan with melted butter. Place one sheet of phyllo dough on the bottom of the pan and brush it lightly with melted butter. Add a second sheet of phyllo and again brush lightly with butter. Continue this procedure until one pound of dough is used up. (To keep the unused dough from drying out, cover it with a damp tea towel.)

Spread the nut mixture evenly over the pan of dough. Cover it with the remaining dough, using the same procedure as before. With a sharp knife, cut the baklawa into 1½-inch diamond shapes, cutting to the bottom of the pan. Pour any remaining warm butter evenly over the top of the pan. Place the pan on a rack in the middle of a preheated 400 degree oven and bake for 20 minutes. Reduce the heat to 300 degrees and continue baking until the baklawa is golden brown (approximately 1½ hours). While the baklawa is still hot, pour the cold syrup slowly and evenly over it. Allow it to cool, then cut it along the diamond shapes and remove each from the pan. Store them in a tightly sealed container, placing wax paper between the layers.

Lebanon took its name from the snow-capped peaks ("Laban" is Aramaic for "white") in the mountainous region where many of the country's Maronites scratched out a meager living by farming. A sect of Christianity, the Maronites had become a distinct religious community in the seventh century. Conflicts between them and their Druze neighbors were a constant part of the region's history; a particularly sad episode was a massacre of the Maronites by the Druze in 1860. The Druze religion is rooted in Islam, and struggles between the two groups for supremacy continue to the present day. This religious strife, combined with poverty and the general difficulty of life in Lebanon's mountains, made emigration attractive—especially to the Maronites, although they were by no means the only Lebanese to look elsewhere for a better life.

In the late 1800s when the Maronites were making their move to the United States, Tupper Lake was coming into its own as a center for the logging industry. The Lebanese immigrants, most of whom spoke no English and had no skills besides subsistence farming, often ended up in Utica or Watertown, terminal points for trains out of New York City, where they went to work in factories. Often they would share a room and sleep in shifts—at first because they could afford nothing else, later because they wanted to save every penny they could so that they could establish real lives in this country.

As these men began to acquire some money and some command of the language, they heard of the burgeoning lumber industry in the Adirondacks. Although they were not merchants by background, they filled packs with articles to appeal to the lumberjacks, and set off for the camps. Some traveled on foot; others bought old cars and traveled together from camp to camp. They were welcomed by the lumber-jacks, who were eager to buy gifts for their wives and girlfriends at home, but those camps with company stores would not allow the peddlers onto the premises.

The itinerant life of the peddler is one that gets old quickly, especially when the choice of sleeping accommodations is between a louse-ridden bunk in a lumber camp and a blanket on the ground with your pack for a pillow. As the young men acquired a bit more wealth, they began to think of putting down roots and marrying, or of sending home for families left behind. They moved into Tupper Lake and opened businesses with their newly-earned capital—clothing or jewelry stores, groceries, hotels, and even a skating rink. In most cases they and their families lived in rooms or apartments on the premises of the new business.

With the exception of one family who were Druze, all the Lebanese who moved to Tupper Lake were Maronite Christians from two extended families in a mountain village called Batuta. The fact that they all shared the same background, religion, and family ties made it easy for the community to remain quite isolated socially for a long time. There was much intermarriage among the immigrants and even among their children, but as the generations passed and more marriages with non-Lebanese took place, the isolation eventually broke down. Although many descendants of the original Lebanese immigrants have remained in Tupper Lake, they have now been absorbed into the larger community, many holding public offices and others playing an active role in local civic and social organizations.

* * *

Adapted from an article by Ellen Maroun entitled "The Lebanese Community of Tupper Lake," which appeared in the *Franklin Historical Review,* vol. 23, 1986.

MENNONITES

Members of the Martin family, German Mennonites who have settled near Philadelphia, Jefferson County, boil pretzel dough in soda water before baking the pretzels in ovens in their small factory. *Norm Johnston Photo/Watertown Daily Times*

Beaver Camp Auction
Lowville

The word is that you have to get there early to get the best pies at the Beaver Camp auction. But it's Saturday! I crawl out of bed at what seems to be the crack of dawn and point the Chevy south. No problem finding the auction once I get to town; cars are parked deep around the fairground. The aroma of chicken barbecue reaches out to meet me as I get out of the car, but I'm not seduced. After all, it's not even 10:30 yet.

I hustle over to the bake tent, eager to choose the perfect pie from mounds of succulent candidates. The tent is empty of customers; a few women bustle around throwing away paper tablecloths, breaking down cardboard boxes and generally tidying the area. The bake sale is over and 300 pies have gone home to the tables and freezers of more enterprising shoppers. I've learned my lesson—next year I'll drive down the night before with my sleeping bag.

Pie dreams shattered, I stroll around the grounds, determined not to let my early disappointment spoil the rest of the day. Fortunately there are plenty of distractions. In one tent I find a wealth of fascinating items from around the world. Ever on the lookout for the perfect Christmas present, I spend a happy half-hour selecting note cards from Bangladesh with straw cutouts glued on them, small wooden animals from Africa, and some shells with scenes carved into them that will make great necklaces for my nieces. I feel doubly good about my purchases when the woman behind the table tells me the Mennonites will be sending the money from the sale of these things back to the villages where they were made as part of a self-help program. I've always liked the idea of "giving a hand, not a handout".

The main event is clearly the auction. Prospective buyers stroll through the barn where items waiting to be sold are spread temptingly. Outside a crowd sits in chairs in front of a raised platform where the auctioneer is busy working his way through assorted pieces of furniture, kitchen ware, and even a box of men's neckties. Caught up in auction fever, I buy a fine-looking red one—my father's favorite color—without realizing that I've bought my standard-sized father an extra-long tie.

The real treasures of the day—quilts handmade by Mennonite women's sewing circles from around the state—are sprinkled among these miscellaneous lots like brightly colored flowers. The bidding quickly moves out of my range whenever one of these beauties comes on the block, so I simply sit and marvel at the intricate patterns, the fine stitching, and the bright colors. It seems that each is prettier than the last.

The smell of the cooking chicken is more attractive now than it was earlier. I find a spot at the table in the food tent with my friend Pat Falton and tear into an enormous piece of chicken* and a mound of potato salad. While we eat, Pat explains that most Mennonite families avoid the Lewis County Fair with its various worldly temptations. They prefer to spend their money here instead, knowing it will go to support the Mennonite camp in the Adirondacks. She tells me it wouldn't be the Beaver Camp auction without a whoopie pie* or an apple fritter* to finish off the meal. I can't decide, so I have both.

Sauce for Barbecued Chicken

This is the recipe used by Ezra Widrick for his chicken barbecues at the Beaver Camp auction.

2	cups vinegar	1	cup salad oil
2	tablespoons salt	1	egg
1	tablespoon poultry season-ing	½	teaspoon pepper

Mix all the ingredients. Marinate the chicken overnight in the sauce. Barbecue it on the grill, basting with the sauce while it cooks.

Marjie Zehr

Whoopie Pies

Cookies

1	cup butter	2	eggs
2	cups sugar	1	cup sour milk
4	cups flour	2	teaspoons vanilla
2	teaspoons salt	2	teaspoons baking soda
1	cup cocoa	1	cup hot water

Filling

2	egg whites	2	teaspoons vanilla
4	tablespoons flour	4	tablespoons milk
4	cups confectioners' sugar	1½	cups shortening

To make the cookies, cream together the butter and sugar. Combine the flour, salt and cocoa. Beat them into the butter and sugar along with the eggs, milk and vanilla. Mix the baking soda and the hot water; add them to the batter and mix well. Drop the dough by teaspoons onto an ungreased cookie sheet. Bake the cookies at 350 degrees for 8 to 9 minutes. Cool.

To make the filling, cream together all the ingredients. Separate the cookies into two equal groups. Spread the filling on the flat side of each cookie in one group. Place the remaining cookies on top to make whoopie sandwiches.

Ginny Moser

Raisin Nut Pie

This pie is an excellent seller at the Beaver Camp pie stand.

3	eggs	½	cup milk
1	cup sugar	1	cup raisins
½	teaspoon cinnamon	¾	cup walnuts, broken up
¼	teaspoon nutmeg	1	(9-inch) unbaked pie shell
6	tablespoons butter, melted		

Beat the eggs and add the sugar, cinnamon and nutmeg. Add the butter and milk; mix well. Sir in the raisins and nuts. Pour the mixture into the unbaked pie shell. Bake at 400 degrees for 10 minutes, then lower the temperature to 350 degrees and bake for 30 minutes more.

Gladys Moshier sometimes substitutes maple syrup for some of the sugar.

Gladys Moshier

Apple Fritters

1	cup flour	1	egg, beaten
1½	teaspoons baking powder	1½	cups apples, pared and
½	teaspoon salt		diced or sliced very thin
2	tablespoons sugar		Vegetable oil for frying
½	cup milk plus 1 tablespoon		

Sift the flour, baking powder, salt and sugar together. Combine the milk and the beaten egg, then pour them into the flour mixture, stirring until the batter is smooth. Add the apples to the batter and blend them together.

Drop the fritters by spoonfuls into deep hot fat (370 to 375 degrees). Fry them until they are golden brown on all sides.

Aleta Zehr

This favorite of the Zehr family comes from The Mennonite Community Cookbook: Favorite Family Recipes *by Mary Emma Showalter. Scottsdale PA: Herald Press, 1978.*

Shoo Fly Pie

1   unbaked 9-inch pie shell

Bottom Part

½	teaspoon baking soda	½	cup corn syrup or maple
¾	cup boiling water		syrup
½	cup molasses	1	egg, beaten

Top Part

1¼	cups flour	2	tablespoons butter
½	cup brown sugar		

Dissolve the soda in the boiling water. Stir in the molasses and syrup, then add the egg.

In a separate bowl make the topping by combining the flour and sugar, then rubbing in the butter to make a crumbly mixture.

Pour one-third of the liquid into the pie shell. Sprinkle one-third of the crumbs over it. Continue to alternate layers, ending with crumbs on top. Bake at 375 degrees for 35 minutes.

Cindy Zehr

Pie Plant Pie (Rhubarb Pie)

It was Sunday, January 6, 1918, when Ellen and Arlene Yousey's mother copied this recipe into her "Record" book, started in 1909, two years before her marriage. Her uncle, Chris Moser, once went on a trip and was attracted by a mysterious offering on a restaurant menu: rhubarb pie. He was quite indignant to discover that he had spent money on his least favorite food—pie plant pie.

2 cups pie plant, diced
1 cup sugar
2 tablespoons flour
1 egg, beaten
⅛ teaspoon salt
1 unbaked 9-inch pie shell— no top crust needed

Mix all the ingredients in a dish. Place them in the unbaked pie shell. Bake at 425 degrees for 15 minutes, then reduce the heat to 350 degrees and bake until the pie plant is soft and liquid set (approximately 30 minutes more).

Ellen and Arlene Yousey

Mincemeat

This recipe was that of Kathryn Forrester's aunt, Lydia Gingerich; it has remained a family favorite.

3 bowls cooked beef, ground
5 bowls apples, chopped
1 bowl suet, ground
½ bowl molasses
1 bowl vinegar
3 lemons
1 tablespoon salt
1 bowl cider
1 bowl raisins
4 bowls sugar
2 tablespoons cinnamon
1 tablespoon cloves
2 oranges
1 teaspoon pepper

Use the same size bowl for measuring all the ingredients. Mix everything together, then cook over medium heat until the apples are soft, stirring occasionally. This mixture will be thick; when you make pies, you will need to add a little water.

Kathryn Forrester

Applesauce Cake

Edna Yousey learned this recipe from her mother-in-law, Molly Yousey.

1	cup sugar	½	teaspoon cloves
½	cup shortening	½	teaspoon nutmeg
1	teaspoon baking soda, dissolved in ¼ cup water	1	teaspoon cinnamon
		⅛	teaspoon salt
1	cup unsweetened apple-sauce	1	cup raisins
		1¾	cups flour

Cream the sugar and shortening together. Blend the soda water into the applesauce and thoroughly mix in the cloves, nutmeg, cinnamon and salt. Dredge the raisins in the flour. Add the flour mixture to the sugar mixture alternately with the applesauce mixture, stirring just until it is well combined. Pour into a greased 9 x 13-inch pan and bake at 350 degrees for 45 minutes.

Edna Yousey

Sauerkraut Salad

½	cup white vinegar	1	cup onion, finely chopped
½	cup water	1	cup celery, finely chopped
1	cup sugar	1	cup red or green pepper, finely chopped
½	cup salad oil		
1	large package raw sauerkraut		

Boil the vinegar, water and sugar together, then remove them from the heat. Add the salad oil. Pour this dressing over the vegetables and refrigerate the bowl.

This salad is best made 24 hours ahead.

Beulah Roggie

Scalloped Peas and Onions

Annie Noftsier learned this recipe from her sister Nancy, who she says is one of the best cooks in Lewis County.

¼	cup butter	4-5	medium onions
3	tablespoons flour	1	(10-ounce) package frozen
½	teaspoon ground mustard		peas
½	teaspoon salt		Paprika
⅛	teaspoon pepper	3	tablespoons Parmesan
1	cup milk		cheese

In a saucepan over medium heat, melt the butter. Stir in the flour, mustard, salt and pepper. Cook, stirring, until the butter is bubbly. Add the milk and stir until the sauce thickens. Gently stir in the sliced onions and peas. Place the mixture in a 2-quart casserole. Sprinkle the top with paprika and Parmesan cheese, then bake it at 350 degrees for 30 minutes.

Annie Noftsier

Kuchen Bread

This is an old-fashioned German loaf. The Moser family often bakes it in pie plates and enjoys it as a pull-apart bread.

1	cup milk	1	teaspoon nutmeg
1	cup water	1	egg, beaten
⅓	cup shortening	1	cup raisins
1	tablespoon yeast	2	tablespoons butter, melted
1	cup sugar		Cinnamon sugar
5	cups flour, divided		

Heat together the milk, water and shortening until the shortening is melted and the mixture is warm. Add the yeast, sugar, two cups of the flour and the nutmeg; mix them well. Dredge the raisins in the remaining three cups of the flour. Add the egg and the raisin/flour mixture to the yeast mixture. Knead the resulting dough on a floured board for 10 minutes. Form the dough into a ball and place it in a greased bowl, greasing the top of the dough lightly. Let it rise until it doubles in bulk. Punch it down and form it into two loaves. Let it rise again until it doubles. Brush the tops of the loaves with melted butter, then sprinkle them with cinnamon sugar. Bake in a preheated 350 degree oven for 10 minutes, then turn the heat down to 300 degrees and bake for 20 to 25 minutes more.

Ginny Moser

On June 19, 1833, the *Barque Statera* arrived in New York City from Le Havre, bearing a load of immigrants hoping to start a new life in Pennsylvania and Ohio. The Michael Zehr family—father, mother and nine children ranging in age from one to nineteen—were among those crowded at the rail for a first welcome glimpse of land. They had listed Ohio as their destination while they were still on the ship; no one knows why they changed their minds once they reached America and decided to settle in Lewis County instead. We do know that they ended up in Croghan, then called French Settlement, the area of land owned by James LeRay de Chaumont. And we know that they were Mennonites from Alsace-Lorraine.

Between the time of the Zehrs' arrival and the mid-1850s, many Mennonite families made their way from Alsace to upstate New York. They came, like many other immigrant groups, to find freedom from religious persecution. One of the major tenets of the Mennonite faith is pacifism. In France at that time, military service was compulsory, and those who refused to participate were dealt with harshly. But this was not their first experience with oppression.

The Mennonite religion had developed in Switzerland at the time of the Protestant Reformation. It held that those who wished to join its ranks should do so voluntarily as adults, signifying their choice by baptism and by nonconformity to the outside world. Unfortunately, the mainstream culture surrounding the Mennonites viewed them with suspicion and they suffered such persecution that they left Switzerland and moved to Alsace.

The history of the Mennonite religion in Lewis County is complex. The Amish and the Mennonites are separate, though related, religions. (The Amish broke away from the Mennonites in 1693 over the question of whether to shun members of the religious community who did not adhere strictly to all its rules.) The families who moved here from Alsace included some Amish and some Mennonites, but the community was so small that they set aside their differences and worshipped together, calling themselves Amish. Around 1912, they affiliated themselves with the Conservative Amish Mennonite Conference. In 1955, the conference eliminated the term "Amish" from its name, and now its members are known as "Mennonites." Thus the original Croghan Amish were in effect assimilated by the Mennonites there; today there are 10 Mennonite congregations in Lewis County that are offspring of the original nucleus of Croghan Amish and Mennonites.

Present-day Mennonites are less conservative than their Amish neighbors in St. Lawrence County. They drive cars, own electric appliances, and wear mainstream—but modest—clothing. In accord with their nonviolent beliefs, many performed alternative duty as conscientious objectors during the various wars of the 20th century. They have a strong outreach program and have become specialists in disaster relief. The Lewis County Mennonites played a large role in aiding the victims of the Corning-Elmira Flood of 1972.

* * *

Adapted from Arlene Yousey's Strangers and Pilgrims: History of the Lewis County Mennonites. *Croghan NY: Arlene Yousey, 1987.*

MOHAWKS

Julius Cook displays braided Indian white corn from his garden, prepared to dry in bunches from the rafters of his garage at Akwesasne. *Varick Chittenden Photo/ TAUNY Archives*

Mohawk Weddings

by Emily White and Harriet LaFrance

as told to the production staff of TAUNY's
radio program "Home Cooking"

and by Florence Cook

as told to Lynn Ekfelt

Wedding hash* is the traditional food for Mohawk weddings. Even when a reception is catered, someone from the reservation always makes the hash. When my nephew got married, they had a catered buffet. I brought a canner full of hash and put it down on the end of the table. Everyone walked around it; they didn't know what it was. Then my nephew came in. He piled his plate high and gave some to the others. Do you know they ate every bit of that canner of hash!

For the weddings where there's no caterer, the women who've been cooking for a long time, the experienced cooks who are relatives of the bride and groom, come over the night before to do the cooking. They make lots of pies, hams, turkeys and hash the night before. All weddings have to have a dish of pickled beets*. The bride and groom have to eat those, and there's always a lot of joking. They say that if young people eat the beets, they'll be the next to get married. Nowadays people aren't so fond of them, but we still put a dish of them out. The wedding cake is always a carrot cake in tiers with lots of white icing and little silver beads. Have you seen the wedding cake basket in the Akwesasne Museum? It's beautiful—a basket shaped like a wedding cake, 3 tiers high, with three tiny basket bells on top. In the old days a dish of rice and raisins was a wedding tradition for dessert. I don't know how they made it, but it was so good.

Nowadays wedding receptions are always smorgasbords, but in the old days they'd set the table the night before with a nice cloth. They always put the plates upside down to keep the dust off them. Sometimes a guy would have a little too much to drink at the reception and he'd end up putting his hash on the bottom of his plate! They always used to have square dancing at receptions but now there's a band, the Little River Mohawks, because not so many people square dance anymore.

Many of the Mohawks are Catholic, so we have church ceremonies. But some of us are traditional Longhouse People. My niece got married a couple of years ago in a traditional ceremony. She made her own deerskin dress. It came below the knee and she wore high moccasins— like boots—with it. The groom wore black slacks and a traditional ribbon shirt; it's a calico shirt with ribbons hanging from the shoulders and the yoke. They each carried a basket. Most people nowadays don't know how to make the baskets so they have to buy them. They are shallow, square baskets with handles, and the bride and groom exchange them during the ceremony. The bride has material or clothing in hers to symbolize her promise to mend and keep clean the clothes of her future family. The groom's basket holds a cake of white corn bread mixed with strawberries; he gives it to the bride as a symbol of his promise to provide food for her and their future children.

In the Western tradition, the father is the one who gives away the bride. For the Mohawks, the mother is the important one because the line of descent is through the female side. The speaker asks the mothers if their children are ready to assume the responsibilities of marriage. He also asks if the mothers would be willing to open their homes to the young couple and their children should hard times make them homeless. If they say "yes" to both questions, the wedding proceeds.

The speaker then asks the bride the following questions:

1. You have chosen this man to be your husband. This means that you are prepared to be his wife for the rest of your life. Is this the way you understand?

2. In all communities there are men and women who gossip and carry rumors; this the Creator forbids. In your marriage, when your husband may be away hunting or working and you are home alone, it may be then that men or women may come to your house and say that your husband is away and he has another woman. This you will not listen to as it is said for the purpose of attacking and destroying your good marriage. You will use a good mind and kind words, whenever a doubt is brought to you by someone. You will talk with

your husband so that there will be no room for doubt or conflict between you. Do you understand and accept what I have told you?

3. Now when your husband has been working hard for you and your children, you will have food prepared for him and the children. Do you accept this responsibility?

4. If you are lucky, the Creator will allow children to be born for you and your husband. Sometimes your children will be playing outside with other children from the community. It is dinner time. You will call your children and all the children playing with them to eat. If the neighbor children have soiled faces, you will wash their face and feed them as though they were your own children. You must never send them away as our Creator would be most displeased! Do you understand and accept this practice of our people?

5. It may be that in the future a sickness may fall upon your husband. This will change things that you were used to before. You must not get angry with him because he cannot work or do his normal duties. You will look for medicine that will make him well. You will bathe him, comb his hair and fix his pillow, in the event he can't do it because of sickness. Do you accept this responsibility?

6. You will also act as a team, consulting with your husband on all matters and agreeing or using one mind. This marriage is a partnership and no one is of more authority. You will not dominate your husband nor will he do this to you. Do you accept to do this in your marriage? [1]

The groom then answers the same questions. All the wedding guests are witnesses to these pledges. If the couple should fail in the future to live up to their promises, then any of the witnesses can approach them and remind them of their vows.

[1] Porter, Tom. *Mohawk Marriage.* Hogansburg NY: North American Indian Travelling College, pp. 6-7.

* * *

Emily White was born on Cornwall Island and taught school there. Harriet La France taught the Mohawk language and did beadwork on slippers at Bombay. Florence Cook works at the Akwesasne Cultural Center.

The foods in this section were described by Emily White and Harriet La France. Unless otherwise indicated, the actual recipes came from a cookbook entitled Grandmother's Recipes of Yesteryear, *put out by the Franklin County Senior Citizens Nutrition Program (Kansas City, Kansas: Cookbook Publishers, Inc., 1977) loaned to me by Carol White of the Akwesasne Cultural Center.*

According to the Iroquois creation story, as Sky-Woman fell through a hole in the sky, she grabbed a strawberry plant and some tobacco leaves. She landed on the back of a giant turtle in the ocean. Various creatures tried to help her find some soil to plant her strawberry and tobacco, but only the otter could dive deep enough to bring some up. The turtle's back and the earth began to grow and the woman planted her plants, then eventually gave birth to a daughter. When the daughter died while giving birth to twin boys, Sky-Woman buried her. From the earth over her head grew corn, beans, and squash—the Three Sisters. Over her heart grew the sacred tobacco plant, and at her feet grew the strawberry and medicinal plants.

As a gift of the Creator, the Three Sisters play a very important role in Mohawk cuisine. Even the Mohawks who are Catholic retain a reverence for these three foods. Corn, particularly, is a staple in their diet. Indian corn is not the sweet corn that most of us are used to. It is more like field corn—quite hard—so it needs to have its hard outer coating removed before it can be eaten. This is done by soaking the dried kernels in a caustic soup of wood ash. The result is much like hominy—white and puffy.

Hulled Indian Corn (Old Method)

1½ quarts clean hardwood
    (maple or oak) ashes
2   gallons water

1½ quarts dried Indian corn
    (removed from the cob
    before drying)

Sift the ashes well before mixing them with the water in a large enamel or stainless steel kettle (do not use aluminum); bring the water to a boil, stirring frequently, and continue boiling for about an hour. The water will feel soapy. Test a handful of corn in the boiling solution. If the corn turns red, the solution is ready. Add the corn and continue boiling, stirring well and frequently, until the hulls and the black hearts of the corn loosen and can be removed easily. Skim these off. Using a basket with coarse openings as a strainer, wash and rinse the corn several times to remove the remaining loose hulls and hearts. After the corn has been thoroughly cleaned, it may be dried for future use or it may be prepared for corn soup.

Emily White puts her ashes into a cloth bag so they are easier to separate from the finished corn. She rinses her corn ten times, until the water comes clean. At that point, she knows it is safe to eat.

Tom Jacobs
St. Regis, Quebec

Hulled Corn (Modern Method)

Today it is harder to produce the traditional hulled corn, since fewer people have wood stoves to produce the ashes. Nancy Terrance uses this method to get the same effect. The white corn flour is also available in stores at Caughnawaga, if you would rather leave the production to someone else altogether.

1½ gallons water
3   tablespoons baking soda

3   cups Indian corn

Bring the water to a boil; add the baking soda, then the corn. The corn will turn a deep orange. Boil, stirring frequently, until the corn turns white again. Wash and rinse it several times, then spread it on papers to dry. It must be completely dry before you try to grind it. Grind and sift the corn several times until the flour is the desired fineness.

Nancy Terrance
Hogansburg

Corn Soup

This is the quintessential Mohawk dish, with as many variations as there are cooks. If you do not feel up to producing your own hulled corn, canned hominy is a reasonable substitute.

3	pork hocks or 1 pound country-style spareribs	1	quart hulled corn, cooked and drained
2	medium carrots, sliced thin	1	can red kidney beans, drained
2	potatoes, diced		Salt to taste
½	medium-sized head of cabbage, chopped		

Cook the meat in plenty of water until it is well done. Remove any bones, then chop the meat. Add the carrots, potatoes and cabbage and continue cooking until they are tender. (Add the cabbage at this point only if the soup is to be served immediately. If not, add it when you reheat it for serving.) Add the kidney beans and corn, then reheat the soup to serving temperature.

This recipe combines ones from Nancy Terrance and Ruth Herne
Hogansburg

Salt Pork Soup

Another staple of the Mohawk diet has been salt pork. Emily White remembers that her family always had barrels of it set aside for winter cooking.

3	quarts water	Carrots, cut into bite-sized pieces
1	pound lean salt pork, cut into bite-sized pieces	Rice
	Celery, cut into bite-sized pieces	Tomatoes, cut into chunks
	Onions, cut into bite-sized pieces	Salt and pepper to taste

Boil the pork in the water for about ½ hour. Add the celery, onions and carrots and boil until the vegetables are cooked. Add the rice and tomatoes and simmer until the soup is well done. Season it with salt and pepper.

Cornmeal Potatoes

The traditional Sunday brunch at Caughnawaga, served after church, is this cornbread—actually more like dumplings—and cube steaks. At Caughnawaga, the cooks add whole red kidney beans to the bread.

1	cup cornmeal (white corn flour made from dried hulled corn)	2	teaspoons salt Boiling water

Mix the cornmeal and salt in a bowl. Add boiling water gradually until the mixture is of a consistency to be handled and formed into cakes. With wet hands, form into cakes about 2½ to 3 inches in diameter. Place a rack in the bottom of a kettle with a lid. Bring to a boil enough water to cover the cakes when they are set on the rack. Reduce the heat so the water is just simmering; put the cakes on the rack. Cover the kettle and simmer the cakes for about 20 minutes. Do not allow the water to boil vigorously, as the cakes may tend to come apart.

Mrs. Moses J. White
Akwesasne

Fried Bread

2	cups flour	½	cup warm water
1	teaspoon salt	½	cup milk
3	teaspoons baking powder		Cooking oil for frying

Combine the flour, salt and baking powder. Gradually stir in the water and milk until you have a soft dough. Let the dough mixture rest for an hour. Knead it for a few minutes then roll it out to ½ inch in thickness. Cut rounds with a biscuit cutter. Fry the bread in a large frying pan in about ¼ inch of very hot oil. (The oil needs to be about 375 degrees or the bread will become soggy.) Turn the pieces so they are golden brown on both sides.

C. Cook
Hogansburg

This recipe was found in Kakhwakon (Good Food) *sponsored by the Mohawk Indian Housing Corporation, 1998.*

Wedding Hash

5	pounds potatoes	3	stalks celery, chopped
3	pounds hamburger	2	tablespoons poultry
1	pound mild bulk sausage		seasoning
2	onions, chopped		

Cook the potatoes until they are tender. Cook the hamburger and sausage together in a small amount of water, stirring to break up the meat. Cook the onions and celery in a little water, just until they are clear. Mash the potatoes and add all the remaining ingredients. Mix them together thoroughly.

Christie Bigtree
Akwesasne

Spiced Winter Squash

Obviously the earliest Native Americans did not have coriander and mace to add to their squash. In this recipe, a Mohawk cook has taken a traditional favorite food and given it a modern twist— a perfect example of how foodways evolve.

4	cups cooked, puréed winter squash	2	tablespoons flour
½	teaspoon salt	5	tablespoons melted butter or margarine, divided
¼	teaspoon coriander	½	cup brown sugar
¼	teaspoon ground mace	¼	cup fine bread crumbs
¼	teaspoon ground ginger		

Combine the squash with the salt, coriander, mace, ginger and flour then turn the mixture into a buttered 1-quart shallow casserole. Drizzle with 2 tablespoons of the melted butter. Sprinkle the brown sugar evenly over the top. Mix the bread crumbs with the remaining 3 tablespoons of butter and sprinkle them evenly over the squash. Bake at 325 degrees until the crumbs are golden and the sugar has melted (approximately 30 minutes).

The recipe may be combined ahead of time and refrigerated for later baking.

Mary Jo Terrance
Hogansburg

This recipe was found in Kakhwakon (Good Food) *sponsored by the Mohawk Indian Housing Corporation, 1998.*

Pickled Beets

3	pounds of tiny beets	½	teaspoon cloves
1	cup sugar	½	teaspoon salt
1	teaspoon cinnamon	2	cups vinegar
1	teaspoon allspice		

Wash and drain the beets. Cover them with boiling water and cook them until they are tender (approximately 20 minutes), then drain them. When they are cool enough to handle, remove the skins, stems and root ends.

Combine the sugar and spices in a saucepan, then add the vinegar. Bring the mixture to a boil and simmer it for five minutes. Pack the warm beets into hot sterilized canning jars and pour the boiling vinegar mixture over them. Cap the jars and process them in a water bath for thirty minutes.

Harriet La France
Hogansburg

Blueberry Batter Cake

2	cups blueberries	1	teaspoon baking powder
½	lemon, juice only	½	teaspoon nutmeg
1¾	cups sugar, divided	½	teaspoon salt, divided
3	tablespoons butter	1	tablespoon cornstarch
½	cup milk	1	cup boiling water
1	cup flour		

Sprinkle the berries with the lemon juice and place them in an even layer in a well-greased 8-inch square pan. Cream ¾ cup of the sugar with the butter. Combine the milk, flour, baking powder, nutmeg and ¼ teaspoon of the salt. Add this mixture to the creamed sugar and butter and pour the resulting batter evenly over the berries.

Combine the remaining cup of sugar with the cornstarch and the remaining ¼ teaspoon of the salt; sprinkle them over the cake. Pour the boiling water over everything and bake at 375 degrees for 1 hour.

Louise W. Cooke
Hogansburg

This recipe was found in Kakhwakon (Good Food) *sponsored by the Mohawk Indian Housing Corporation, 1998.*

Native Americans were the first residents of the North Country, of course; but even they were not always here. There is some evidence that the ancestors of the present-day Mohawks came from the lower Mississippi Valley. Be that as it may, we know for certain that before any Europeans discovered the area a powerful Algonquin tribe called the Adirondacks drove the Mohawks south from their homes in the St. Lawrence River valley to the banks of the Mohawk River where they settled.

That was a time of considerable unrest among the various tribes living in New York State. The Mohawks, Oneidas and Ononadagas on one side were constantly fighting the Senecas and Cayugas on the other, not to mention the Mahicans to the east, the Hurons to the north, and the Eries and Susquehannocks to the south.

Then around 1570, two men were adopted into the Mohawk tribe: Deganahwidah, a Huron, and his disciple Hiawatha, an Onondaga. They spent five years working to bring peace to the five nations—the People of the Great Mountains (Senecas), the People of the Mucklands (Cayugas), the People of the Hills (Onondagas), the People of the Upright Stone (Oneidas), and the People of Flint (Mohawks). The result was the Iroquois Confederacy. Because the members of these tribes lived in palisaded villages in rectangular, bark-covered houses, they used the image of the longhouse to describe their alliance. The Mohawks became the keepers of the eastern door, the Senecas the keepers of the western door, and the Onondagas, geographically the central one of the five tribes, were the keepers of the council fire. The Iroquois Confederacy became extremely powerful not only militarily, but also politically.

Unfortunately for the French, their first contacts with the Iroquois were not successful ones; Cartier took prisoner a Mohawk chief who had welcomed him during his explorations of the St. Lawrence River, then Champlain killed three Mohawk chiefs while he was in Iroquois Country. These first encounters with Europeans and with firearms left the Mohawks with a lasting hatred for the French. Consequently, they allied themselves with the Dutch, and later the English, in those nations' battles against the French and against those Indians, such as the Hurons, who were on the side of the French.

In an effort to lure the Iroquois away from their friendship with the English, the French sent Jesuit missionaries to the five nations; by

1668 all five had missionaries living with them. A village called Laprairie was set up across from Montreal on the St. Lawrence River for the Christianized Indians, and by 1677 there were more Mohawks living there than there were in the Mohawk Valley. (The Mohawks were not the only Indians living at Laprairie; old records indicate that over twenty-two nations were represented there.)

Unscrupulous fur traders introduced alcohol to the Indians, in spite of the missionaries' efforts to combat such bad influences. Over the next few years, several groups of Indians and missionaries moved west to try to escape the drunken atmosphere at Laprairie. Finally, in 1716, a small group moved to Caughnawaga, a new village site along the river. Even there the problem of alcohol plagued them. In 1754, some of the Caughnawaga Mohawks, led by fathers Billiard and Gordan, traveled west along the river until they came to a spot where their ancestors had lived before being driven south by the Algonquins. They named it Akwesasne, "Place Where the Partridge Drums," and placed it under the patronage of St. John Francis Regis, an 18th-century Jesuit. The Mohawks were home again and have been at Akwesasne ever since.

YANKEES

Farm families of Crary Mills Grange No. 54—many of them descendants of pioneer settlers to this region from Vermont and Connecticut—gathered for a meeting and "dinner" at noon each month in their new hall in Crary Mills, St. Lawrence County, 1909. *Photo courtesy of Herbert Judd*

Yankee Food

When our Yankee forebears made their way from New England to the North Country, they spent a much greater proportion of their time acquiring food, caring for food, and preparing food than we do today. The settlers could not produce white sugar, molasses, wheat flour, spices, tea, or coffee in their new homes in the North Country any more than they could have in their old ones in Vermont, Connecticut, or Massachusetts. But here they had no stores, and no trains to transport goods to the area. Every time they needed non-local foods they had to make a lengthy and arduous journey with a wagon to some population center. Clearly, early North Country settlers had to be to all intents and purposes self-sufficient.

Fresh food came only from one's own garden or from the neighboring woods and fields. The settlers did not garden for recreation or because they particularly liked the taste of a fresh-from-the-vine tomato; they gardened to survive. But growing and gathering the crops was only the beginning. Canning technology did not become available to housewives until after the Civil War. Before that, perishable fruits and vegetables were part of the daily meals only when they were in season. Otherwise people lived on food that they could store in a root cellar: potatoes, squash, carrots, turnips, and parsnips. The root cellar had to be built just right if you wanted your family to live to see the spring. On the one hand, it had to be cool enough to preserve the foods, but it also had to be warm enough to keep them from freezing on long North Country winter nights. It had to be dry so the food would not mold, and it had to be secure enough to keep out rodents looking to share the garden's bounty.

There were two other methods of preserving garden produce available to the settlers. They could dry foods in the sun or by the fireside, depending on how late in the season the crop ripened. This technique worked for beans, corn, apples, and herbs. They could also pickle in brine or preserve using sugar. Winter meals included an amazing variety of pickles, relishes, and jams because that was the only way to continue to enjoy the crops grown so laboriously over the summer. Today sauerkraut, Indian relish, green tomato pickles, and blackberry jam are side dishes for most of us; they played a much larger role in the diet of the 19th century. Since home canning was not yet an option, the pickling was done in large crocks, using homemade cider vinegar, and the preserves went into jars sealed with paraffin.

The short growing season in the North Country meant that wheat flour was something to be purchased. Such a valuable commodity was not used for daily baking but saved for special treats. The everyday grain for the Yankee settlers was corn, to which their colonial ancestors had been introduced by Native American neighbors. In fact corn was the mainstay of their diet. A bowl of popcorn with milk was a standard breakfast before the days of Cocoa Puffs, and it remained one well into this century. Corn appeared in bread, soup, side dishes, and even desserts such as Indian pudding. However, this was not corn as we think of it—succulent butter-and-sugar corn, eaten from a cob dripping with butter. Modern-day sweet corn was not really grown much until the very end of the 19th century. Before that, the farmers ate the same field corn that their animals did.

White sugar was as rare and precious as white flour. North Country settlers used maple sugar and maple syrup for sweetening their daily foods—another practice learned from the Native Americans—and saved the white sugar for making special dishes in which the cook did not want the dish overwhelmed by the more strongly-flavored maple syrup. When a housewife wanted to bake something, she could not automatically reach for a can of baking powder. Commercial baking powder did not exist until the middle of the 19th century. Even then it was quite unreliable, so it was not until the end of the century that it began to appear in recipes. Instead cooks used yeast or homemade mixtures involving saleratus, cream of tartar, or carbonate of ammonia to make their baked goods rise.

Meat was either hunted in the woods and fields or raised and butchered at home. Again, the problem of preserving the meat arose quickly in a time without refrigeration. Smoking, salting, drying, and pickling were used to extend the life of meats as well as vegetables. Salt pork and corned beef were staples of the settlers' diet; both were stored in a salt brine. Venison was often dried into jerky. Fish were salted or dried. Hunting game or raising animals was work, so farmers did not want to waste any of the hard-earned carcass. Head cheese, sausage and mincemeat are all products that attest to the need to use every scrap of the animal.

Even eggs had to be preserved, for in the days before hen-houses with artificial lights to control the laying cycles, hens did not produce eggs year-round. Farmers would cover the eggs with lard to seal the pores, then store them buried in crocks full of lard. Sometimes they covered the eggs with isinglass, a form of gelatin made from dried sturgeon air bladders.

When one considers the effort these people had to put into every meal, it is amazing that they had as varied a diet as they did. Although many of their dishes are too high in fat to fit into today's less active lifestyles, some others remain favorites—a legacy from our Yankee ancestors.

Corn Chowder

3	slices salt pork, cubed	1	cup milk
1	large onion, sliced	2	cups corn, canned or
4	large potatoes, cubed		frozen
2	cups water	1	teaspoon salt
6	large soda crackers		

Fry the salt pork until it is crisp and lightly browned. Stir in the onion and cook until it is golden. Add the potatoes and water; continue cooking until the potatoes are tender. Crumble the crackers into a bowl, pour in the milk and let the crackers soak. Add the crackers to the cooked potatoes, then add the corn and salt. Simmer the soup over a low heat for 8 to 10 minutes.

Serves 4.

Beverly Markkula
Canton

Corn Pudding

3	slightly beaten eggs	⅓	cup finely chopped onion
2	cups drained cooked or	1	tablespoon butter, melted
	canned whole kernel corn	1	teaspoon sugar
2	cups milk, scalded	1	teaspoon salt

Combine all ingredients and pour into a greased 1 ½-quart casserole. Set the dish in a shallow pan. Fill the outer pan with boiling water to 1 inch from the top. Bake at 350 degrees for 40 to 45 minutes, or until a knife inserted off the center comes out clean. Let the pudding stand for 10 minutes at room temperature before serving.

Judy Gutekunst
Canton

Boiled Dinner

4	pounds corned beef	6	medium carrots
4	peppercorns	6	medium onions
1	bay leaf	1	medium head cabbage
6	small potatoes		

Place the meat, the peppercorns and the bay leaf in a large, heavy kettle with enough cold water to cover them. Bring the water to a boil, then reduce the heat to simmer. Cook, covered, about three hours or until the meat is tender. About 30 minutes before the meat is done, add the potatoes, carrots and onions. About 15 minutes before the meat is done, add the cabbage, cut into wedges. Place the meat on a warmed platter and surround it with vegetables.

Betty Dean Reed

Johnnycake

Early North Countrymen often made a meal of johnnycake with maple syrup or milk. According to Barbara Walker in The Little House Cookbook, *"johnny-cake" comes from "journey-cake," a brick of cornmeal and water baked over an open fire by travelers in Colonial days. This recipe is straight out of the recipe collection of Varick's grandmother.*

½	cup sour milk or buttermilk	½	cup stone-ground yellow cornmeal
1	teaspoon baking soda		
1	egg	2	large tablespoons sour cream or melted butter
½	cup sugar		
½	cup flour	⅛	teaspoon salt

Beat the milk and baking soda together until frothy. Add all other ingredients and blend them well. Pour the mixture into an ungreased 8-inch square baking pan. Bake at 400 degrees until the center is firm (approximately 30 minutes). Good served hot with butter as a bread, or cold with jelly or preserves for breakfast.

Varick Chittenden
Canton

Brown Bread

Barbara Walker in The Little House Cookbook *says this was sometimes called "thirded bread" for the three grains used in it. In older days this bread would have been cooked slowly in the oven along with the baked beans rather than steamed as in this recipe from my husband's family.*

1	cup rye flour	1½	teaspoons salt
1	cup whole wheat flour	1	cup raisins
1	cup cornmeal (stone-ground is best)	2	cups buttermilk
1½	teaspoons soda	¾	cup molasses

Mix the flours, cornmeal, soda and salt. Mix in the raisins. Combine the milk and molasses and add them to the flour mixture, mixing well. Fill two well-greased 1-pound coffee cans no more than ⅔ full. Cover each with tin foil and tie the foil on tightly with a string. Put the cans on a rack in a large kettle with water coming about ⅓ of the way up the cans. Cover the kettle. Bring the water to a boil and continue to boil gently for 3 hours. Serve the bread hot with baked beans for Saturday night supper or cold the next morning with cream cheese and jelly.

Lynn Ekfelt
Canton

Fried Parsnips

Parsnips	Pepper to taste
Butter	Nutmeg to taste
Salt to taste	

Wash the parsnips and cover them with boiling salted water in a large kettle. Simmer them for 30 minutes or until you can just penetrate them with a fork. Plunge the cooked parsnips immediately into cold water and remove the skins. Cut each into six pieces, lengthwise. Sauté the pieces in butter in a skillet until they are delicately browned. Flavor with salt, pepper, and nutmeg.

Jane Eaton
Canton

Jane Eaton found this recipe in an old Boston Cooking School Cookbook *by Fannie Farmer, first published in 1896.*

Switchel

This drink was taken to the fields to slake the thirst of the hard-working haymakers in the days before bottled soft drinks were readily available. In The Long Winter, *Laura Ingalls Wilder says this of switchel: "Ma had sent them ginger-water. She had sweetened the cool well-water with sugar, flavored it with vinegar, and put in plenty of ginger to warm their stomachs so they could drink till they were not thirsty. Ginger-water would not make them sick, as plain cold water would when they were so hot."*

3	tablespoons ginger	½-1	cup vinegar
4	cups brown sugar		Cold water to make one gallon

Mix all ingredients together.

Jessie Collins

Nana's Cottage Pudding

1   baked white cake

Sauce

1	cup sugar	3	cups water
½	cup butter	2	teaspoons vanilla
½	teaspoon salt		Nutmeg to taste
2	tablespoons flour		

Place all the sauce ingredients in a double boiler. Cook the mixture until it thickens. Cut individual serving pieces of the cake and pour the sauce over the top.

Judy Liscum
Morristown

"By Guess and by Gosh" Bread Pudding

Pudding

3	cups ½-inch bread cubes	½	teaspoon nutmeg
2	eggs	¼	teaspoon apple pie spice
2⅛	cups milk		or cinnamon
1	teaspoon vanilla		

Maple Hard Sauce, optional

¼	cup butter	½	teaspoon vanilla
1	cup plus 1 tablespoon	¼	teaspoon nutmeg
	powdered maple sugar,		
	divided		

To make the pudding, place the bread cubes in a greased ovenproof glass casserole. Beat the eggs and gradually add the milk. Mix in the vanilla, nutmeg and pie spice, then pour this mixture over the bread cubes. Place the casserole in a shallow pan, and pour boiling water into the outer pan to the level of the mixture in the baking dish. Bake for at 350 degrees for one hour. Test to see if the pudding is done by inserting a clean knife into the center. If the knife comes out clean, the pudding is done. Serve it warm with maple syrup or maple hard sauce.

To make the sauce, work the butter, the cup of powdered maple sugar and the vanilla together until they are smooth. Mix the nutmeg with the one tablespoon powdered sugar and sprinkle over the top.

If you can not find maple sugar, you can make your own. Put ½ gallon of last year's syrup into a 2 gallon pan. Boil it to 232 degrees. Pour it into a bowl and stir until it is a pale beige color. Keep working until coarse grains develop. Pour it into a mold.

Mary Smallman
Hermon

Vinegar Pie

This recipe is an old standard for holidays and fairs. According to Barbara Walker of The Little House Cookbook, *it was sometimes called "poor man's pie," and it took the place of lemon pie in areas where lemons were unavailable.*

1	stick margarine, melted and cooled	1	tablespoon vanilla
2	tablespoons vinegar	1½	cups sugar
3	eggs	2	tablespoons flour
		1	Unbaked 9-inch pie shell

Blend all ingredients well and pour into the pie shell. Bake at 300 degrees for 45 minutes.

Gail Baldwin
Canton

Lemon Crackers

2½	cups sugar	1½	teaspoons carbonate of ammonia (available at drug stores)
1	cup lard or other shortening		
2	cups milk	2	eggs
¼	teaspoon salt	3	cups flour, approximately
½	teaspoon lemon oil		

Mix the ingredients in the order given, adding flour until the dough is stiff enough to roll. Roll it thin, then cut into squares. Prick the squares with a fork, as for crackers. Bake the crackers on a greased cookie sheet at 350 degrees for 10 minutes.

The carbonate of ammonia is a leavening agent which would have been more familiar to early North Country settlers than it is to us. It gives a different taste to baked goods from our modern baking powder and baking soda.

Emily Lyon Perry

Steam Pudding

Pudding

1	pint bread crumbs, preferably home-dried	1	teaspoon soda
1	cup flour	¼	teaspoon salt
1	teaspoon cinnamon	1	egg, well beaten
1	teaspoon ground cloves	1	cup cold water
1	teaspoon allspice	1	cup maple syrup

Sauce

1	cup butter	1	cup water
1	egg	4	tablespoons boiling water

To make the pudding, mix the crumbs, flour, cinnamon, cloves, allspice, soda and salt together. Combine the egg with the water and the syrup. Add this mixture to the flour mixture to create a thin batter. Steam for three hours in a pudding mold (or a tightly covered can or ovenproof glass bowl) in a large covered kettle with boiling water coming half-way up the sides of the pudding mold.

To make the sauce, combine all the sauce ingredients and cook them in a double boiler for 15 minutes. Remove the pan from the heat immediately. Once it has cooled, beat the mixture with an egg beater until it is thick and smooth (approximately 10 minutes).

Serve the pudding warm, topped with the sauce.

Beth Gibbo
Canton

The first Europeans to see the North Country were fur traders who knew the St. Lawrence River and its shores, but never ventured inland. Cartographers of the day settled for writing "hunting ground of the Iroquois" over the whole area, focusing their energy on more populated regions. After the American Revolution, however, things changed. The government of New York State, worried about the proximity of the British on its northern border, decided that a buffer was needed to protect against sneak attacks. Consequently it decided to divide the land in St. Lawrence County into ten towns, five along the river and five inland, which it would then subdivide and sell at a price calculated to encourage settlement. The price was so attractive that Alexander Macomb, a wealthy fur trader, bought not only all the land in all ten of the towns, but also all of Franklin County and parts of Jefferson, Oswego, Lewis, and Clinton counties—4,200,000 acres in all. His greed had the result that inspired the adage about biting off more than one can chew; he went bankrupt. His lands were divided among his many creditors and they, in turn, sold parts to friends. It was these men, dreaming of establishing English-style estates for themselves, who finally subdivided the vast lands of the North Country, built the roads and mills that encouraged settlement, and left their names on our maps—Gouverneur Morris, Samuel Ogden, William Constable, George Parish.

One might wonder why anyone, especially a farmer, would be attracted to the rocky soil and short growing season of the North Country. The answer was, then as now, cheap land. The proprietors were willing to sell their land for $2 an acre, so eager were they to attract settlers to their towns. Newspapers in Vermont trumpeted the glories of the land to the west, and some New Englanders, unhappy with high taxes and the oppressive morality of their neighbors, began to heed the call. By 1820, President Timothy Dwight of Yale was calling New York "a colony from New England," and estimating that 60-67% of the people here had New England origins.[1] By 1850, about 52,000 Vermonters, or one fifth the population of Vermont itself, were living in New York, so many that early maps sometimes call the North Country "New Vermont".[2]

There were two main routes of immigration from New England to northern New York. The first was the Chateaugay Trail which crossed Lake Champlain, then passed north of the mountains through Clinton and Franklin counties. It took six to ten days to travel to St. Lawrence County this way, the route immortalized by Irving Bacheller in *Eben Holden*. Most settlers tried to make the trip in winter, preferring the deep snow and the cold to summer's bugs, rains, and mud.[3] The other route, equally strenuous, passed up the Mohawk valley and the Black River valley into the southern and western parts of the North Country. The first settlers came on foot, following a trail of blazed trees. The land agents built roads as quickly as they could to encourage settlement. The St. Lawrence Turnpike, built between Carthage and Malone in 1810, did much to aid the growth of the towns along its route—Hopkinton, Parishville, Russell, and Edwards. Pioneers could now haul their pots and pans, beds, and tools in ox-drawn wagons. Children and old people could ride, but the able-bodied walked with the oxen or herded the family's cow and sheep.

The old Puritan virtues were transported to the North Country along with their corresponding vices as part of the pioneers' baggage. Thrift verging on stinginess, self-esteem verging on arrogance, and a morality that often led to meddling in the lives of one's neighbors characterized the early settlers. It is no surprise that John Brown built towns in the Adirondacks called Frugality, Industry, Enterprise, and Sobriety.[4] Accustomed to hard work and few luxuries, the settlers were the perfect people to subdue the wilderness. They hacked clearings into the forests to make room for their farms, then turned the felled trees into the North Country's first crop—potash. Although many were unschooled themselves, they had a respect for education. We have the Yankees to thank for the private colleges and academies that were set up in this area, many of which drew their faculties from New England and modeled their curricula on those of Harvard and Yale.

David Ellis calls the migration of New Englanders to New York "a thrilling chapter in one of the great folk migrations of all time."[5] It left a lasting mark on the North Country, shaping everything from the layout of our towns to the way we govern ourselves.

[1] Dwight, Timothy. *Travels in New-England and New-York.* (New Haven, 1921-18220, III, 266-267. Cited in Ellis p. 105.

[2] Ellis, p. 110.

[3] Webster, p. 19.

[4] Ellis, p. 106.

[5] Ellis, p. 107.

Hundreds of chicken halves, basted with a sauce from a carefully-guarded recipe, are barbecued by men of several Mennonite churches at the annual Beaver Camp Auction in Lowville, Lewis County. *Varick Chittenden Photo/ TAUNY Archives*

BUILDING COMMUNITY

COUNTY FAIRS

Bea Reynolds, Burke, repeatedly the Grand Champion Cook of the annual Franklin County Fair in Malone, exhibits some of her prize-winning pies, cakes, and preserves, 1997.
Martha Cooper Photo/TAUNY Archives

Franklin County Fair
Malone

Outside, all is noise and bustle. On the midway, barkers on all sides offer enticements to part the strolling crowd from its money: throw a ping- pong ball into a fish bowl and win an iguana; see Tiny Tim, the world's smallest horse; buy a tie-dyed t-shirt; get a removable tattoo. In the barn area, competitors groom loudly protesting goats, exercise saddle horses with elaborately braided manes, and lead reluctant Holsteins to the judging arena, while roosters try tirelessly to out-crow each other for mastery of the poultry house. Cacaphonous as this chorus may be, it totally disappears every few minutes under the mind-numbing, skull-pounding roar of the REALLY BIG competitors in the tractor pull—shocking pink and turquoise blue machines that clearly have never pulled a load of manure or hay in their pampered existences.

Inside the vegetable building, the room is hushed. Not even the sound of the behemoths competing at the grandstand penetrates the closed doors of the judging area where three judges sit, methodically working their way through seemingly endless categories—angel cake unfrosted, sponge cake unfrosted, jelly roll unfrosted, chocolate layer unfrosted, white layer unfrosted, white layer frosted, yellow layer frosted, chocolate layer frosted, coconut layer frosted, any other frosted layer cake, nut loaf cake unfrosted, fruit cake loaf unfrosted, applesauce cake unfrosted, gingerbread, cupcakes frosted, doughnuts plain, doughnuts raised, cream puffs unfilled, cheesecake, strudel, coffee cake, pumpkin chocolate cake, any other cake…and that's just the cakes. Earlier this morning they finished the yeast breads and the quick breads, and after a lunch break they'll go on to the decorated cakes, the cookies, the pies, and the candies. Friday, before the fair officially opened, the same three women put in a correspondingly long day judging the canned goods. Now the ribbons on the jars of jams, relishes, and pickles form an odd, abstract red-white-and-blue crazy quilt behind them as they work.

All judging is done blind; the entries are identified only by a number. Like wine tasters, the judges consume little. They take only a small slice from each cake, then cut that into thirds; then each samples only a bite of her third, discarding the remainder of the slice. UNLIKE wine tasters, they keep a take-home goodie plate for the remnants of favorite treats, unable to consign even a crumb to the trash. Before tasting, they carefully examine the color and texture of each entry, turning it over to see if it is scorched or overly moist. Every item must be tasted except the decorated cakes; there the emphasis is entirely on the decoration. Not coincidentally those are the only baked goods which may be made from a mix. One of the judges casts a suspicious eye on a doughnut and remarks, "This looks a lot like a Freihofers." Another recalls a contestant from the past, famous for her angel food cakes, who was spotted emerging from a grocery store carrying a box of angel food cake mix. Did she, or didn't she? All the judges agree that it is often very difficult to detect a "plagiarized" entry; in most cases they have to rely on the honesty of the contestants.

Slowly the baked goods shelves take on the red, white, and blue appearance of the canned goods section. I have always assumed that a blue ribbon means first place, a red means second place, and a white third, so I am surprised to learn that there can be more than one blue ribbon in a given class. I realize that of course this system makes perfect sense—just as a teacher can give more than one "A" on a test if the performance of her students warrants it, the judges can bestow blue ribbons on all deserving bakers.

Noon has arrived, and even though the judges look slightly queasy at the prospect of lunch, I've developed quite an appetite as a bystander at the parade of treats. Fortunately the midway offers plenty of opportunity to satisfy my growling stomach. I settle for a Michigan* (gladly paying the 25 cents extra to have it made with a Glazier hot dog), a cup of poutines, a slab of fried dough (I fight off the yellow jackets jealously hovering over the huge jars of honey that I want to drizzle over it), and—to top off my feast—a frozen banana dipped in chocolate and rolled in peanuts*. If only I had room for a funnel cake*! Fortunately I am saved from myself; the humidity has affected the batter, and the cakes are temporarily unavailable.

This is the 147th fair put on by the Franklin County Agricultural Society. According to the program, the society's mission is "the promotion of agriculture, mechanics, horticulture, and household arts." I imagine myself in 1850 wandering around the fairground, and I find that not much has changed. Quilt competitions—sure. Cattle judging— definitely. Prize vegetables—of course. Even the tractor pull has its roots in the old-time horse pulls. But shocking pink? And turquoise?

Michigans

*These hot dogs are a specialty of the eastern half of the North Coun-
try. Local legend says that the name was coined by Mrs. Eula Otis,
who learned to make the sauce in Detroit and brought the recipe
with her when she moved to Plattsburgh in the 1920s. In turn, she
passed on the recipe to Irving "Nitzi" Rabin, when he opened Nitzi's
Hot Dog Stand in 1935. Today Michigans are a staple of several
long-standing hot dog businesses in the Plattsburgh area, and each
has its own secret recipe. This version is said to be close to Mrs.
Otis's original.*

1 pound ground round or chuck	1 pound hot dogs—
1 (8-ounce) can tomato paste	Glazier's, from Potsdam,
1 cup water	are a local favorite
1 tablespoon prepared	Buns—a good choice is a
mustard	large roll made by
½ teaspoon dried oregano	Bouyea Fassett baking
and/or sweet basil	company of Plattsburgh
½ teaspoon curry powder	Chopped onions
½ teaspoon chili powder	Mustard and grated
Garlic salt or onion salt to	cheese, optional
taste	

Brown the ground meat and drain off the fat. Add the tomato paste and
water; mix them into the meat. Add the mustard, combine the other spices,
and blend them in thoroughly. Steam or grill the hot dogs. Warm the bun.
Bury chopped onions in the roll under the hot dog, then ladle a generous
layer of sauce over the top. Top with mustard and grated cheddar if desired.

Stanley Ransom
Plattsburgh

Frozen Chocolate-Coated Banana

1 banana	Sprinkles or chopped nuts,
Shell topping for ice cream	optional

Peel the banana. Insert a wooden popsicle stick into one end and place
the banana in the freezer. When it is hard, take it out and, holding it by the
stick, squirt the shell topping onto it until it has a thin coat adhering to it. If
desired, roll it quickly in sprinkles or chopped nuts. Eat it immediately.

Funnel Cakes

2	eggs, beaten	1½	teaspoons baking powder
1⅓	cups milk	¼	teaspoon salt
3	tablespoons sugar		Vegetable oil for frying
2½	cups flour, sifted		Confectioners' sugar

Combine the beaten eggs, milk and sugar. Sift together the flour, baking powder and salt and add them to the egg mixture, beating to make a smooth batter. Heat the oil to 375 degrees. Place your finger over the hole in a regular household funnel with a ½-inch hole and fill the funnel with batter. Holding the funnel as close to the surface of the fat as possible, remove your finger from the hole, releasing the batter. Make patterns or swirls with the stream of batter as it flows into the hot fat. When you have created a cake the size you want, cover the hole again. Make as many cakes as can float in the fat without touching. Fry the cakes until they are golden brown, turning each once. Drain them well, sprinkle them with confectioners' sugar, and serve immediately.

Pumpkin Muffins

This recipe won a blue ribbon at the 1998 Jefferson County Fair.

2⅔	cups sugar	2	teaspoons soda
⅔	cup shortening	1½	teaspoons salt
4	eggs	½	teaspoon baking powder
1	pound pumpkin purée	1	teaspoon cinnamon
⅔	cup water	1	teaspoon cloves
3⅓	cups flour		

Cream the sugar and shortening together and beat in the eggs until well mixed. Add the pumpkin and water. Combine the flour, soda, salt, baking powder, cinnamon and cloves. Blend the flour mixture into the pumpkin mixture just until all the dry ingredients are moistened. Spoon into prepared muffin tins. Bake at 350 degrees for 25 minutes.

Makes 4 dozen muffins.

Alexis Swan
Watertown

Fried Dough

1½	cups milk	2	packages yeast
2	tablespoons sugar	4	cups flour
1	teaspoon salt		Vegetable oil for frying
6	tablespoons shortening		

In a saucepan, combine the milk, sugar, salt and shortening. Heat until the shortening is melted. Do not let the mixture boil. Cool it to lukewarm before adding the yeast. Stir until the yeast is dissolved. Mix in the flour, two cups at a time. Beat until the mixture is smooth after each addition.

Put the mixture into a greased bowl, cover the bowl with a damp cloth, and let the dough rise until it doubles in bulk. Pinch off pieces of dough about the size of a golf ball. Stretch each piece into a thick 6 to 8-inch circle. Fry one at a time in oil heated to 350 degrees, until the dough rises to the surface. Turn the dough over and fry it on the other side until it is light brown. Drain it on a paper towel, then shake on cinnamon sugar, or top with honey or maple syrup.

This recipe appeared in the Kitchen Exchange section of the Watertown Daily Times *on February 6, 1999.*

In 1997, Beatrice Reynolds, many times the Grand Champion Cook at the Franklin County Fair, won a North Country Heritage Award from TAUNY. According to director Varick Chittenden, the awards are given to "people who quietly go about their business of making life better and richer in their families and communities." Selection criteria include "evidence of traditionality, mastery, and creativity; commitment to the art form over time; and a commitment to the community and the teaching of others."

Carrot Cake

Cake

1½	cups sugar	1	teaspoon salt
1	cup oil	1½	teaspoons cinnamon
3	eggs	2	jars Junior baby food
2	cups flour, sifted		carrots
1½	teaspoons baking powder	¾	cup walnuts
1½	teaspoons soda		

Icing

3	cups confectioners' sugar	¼	cup milk (approximately), heated
2	large tablespoons peanut butter	¼	teaspoon salt
1	large tablespoon shortening	1	teaspoon vanilla
			Walnuts, ground

To make the cake, mix the sugar and oil. Beat in the eggs one at a time. Sift the flour with the baking powder, soda, salt and cinnamon; add them to the above mixture. Add the carrots and walnuts last. Do not overbeat. Pour the batter into two greased layer cake pans or a 9 x 13-inch pan. Bake at 350 degrees for about 40 minutes. Cool the cake before making the icing.

To make the icing, make a well in the sugar for the peanut butter and the shortening. Add about ¼ cup hot milk to melt the shortening and peanut butter. Add the salt and vanilla. Mix with the electric beater, adding more hot milk until the icing is smooth enough to spread on the cake. Sprinkle with ground walnuts.

Beatrice Reynolds
Burke

Coffee Cake

Batter

1	stick margarine	1	teaspoon baking powder
1	cup sugar	¼	teaspoon salt
2	eggs	1	cup sour cream
2	cups sifted flour	1	teaspoon vanilla
1	teaspoon soda		

Streusel Mixture

¼	cup sugar	½	cup ground walnuts
1	teaspoon cinnamon		

To make the batter, beat the margarine and sugar together until they are light and creamy. Add the eggs one at a time, beating after each one. Sift the flour, soda, baking powder and salt together, then add them to the above mixture alternately with the sour cream. Add the vanilla.

To make the topping, mix the sugar, cinnamon and walnuts together.

To assemble the cake, pour half of the cake batter into a greased Bundt pan and spread half of the streusel mixture over it. Pour on the remaining batter and top with the remaining streusel mixture. Bake at 350 degrees for 40 minutes or until a cake tester comes out clean.

Beatrice Reynolds
Burke

Baking Powder Biscuits

2	cups flour	½	cup shortening
3	tablespoons sugar	1	egg, beaten
5	teaspoons baking powder	⅔	cup milk
½	teaspoon salt		

Sift the flour, sugar, baking powder and salt together; cut in the shortening until the resulting mixture is crumbly. Combine the beaten egg with the milk and add them to the flour mixture all at once. Stir just until a dough is formed that will follow the spoon around the bowl. Turn the dough onto a lightly floured board and knead gently. Roll the dough to ¾ inches thick. Cut the biscuits with a 2-inch cutter and place them on an ungreased cookie sheet. Bake at 425 degrees until they are golden brown (approximately 10 minutes).

Beatrice Reynolds
Burke

Filled Cookies

Dough

½	cup shortening or 1 stick margarine	2	cup flour, sifted
¾	cup sugar	1½	teaspoons baking powder
1	egg	½	teaspoon salt
		¼	cup milk

Filling

½	pound raisins or dates	¼	teaspoon salt
½	cup brown sugar	1	cup water
1	heaping tablespoon flour	1	teaspoon vanilla

To make the cookie dough, cream the shortening and sugar until they are light and fluffy. Add the egg and beat well. Sift the flour, baking powder and salt together, then add them to the creamed mixture with the milk. Chill the dough until it is firm enough to roll. (You may need to add a little more flour.)

To make the filling, grind up the fruit. Add the remaining ingredients except for the vanilla and cook them over low heat, stirring constantly, until the mixture thickens. Add the vanilla and let the mixture cool.

To assemble the cookies, roll out the dough on a floured board and cut with a 3-inch round cutter. Place half the discs on an ungreased cookie sheet. Place 1 teaspoon of the filling on top of each cookie, cover it with a second cookie, and press the edges together to seal them. Bake at 350 degrees until they are light brown on top (approximately 10 minutes).

Both the dough and the filling can be made ahead and left in the refrigerator overnight. If any filling is left over, it can be frozen.

Beatrice Reynolds
Burke

Honey Graham Nut Loaf

This recipe won Best of Show in quick breads at the 1998 St. Lawrence County Fair.

2½ packages graham crackers (approximately 50-55 squares)	2 cups chopped nuts
1 cup flour	4 tablespoons soft butter
1 cup sugar	1½ cups milk
5 teaspoons baking powder	1 teaspoon vanilla
	2 eggs

Crush the crackers to crumbs. Place 4 cups of the crumbs in a mixing bowl. Add the flour, sugar and baking powder; mix well. Add the remaining ingredients. Beat for two minutes. Spoon the mixture into a greased and floured 9 x 5-inch loaf pan. Bake one hour at 350 degrees. Cool the loaf in the pan for 10 minutes, then remove it and continue cooling it on a rack. When it is cool, glaze the top with a confectioners' sugar glaze if desired.

Noreen La Vack
Gouverneur

Red Raspberry Jelly

This recipe won Best of Show in jams and jellies at the 1998 St. Lawrence County Fair.

4 cups juice (about 2½ quarts of fully ripe berries)	2 (3-ounce) pouches liquid pectin (Certo recommended)
7½ cups (3½ pounds) sugar	

Prepare the juice by crushing 2½ quarts of fully ripe berries. Place the berries in a jelly bag and allow them to drip. Place the opened pouches of pectin in a glass or cup of hot water to make it flow more freely. Measure 4 cups of juice into a 6- to 8-quart saucepan and add the sugar. Place the pan over high heat and bring the mixture to a full boil, stirring often. Stir in the pectin. Bring it to a full, rolling boil and boil hard for one minute, stirring constantly. Remove the pan from the heat. Skim off the foam.

Fill hot, sterilized, half-pint jars with jelly leaving ¼ to ½ inch of head space. Wipe the jar tops and threads clean. Place hot lids on the jars and screw the bands on firmly. Process in a boiling-water canner for 5 to 10 minutes.

Yvonne Lewandowski
Heuvelton

Peach Marmalade

Celeste Sweet is a winner of multiple blue ribbons at the Malone Fair. Her specialty is canned goods.

4½ cups prepared fruit (approximately 1 orange, 2 lemons, 2 pounds ripe peaches)	7 cups sugar ½ bottle or 1 package of Certo fruit pectin

Cut the orange and the lemons in quarters; remove the seeds, then grind them or slice them very thin. Add 1 cup of water and simmer, covered, for 20 minutes. Peel and pit the peaches. Chop or grind them. Combine the peaches and the citrus fruits and put 4½ cups of the mixture into a very large pan. Add the sugar and mix well. Place the pan over high heat and bring the mixture to a full rolling boil. Boil hard for 1 minute, then stir in the fruit pectin at once. Skim off the foam. Stir and skim for 5 minutes to cool slightly and prevent floating fruit. Ladle the mixture into hot jars, wipe off the rims, and seal with hot lids.

Makes about 9 cups.

Celeste Sweet adds ¼ teaspoon margarine or butter to all her jams, jellies, and marmalades when they are cooking, to keep the foam from forming on top.

Celeste Sweet
Bangor

Zucchini Relish

10	cups zucchini, ground coarse	1	tablespoon turmeric
4	cups onions, ground coarse	1	tablespoon cornstarch
		2	teaspoons celery seed
5	tablespoons salt	2	teaspoons mustard seed
2½	cups vinegar	1	teaspoon pepper
6	cups sugar	1	red pepper, chopped
1	tablespoon dry mustard	1	green pepper, chopped

Place the ground zucchini, onions and salt in a pan; cover the pan and let it stand overnight. Rinse the mixture and drain it well. Add the remaining ingredients. Cook over medium heat for 30 minutes. Pour the mixture into hot jars which have been in boiling water for at least 10 minutes. Seal with lids.

Makes 9 pints.

Celeste Sweet
Bangor

Corn Relish

This recipe won Best of Show in pickles and relishes at the 1998 St. Lawrence County Fair.

4	medium red peppers, diced	2	tablespoons salt
4	medium green peppers, diced	2	teaspoons celery seed
		2	tablespoons dry mustard
1	large celery bunch, chopped	1	teaspoon turmeric
8	small onions	2	quarts whole kernel corn
1½	cups sugar	¼	cup flour, blended with ½ cup water
1	quart vinegar		

Combine the peppers, celery, onions, sugar, vinegar, salt and celery seed. Heat the pan, covered, until the mixture boils, then uncover it and boil for five minutes, stirring occasionally. Mix the dry mustard with the turmeric and blend them with some of the liquid from the boiling mixture; add the resulting paste along with the corn and the flour/water mixture to the boiling mixture. Cook for five minutes, stirring occasionally. Pack in jars, filling to within ½ inch of the top. Adjust the lids. Process in boiling water. Remove from the water and cool.

Makes 7 pints.

Cathy La Vack
Gouverneur

Historian Wayne Neely refers to the years between 1850 and 1870 as the "golden age of the agricultural fair."[1] Farmers were beginning to move away from the individual subsistence agriculture that had marked the nation's early years. Improved transportation was opening up distant markets. In July of 1851, the Northern Railroad instituted its "butter train," which carried tons of butter every Monday from the North Country to Boston. Within two years the value of dairy farms along its route had doubled,[2] and their owners began to enjoy the cash flow that specialization made possible.

As they moved into this new agricultural world, farmers were eager to learn the latest methods of improving their crops and increasing their output. Agricultural societies were established to aid them in this endeavor. These societies quickly realized the usefulness of the fair as an educational tool. By keeping admission fees low, they encouraged farmers to come to see the latest equipment displayed and demonstrated, to attend evening lectures on farming methods, and to gain inspiration from observing and trying to emulate the practices of blue ribbon winners. In the earliest days, even the prizes were educational: subscriptions to farming journals. Fairs became major venues for the development of standards of excellence for livestock and farm crops; the judging and awarding of ribbons constituted the public application of those standards. Fairs also acted as expositions to show off the latest advances in areas beyond agriculture. Many farm families from remote rural areas saw their first airplanes and automobiles at the local fair.

The St. Lawrence County Agricultural Society held its first annual fair in Canton on September 15, 1852. That was followed by ones in Ogdensburg beginning in 1856, Hammond in 1857, Gouverneur in 1859, Waddington in 1869, and Potsdam in 1870. Shortly after the "golden age" ended in 1870, the fairs in Hammond and Waddington fizzled out. The others continued into the twentieth century, competing with each other for attendees, until finally in 1934 the two remaining fairs, Canton and Gouverneur, merged and gave birth to the present-day St. Lawrence County Fair in Gouverneur.

The multiplicity of fairs meant that each was engaged in a constant struggle for money. Although they had been founded for educational purposes, they quickly developed an entertainment component to provide financial support. Horse races played a major role in all the fairs except the one at Hammond. Baseball games were a big drawing card, especially when professional teams came to play the locals, and so were speeches by politicians—difficult as this may be to believe in these times of disillusionment with politics. Of course the midway with its dancing bears and acrobats, its games of chance, and its concessions also helped swell the coffers. In 1912 the Potsdam fair sold concessions for soft drinks, ice cream, popcorn, and taffy.[3] At most of the fairs, church women's groups ran dining halls, paying rent to the fair in return for a chance to earn money for church projects.

At first fairs were held in autumn, providing a holiday after the heavy work of summer and harvest—a time for farmers to relax and visit with neighbors. As mass media, extension courses, and better transportation opened other educational doors to farmers, the fairs gradually shifted their emphasis to the recreational and social. With this change came others. Most fairs moved from fall to summer, with its greater likelihood of good weather. They also increased in length to six days, lessening the chance of financial disaster should there be a rainy day or two during their run.

Although they have changed over the years, today's county fairs would certainly be recognizable to a farmer of the 1860s. The political speeches may have gone by the wayside, but church groups still give dinners, hearts still swell with pride as a blue ribbon is clipped to the stall of a favorite cow, various organizations still provide booths to educate fairgoers, grandstand events still pack in the crowds, young men still try to impress their dates by winning games of skill, and children still stuff themselves to the bursting point with popcorn and cotton candy.

* * *

Adapted from an article by Judith Becker Ranlett entitled "And Then There Was One: the Fairs of St. Lawrence County" which appeared on pages 3-29 of the July 1987 issue of The Quarterly *of the St. Lawrence Historical Association.*

[1] Neely, Wayne. *The Agricultural Fair,* p. 81.

[2] Shaughnessy, Jim. *The Rutland Road* (Berkeley CA, 1964), p. 58-59.

[3] "Potsdam Fair Privileges," Courier & Freeman, July 31, 1912.

CHURCH SUPPERS

A volunteer passes a tray of homemade pies to guests at the Brick Chapel annual fall chicken and biscuit supper in the church basement dining room, Canton, St. Lawrence County. *Mark Sloan Photo/TAUNY Archives*

Church Supper
DePeyster United Methodist Church

Our jack o'lantern is still fresh on the window sill, and there is a lingering feel of Halloween as we drive through drizzle and wispy fog to DePeyster. Suddenly my stomach squeezes as I look down a side road and see a ghostly three-sided square floating away from us, about three feet in the air. A moment later rationality reasserts itself and I realize that my apparition is simply the back of an Amish buggy outlined in silver reflective tape—I think.

We park the car behind the church and pick our way through the mud to the front door. In between the ruts our wheels made in the drive I see a huge dark object and wonder if someone has lost a vital chunk of car. As we approach, I realize this particular bit of litter is very much alive; it is a huge snapping turtle with a shell at least a foot long, and he's looking at me and licking his lips.

The light and warmth of the church hall are a welcome antidote to the spookiness abroad. Although we sit down on the dot of six, we are the last to arrive. Remembering the atmosphere outside, I can understand people who wanted to be there when the doors opened at 4:30 so they could get home before dark. We find seats at one of the long tables and help ourselves from the platters of rolls and roast beef and from the bowls of mashed potatoes, green beans, and cole slaw. As we eat we strike up a conversation with the couple across the table from us. Outsiders too, they are residents of Morristown who come every election night to share the bounty at DePeyster. The time passes quickly as we chat about the Comstock Patent Medicine Company, once one of the largest businesses in Morristown. The company's Dr. Morse's Indian Root Pills were sold both nationally and internationally, bringing a healthy income to the small community. In fact, Comstock continued to sell its products abroad well into the middle of this century, going head-to-head in the marketplace with its competitors from across the river in Brockville—Pink Pills for Pale People.

We agonize over the decisions at the pie table, then return to our seats to find that our friends from Morristown have departed, leaving us as the sole remaining customers. We feel rather Last Supper-ish as we sit back down in a row, backs to the wall, facing out over the ranges of empty tables, from which the cloths have already been whisked away.

On the way out I stop to congratulate the kitchen staff, now enjoying their own dinner at a long table across the room from ours. A nice mix of generations, they have been working all day to get ready for tonight. In fact the work actually began yesterday when the United Methodist Women devoted their meeting time to peeling potatoes. The group tells me this dinner has been held every election night for more than 50 years; the presence of the young chefs and dish washers holds promise that it will continue for the next 50.

Raisin Sauce for Ham Dinner

½	cup raisins	2	tablespoons vinegar
1½	cups water	2	teaspoons lemon juice
½	cup brown sugar	¼	teaspoon grated lemon
2	tablespoons cornstarch		peel
1	teaspoon dry mustard	2	tablespoons butter

Bring the raisins, water and brown sugar to a boil in a saucepan. Combine the cornstarch and mustard; dissolve them in the vinegar and lemon juice. Gradually add this mixture to the hot liquid and cook slowly until it thickens. When it is thick, add the lemon peel and butter. Serve over ham.

Makes 2 cups.

Ortha Sibbitts
Methodist Church, Canton

Corned Beef and Cabbage Casserole
for Lenten Lunch

3	medium potatoes, thinly sliced	1	(10⅓-ounce) can cream of celery soup
1	medium onion, thinly sliced		Milk to fill the empty soup
2	cups shredded cabbage		can
1	can corned beef		

Place the potatoes in a greased shallow baking dish; cover them with the onion slices. Add the cabbage. Crumble the corned beef and sprinkle it over the cabbage. Dilute the soup with the milk, then pour it over the corned beef. Cover the dish and bake it at 350 degrees for 1 hour and 30 minutes.

Serves 6.

Dorothy Wells
Methodist Church, Canton

Tomato-Beef Casserole for Lenten Lunch

1   pound ground chuck
1   onion, diced
1   (28-30 ounce) jar spaghetti sauce —Ragu "thick and hearty" with mushrooms is good

Basil, oregano, salt pepper to taste
16 ounces cottage cheese— low-fat is o.k.
1   green pepper, diced small
8   ounces wide egg noodles, cooked and drained

Sauté the ground beef and onion together until the beef is brown. Drain off the fat. Add the spaghetti sauce and seasonings. Mix the cottage cheese with the green pepper.

In a 2½-quart ovenproof glass dish assemble the casserole in this order: a layer of noodles, the cottage cheese mixture, a thin layer of noodles, the tomato and beef mixture. Pierce the layers with a fork so that the sauce penetrates. Chill the dish overnight. Bake at 350 degrees until hot and bubbly (approximately 30 to 45 minutes).

Judy DeGraaff
Unitarian-Universalist Church, Canton

Three-Bean Salad for Lenten Lunch

Slightly less than ½ cup unpacked brown sugar
¾ cup vinegar
1   small onion, chopped
¾ cup chopped celery
1   green pepper, chopped
⅓ cup corn oil
¼ teaspoon black pepper

1   (14½-ounce) can yellow beans, drained
1   (14½-ounce) can green beans, drained
1   (14½-ounce) can kidney beans, drained
1   (14½-ounce) can pinto beans, half drained

Mix the sugar and the vinegar until the sugar dissolves. Add the onion, celery, green pepper, corn oil and black pepper and mix them together well. Gently stir together the beans and half the juice from the pinto bean can. Pour the vinegar/oil mixture over the beans and stir to combine them. Let the salad sit overnight for the best flavor.

Beverly Walrath
Seventh-Day Adventist Church, Canton

Spinach Soufflé for Church Council Dinner

1	package frozen chopped spinach, defrosted and drained dry	2	eggs, slightly beaten
		2	tablespoons soft butter
1	cup cooked long-grain converted rice (about ½ cup raw)	⅓	cup milk
		2	tablespoons chopped onion
1	cup shredded extra-sharp cheddar	¼	teaspoon Worcestershire sauce
		1	teaspoon salt
		¼	teaspoon thyme or rosemary

Mix all the ingredients together well and pour them into a 10 x 6-inch pan. Bake the soufflé at 350 degrees for 20 to 25 minutes. Test for doneness by inserting a knife near the center; if it comes out clean, the soufflé is done.

Mimi Shields
St. Mary's R. C. Church, Canton

Shepherd's Pie for Free Dinner

1	pound hamburger or other chopped meat	½	cup leftover, canned or homemade gravy
1	onion, diced		Sharp cheddar, grated—to taste
	Salt, pepper, celery salt to taste		
1	(10-ounce) package frozen corn (or you can use canned)	2	cups mashed potatoes

Brown the hamburger with the onion; pour off the fat. Season the mixture with salt, pepper and celery salt. Place the meat mixture on the bottom of a large, greased casserole dish, then cover it with the corn. Pour the gravy over the corn and sprinkle some grated cheddar on top. Cover the dish with a layer of mashed potatoes. Sprinkle a little more grated cheese over the potatoes, or dot the top with butter. Bake the casserole at 400 degrees until it is brown and heated through (approximately 20 minutes).

Carlton Doane
Methodist Church, Canton

Broccoli Special For Lenten Lunch

½ stick margarine, melted
1 onion, finely chopped
1 (10-ounce) box frozen
   chopped broccoli, thawed
1 (10½-ounce) can cream of
   mushroom soup

Milk to fill the empty soup
   can halfway
½ cup cheddar, shredded
½ cup uncooked rice

Sauté the onion in the melted margarine. Add the remaining ingredients and place in a greased baking dish. Bake at 350 degrees for 45 minutes, covered, then 35 more, uncovered.

Beverly Walrath
Seventh-Day Adventist Church, Canton

Peach Pie for Election Night Supper

4 cups sliced canned
   peaches, drained
¾ cup sugar
¼ cup quick-cooking tapioca

1 tablespoon lemon juice
1 tablespoon margarine
Pastry for a 9-inch two-crust
   pie

Mix the peaches, sugar, tapioca and lemon juice in a bowl and let them stand for 15 minutes. Fill a pastry-lined pie pan with the fruit mixture and dot with the margarine. Place the top crust on top, flute the edges, and cut slits in the top to vent the steam. Bake one hour at 400 degrees or until the juices form bubbles that burst slowly.

Lorna Sloan
Methodist Church, DePeyster

Sugar-Free Strawberry Pie for Election Night Supper

5 tablespoons flour
½ cup cold water
1 (16-ounce) package frozen
   whole strawberries
   without sugar

1 small (.32-ounce) package
   sugar-free strawberry
   gelatin
1 (9-inch) pre-baked pie crust
   Whipped topping for
   garnish

Mix the flour and water together to form a smooth paste. Add the frozen strawberries and cook until clear and thick. Add the gelatin. Pour into the pre-baked crust. Refrigerate the pie until the filling is set. Serve with whipped topping.

Ruby Sterling
Methodist Church, DePeyster

Almond Joy Cheesecake
for Chocolate Fantasy Fundraiser

Crust

1½ cups graham cracker crumbs	½ cup sliced almonds, toasted
1½ cups sweetened, flaked coconut, toasted	¼ cup sugar
	½ cup (1 stick) butter, melted

Filling

4 (8-ounce) packages cream cheese, room temperature	1 cup sweetened, flaked coconut, toasted
1 cup sugar	1 tablespoon coconut extract
4 large eggs	1 cup sliced almonds, toasted

Glaze

1 cup semi-sweet chocolate chips	¾ cup whipping cream
	1½ teaspoons vanilla

To make the crust, wrap with foil the outside of a 9-inch springform pan with 2½-inch sides. Finely grind the graham cracker crumbs, coconut, almonds and sugar in a food processor. Add the butter and process until the crumbs are moist. Press the mixture onto the bottom of the pan and one inch up the sides. Bake the crust in a preheated oven at 350 degrees until it is set and beginning to brown (approximately 12 minutes). Cool the crust and turn down the oven to 325 degrees.

To make the filling, beat the cream cheese and sugar with an electric mixer in a large bowl until they are smooth. Add the eggs, one at a time, beating after each addition just until the egg is blended in. Mix in the coconut flakes and extract. Fold in the almonds, then transfer the filling to the crust. Bake at 325 degrees until the cake is puffed and no longer moves when the pan is shaken (approximately one hour and 15 minutes). Cool the cake completely on a wire rack.

To make the glaze, combine the chocolate chips with the cream and vanilla in a small saucepan. Stir them together over medium-low heat until they are smooth. Cool the glaze until it has begun to thicken but can still be poured. Pour the glaze over the cooled cake and spread it evenly. Chill the cake overnight.

To remove the cake from the pan, run a small knife around the sides of the cake to loosen it before releasing the pan sides.

Katie Hardwick
All Souls Unitarian-Universalist Church, Watertown

Katie Hardwick found this recipe in Bon Appétit *magazine.*

Chocolate-Mint Tart for
Chocolate Fantasy Fundraiser

Crust

1	cup unbleached all-purpose flour	½	teaspoon baking powder
½	cup powdered sugar	⅛	teaspoon salt
¼	cup cake flour	1	stick chilled unsalted butter
		1	large egg, lightly beaten

Filling

1¼	cups whipping cream	1¾	teaspoons peppermint extract
3	tablespoons unsalted butter		
2	tablespoons sugar	1½	teaspoons vanilla extract
1½	pounds semi-sweet chocolate		

To make the crust, butter an 11-inch tart pan with a removable bottom. Sift the all-purpose flour, powdered sugar, cake flour, baking powder and salt into a large bowl. Cut the butter into pieces and add it. Using your fingers, rub in the butter until the mixture resembles coarse meal. Add the egg and stir until moist clumps form. Gather the dough into a ball, then flatten it into a disk. Wrap the disk in plastic wrap; place it in the freezer for 10 minutes.

Roll out the dough on a floured surface until it measures 14 inches in diameter. Transfer the dough to the buttered pan and press it in gently. [If the dough tears when you try to lift it, just press the torn pieces together into the pan.] Trim the overhang to ½ inch. Fold the overhang in and press in down, forming double-thick sides. Freeze the crust until it is firm (approximately 20 minutes).

Preheat the oven to 400 degrees. Line the crust with foil and fill it with dried beans or pie weights. Bake it until the sides are set (approximately 15 minutes). Remove the foil and beans and reduce the oven temperature to 350 degrees. Bake the crust until it is golden brown (approximately 20 minutes). Cool the crust completely.

To make the filling, combine the cream, butter, and sugar in a large heavy saucepan. Stir this mixture over medium heat until the butter melts, the sugar dissolves, and the mixture comes to a simmer. Remove the pan from the heat. Chop the chocolate into small pieces and add it to the hot mixture along with both extracts. Stir until the chocolate melts and the mixture is smooth. Pour one cup of the filling into a small heavy saucepan and reserve it for the glaze. Pour the remaining filling into a large bowl. Chill it, stirring occasionally, until it is thickened but still spreadable (approximately 1 hour).

Chocolate-Mint Tart *(continued)*

Whisk the cold filling just until the color lightens (approximately two minutes). Spoon into the crust. Chill the tart until the filling is firm (approximately 30 minutes).

Stir the reserved 1 cup of filling over low heat until it is just lukewarm. Spread it over the filling in the crust to glaze the tart. Chill the tart again until the glaze sets (approximately one hour) before serving. It should be served cold. If it is kept covered and chilled, it can be made up to two days ahead.

Harriet McMillan
All-Souls Unitarian-Universalist Church, Watertown

Harriet McMillan found this recipe in Bon Appétit *magazine.*

It is literally possible to eat out every night of the week in the North Country simply by attending dinners put on by churches and service organizations. Clearly people have found a fund-raising formula that works. To some extent, the menus are seasonal—maple syrup festivals and bullhead feeds in the spring, strawberry or ice cream socials and chicken barbecues in the summer, turkey dinners in the fall, pastry sales around the holidays. But other foods know no season—ham, spaghetti, cabbage rolls, roast beef, and the ubiquitous chicken-and-biscuits can show up any time during the year.

What is it that makes these dinners and bake sales so successful? Their appeal is that they offer something to everyone involved. Sponsoring organizations like them because people are generally more willing to contribute money if they get something in return. It's easier to find 200 people willing to eat a $6.00 ham dinner than it is to find 200 people willing to put $6.00 into a collection jar. Since the labor and most of the food for the dinner are donated, the proceeds go straight to the organization's coffers.

But the money raised is only part of the sponsor's reward; equally important is the way these events act to strengthen the group itself. Many of these fund-raisers have been going on annually for half a century or more. The wise old lady you see tasting the gravy and directing the kitchen operations probably began as a girl helping set the tables, then graduated as a young woman to cutting vegetables and mashing potatoes under strict supervision and quality control. Along the way she had a good chance to learn the traditions of her organization and to build strong ties to the other members—ties that are likely to make her more loyal to the group as a whole.

Members of the sponsoring organization like these meals because they offer an opportunity to work together for a good cause. As anyone who has taken part in a fund-raising supper knows, they involve a lot of plain hard labor and tired feet. But at the end you feel proud because you helped put a bell in the church tower or a gurney in the hospital emergency room. Of course there are also less altruistic rewards: the glory of seeing your pies snatched first from the dessert table, the opportunity to make new friends, and the chance to chat all afternoon with old ones guilt-free—after all, you HAVE to be there to help out.

The customers, like the workers, benefit from these events in a number of ways. These days when take-out and packaged foods are the norm in so many households, it is nice to be able to sit down to a home-cooked meal like those grandma used to make—not elegant fare, but well prepared and tasty food. Most organizations charge $5 or $6 for all-you-can-eat dinners, and even less for lunches, prices that compare very favorably with those of local restaurants. Customers share the satisfaction of supporting a worthwhile cause and being a contributing part of an organization. And again there's the chance for guilt-free sociability. Many of us spend so much time rushing around from one meeting to another that it's a real treat to be able to take a break to visit with friends, a break justifiable because "it's for a good cause". And those of us who are new to the community, sitting at a table with strangers, find that food can smooth the entrance into a group by providing a ready-made, at-hand topic of conversation.

As long as people like to eat and organizations need money, I predict that there will be fund-raiser dinners, lunches, breakfasts, and bake sales. They are simply too rewarding to give up.

FUNDRAISERS

Lay minister Norman Bice mashes potatoes with a heavy duty electric drill and a paint paddle for public suppers in the DePeyster United Methodist Church basement. *Photo courtesy of the DePeyster United Methodist Church*

The Anatomy of an Election Night Supper

by Judy Hoyt

as told to Lynn Ekfelt

Our dinner started many years ago on election day, and it has continued through the years on the same date. People know about us, and some travel for miles to eat our chicken and biscuits. We usually serve 360 to 400 people between the hours of 4 p.m. and 7 p.m.. The dinner includes mashed potatoes, chicken, biscuits, gravy, coleslaw, peas and pearl onions, a raw veggie tray (carrots, celery, radishes, and green peppers), pickles (dill and sweet), olives, cranberry sauce, and cake or pie.

We start with the following grocery list:

potatoes—160 pounds
chicken—225 pounds of fryers cut
    in quarters and 75 pounds of
    boneless breasts
carrots—8 pounds for salad and the
    veggie tray
cabbage—25 heads
Spanish onions—4 large
frozen peas—25 large bags
frozen pearl onions—10 large bags
celery—5 bunches
green peppers—6 large
radishes—12 bags
dill pickles—2 gallons
sweet pickles—1 gallon

Hellmann's mayonnaise—
    4 gallons
cranberry sauce—4 1-pound cans
milk—4 gallons for coffee and the
    potatoes
margarine or butter for the mashed
    potatoes
biscuits—4 dozen ordered from a
    bakery
Worcestershire sauce
garlic powder
chicken base
cornstarch—12 boxes
Kool-Aid
Coffee—regular and decaf

Preparing the dinner is a two-day process. We cook all the chicken the day before our dinner, then at a night work-detail we de-bone it and refrigerate it. I keep all the broth and chicken fat for my gravy. That day we also put the cabbages and carrots for the coleslaw through the food processor (the fine side, not the long shredded side) and mix them together, but we do not mix up the slaw until the next morning. We also clean the veggies for the trays and peel the potatoes.

302

The day of the dinner I spend the whole morning making gravy; it's usually a three-hour job for me. I use large restaurant pots—two full ones for the dinner. First I heat up all the broth and put it through a fine strainer. Then I add garlic powder, Worcestershire sauce, and chicken base; as for how much, I guess I'm not sure since it's done to taste. For thickening the gravy I use cornstarch because I feel that flour makes it too pasty for such a large amount. It will take twelve boxes of cornstarch to make this much gravy. I mix one box at a time in a smaller kettle until it is perfect consistency. Then I mix all the batches together in the big pots so the gravy is all flavored the same. Sometimes after you get it all done, you have to add more of some ingredients; you just have to taste it and keep working until it's right.

We make the coleslaw the morning of the dinner, too, so it can season through. We chop the Spanish onions fine, then add them to the carrots and cabbage we shredded the day before, along with salt, pepper, and sugar to taste. Then we mix the whole thing very well with Hellmann's mayonnaise; don't use any other kind! Finally, we taste it and adjust the seasonings to perfection.

At the same time, somebody cuts up the carrots, celery, radishes, and green peppers for the veggie trays. They also cut the dill pickles lengthwise and put them out with black and green olives and bread & butter sweet pickles. We do many trays of each so we can replenish as needed.

Around noon the chicken is put into the oven in long steam-table pans covered with foil. We add water to it so it won't dry out. For the dinner, we usually have six of these pans.

The potatoes are put on to cook about 1:30, since it takes the big pots quite a while to boil. By 3:15 the potatoes are ready to mash. We keep them in steam-table pans once they are done.

We put the peas and pearl onions on around 2:30 in a big pot. These go over real well cooked together. Then we slice the biscuits in half and get them ready on trays so we can replenish them as needed.

For dessert, we serve pies; each member brings four. When we have our spring dinner we serve cake instead. Then each member brings two 9 x 13-inch cakes.

With all this done, we are usually ready to serve at 3:30 or 3:45 p.m. We use a steam table and people help themselves. We serve the coffee, Kool-Aid and water once people are seated. This is an auxiliary function, but the firemen help us serve. We are proud of our dinner, but we sure are tired at the end!

Judy Hoyt is president of the Pierrepont Fire Department Ladies Auxiliary.

Broccoli-Cheddar Soup

Each spring the E. J. Noble Guild of Canton-Potsdam Hospital holds a soup, salad, bread, and gourmet dessert lunch to raise money to buy equipment for the hospital. This soup is the clear favorite among those attending.

2	small heads broccoli or 1 (16-ounce) bag frozen broccoli	½	cup (1 stick) margarine
		¾	cup flour
		4	cups milk
1	cup chopped onion	½	teaspoon pepper
2	carrots, grated	¼	teaspoon nutmeg
½	cup finely chopped celery	3	cups grated extra sharp
1	teaspoon minced garlic		cheddar (about ¾ pound)
6	cups canned or fresh chicken broth		

Cook the broccoli until it is tender. Drain and cool it, then chop it into small pieces. Combine the onion, carrot, celery, garlic and chicken stock in a large pot. Bring the mixture to a boil, then reduce the heat and let it simmer for 20 minutes or until the vegetables are tender.

Meanwhile, in a large saucepan, melt the butter over medium heat. Add the flour and cook, stirring constantly, for 1 minute. Add the milk gradually, whisking as you add it. Bring this mixture to a boil over medium heat. Reduce the heat and add the pepper and nutmeg. Cook, stirring occasionally, until the sauce is thick.

Stir the sauce into the vegetable/chicken broth mixture. Add the broccoli and simmer on low heat for about 20 minutes. (Do not allow the temperature to become too hot, as the soup will curdle.) Stir in the cheese and serve when it is melted.

Mimi Shields
Canton

Deep-Fried Northern Bullhead

Forget the robins; you know it's spring when the notices of bullhead feeds begin to appear in the Upcoming Events column of the newspaper. These feeds are a long-standing and well-loved tradition in the North Country. In the past sponsoring organizations caught and cleaned their own bullheads, but now they now buy them from northern Canada already skinned. This change is not a result of laziness but rather a response to the fact that our local fish are often infected with trematodes—harmless but visually unappetizing parasites. This recipe is the one used by Dads Post 80 of the Gouverneur VFW at their bullhead feed.

1	cup fine cornmeal	2	pounds bullheads, averaging 6 cleaned fish to a pound
1	cup Italian-seasoned bread crumbs		
½	teaspoon salt (optional)	1	quart water
1	teaspoon lemon pepper		Vegetable oil or shortening for frying

Mix the cornmeal, bread crumbs, salt and lemon pepper in a shallow pan. Place the cleaned bullheads in a pan of water, splitting them in half if they are large. Drain the fish, then while they are still moist, roll them in the crumb mixture until they are completely covered. Shake off the excess coating. Heat the oil in a deep fryer to 375 degrees and gently drop the fish into it. Cook the fish until they are golden brown (approximately 4 to 8 minutes, depending on the size of the bullheads). To test for doneness, insert a fork into the fish and lift the meat from the bone. The fish should be white, with no blood showing.

Curt Serviss
Gouverneur

Scalloped Potatoes

Scalloped potatoes are a staple of fund-raising dinners. Every cook has a favorite addition—a bit of ham, some grated cheese, more onion. It would be possible to eat ten different helpings of scalloped potatoes and never find one that exactly duplicated another.

6-8	medium potatoes, peeled and sliced	4	tablespoons butter or margarine
1	medium onion	2	cups cooked ham, diced
1½	teaspoons black pepper	½	cup flour
1	teaspoon salt	1	cup grated sharp cheddar (optional)
3-4	cups milk		

Mix all the ingredients together in a large greased baking dish. Pour in enough milk to cover the potatoes. If desired, add a cup of grated cheddar. Bake at 350 degrees for 1 hour.

Ruth Trudell
Lisbon

Coleslaw

This recipe, used by the Canton VFW at their dinners, is like the one served at KFC.

⅓	cup sugar	1½	tablespoons white vinegar
1	teaspoon salt	2½	tablespoons lemon juice
¼	teaspoon black pepper	8	cups finely chopped cabbage
¼	cup milk		
½	cup mayonnaise	1	medium carrot, peeled and shredded
¼	cup buttermilk		

Combine the sugar, salt, pepper, milk, mayonnaise, buttermilk, vinegar and lemon juice. Beat them until they are smooth. Add the cabbage and carrots (be sure they are chopped up into fine pieces) and mix well. Refrigerate for at least 2 hours before serving to give the flavors time to blend.

Darlene Leonard
Canton

Most fund-raising dinners and food sales use homemade baked goods to attract customers, an effective tactic now that the pace of life means that most of us find less time to spend in the kitchen.

Blueberry Pie

Crust

½ cup plus 1 tablespoon shortening

1½ cups flour

3 tablespoons very cold water

Filling

⅓ cup all-purpose flour

1 cup granulated sugar

¼ teaspoon nutmeg, optional

2 teaspoons lemon rind

5 cups blueberries, washed and culled

3 tablespoons minute tapioca

2 tablespoons butter

3 tablespoons lemon juice

To make the crust, cut the shortening into the flour until the mixture is crumbly. Add the cold water and toss the dough together with a fork. Divide the dough and roll out half. Fit that into a 9-inch pan to make the bottom crust. Roll the top crust, cover it with waxed paper and wrap it around the rolling pin. Put each crust in a plastic bag in the refrigerator for 20 minutes or longer.

To make the filling, blend together the flour, sugar, nutmeg and lemon rind in a large bowl. Fold in the blueberries. Sprinkle the tapioca evenly over the bottom crust. Pile in the berries. Dot the filling with butter. Spoon the lemon juice evenly over the berries.

Cover the pie with the top crust. Seal and crimp the edges and cover them with narrow strips of foil. Bake the pie in a preheated oven at 450 degrees for 20 minutes, then turn the heat down to 350 degrees and bake until the crust is golden (approximately 35 minutes more).

Note from Sally Van de Water: "I usually use Peter's big, juicy organic berries. Wild ones might need more sugar and less thickening."

Sally Van de Water
Canton

Healthy Homemade Rolls

These rolls won a blue ribbon at the 1998 Jefferson County Fair.

1	package dry yeast	6+	cups unbleached flour, divided
2¼	cups warm water		
3	tablespoons sugar	2	tablespoons oat bran
1½	teaspoon salt	2	tablespoons wheat germ
1	tablespoon honey	2	tablespoons shortening

Dissolve the yeast in the water. Add the sugar, salt, honey and two cups of the flour. Stir until the mixture is smooth. Mix in the wheat germ and oat bran. Add the shortening. Gradually stir in the flour until a stiff dough forms. Knead the dough by hand or machine until it is smooth and elastic—approximately 10 minutes by hand. Place the dough in a greased bowl; cover it and let it rise until it has doubled in bulk. Punch it down and let it rest for 10 minutes. Shape the dough into two dozen rolls and place them in tins which have been sprayed with non-stick cooking spray. Let the rolls rise for 20 minutes, then bake them in a pre-heated oven at 375 degrees for 20 to 25 minutes. Remove them from the tins and cool them on a wire rack.

Andrea Swan
Watertown

Coffee Time Doughnuts

3½-3¾	cups all-purpose flour, divided	1	package active dry yeast
¼	cup sugar	1	cup milk
1½	teaspoons salt	¼	cup shortening
1	teaspoon nutmeg	1	egg
			Vegetable oil for frying

In a large bowl combine 1 cup of the flour with the sugar, salt, nutmeg and yeast. In a saucepan, heat the milk and shortening until the milk is warm. (The shortening does not need to melt.) Add the egg and the warm milk to the flour mixture and beat until smooth. Stir in the remaining flour to form a stiff dough. Cover the bowl and let the dough rise in a warm place until it is light and doubled in size (approximately one hour).

Punch down the dough, then roll it out on a floured surface to ½ inch in thickness. Cut out the doughnuts with a 3½-inch floured cutter. Cover the doughnuts and let them rise in a warm place until they have doubled in size (approximately 30 to 45 minutes). Fry the doughnuts in deep hot fat (375 degrees) about two minutes on each side until they are golden brown. Drain them on absorbent paper.

Ruth Trudell
Lisbon

Custard Pie

Darlene Leonard makes this pie every Thanksgiving from a recipe she found in the Betty Crocker *cookbook. It's a favorite of her husband and son.*

8-inch Pie

1	unbaked 8-inch pie shell	¼	teaspoon nutmeg
3	eggs	1¾	cups milk
⅓	cup sugar	1	teaspoon vanilla
¼	teaspoon salt		

9-inch Pie

1	unbaked 9-inch pie shell	¼	teaspoon nutmeg
4	eggs	2⅔	cups milk
⅔	cup sugar	1	teaspoon vanilla
½	teaspoon salt		

Beat the eggs slightly with a rotary beater, then beat in the remaining ingredients. Pour the egg mixture into the pastry-lined pan. (To prevent spills, place the pie pan on the oven rack before filling it.) Bake in a preheated oven at 450 degrees for 20 minutes, then reduce the oven temperature to 350 degrees. Bake an 8-inch pie for 10 minutes longer or a 9-inch pie for 15 to 20 minutes longer, or until a knife inserted halfway between the center and the edge comes out clean.

Darlene Leonard
Canton

Craisin-Apple Pie

This pie won a ribbon at the 1998 St. Lawrence County Fair.

Pie Crust Mix

4	pounds flour	11	teaspoons salt
		3	pounds shortening

Filling

3	cups apples, peeled and sliced	1	cup sugar
1	package dried cranberries	¼	cup flour
		2	tablespoons butter or margarine

To make the crust mix, blend all the ingredients together until the mixture resembles peas. Store it in a cool place until it is needed.

To make a pie, take 2 rounded cups of the mix and add just enough water to form a ball (about 4 to 5 tablespoons). Place the ball on a floured board and roll it out to the size desired.

To make the filling, combine the apples, dried cranberries, sugar and flour; place them in the crust. Dot with the butter. Put on the top crust and seal. Bake at 425 degrees for 40 to 45 minutes.

Inez Beggs
Ogdensburg

Ola Lowe's Doughnuts

This recipe is from a book used by Tina Houghton-Hopkins' grand-mother when she was a cook for the Evans family of Cherry Island during the 1930's and 1940's. Tina's mother remembers her mother rising early each morning to be taken over to Cherry Island in a small boat, where she made doughnuts for the family along with their breakfast fare.

3½	cups sifted all-purpose flour	1	cup granulated sugar
4½	teaspoons baking powder	2	eggs, well beaten
½	teaspoon cinnamon	1	cup milk
½	teaspoon nutmeg	½	cup minced nuts, optional
½	teaspoon mace	½	cup sifted flour to flour the
1	teaspoon salt		board and cutter
3	tablespoons shortening		

Sift together the flour, baking powder, cinnamon, nutmeg, mace and salt. Work the shortening with a spoon in a medium bowl until it is creamy. Gradually add the sugar, continuing to work the mixture until it is light. Add the eggs; beat the mixture well with a spoon. Add the flour mixture alternately with the milk, blending well with a spoon after each addition. Add the nuts and enough of the ½ cup flour to make a soft, easily handled dough. Chill one hour or longer.

Roll the dough on a floured board to ½ inch thickness; cut it out with a floured doughnut cutter. Form the trimmings of dough into a ball; roll and cut it as above. Drop doughnuts may also be made by dropping heaping teaspoons of dough into the hot fat. Push the dough carefully from the spoon with a rubber scraper to prevent splatters.

Fry the doughnuts in 1½ inches of fat or salad oil, heated to 370 degrees on a deep-fat thermometer, or until a cube of day-old bread browns in 60 seconds. Fry only as many doughnuts at a time as float easily on the fat. As soon as the doughnuts rise to the surface, turn them with a long-handled fork being careful not to pierce them. Turn them often thereafter until they are golden. Remove them from the fat with the fork. Hold them over the fat for a second so that the excess can drip off, then drain them on brown paper. Serve as is, or dust them with granulated or powdered sugar or with cinnamon and sugar. You can also shake them a few at a time in a paper bag containing sugar.

Tina Houghton-Hopkins
Alexandria Bay

When a drive into town meant a much greater time commitment than it does today, election day was, willy nilly, a holiday. People would drive their buggies in to vote, then stay around for the counting of the ballots. Since it was illegal to serve alcohol on election day, people needed a place to eat and socialize while they waited. The local churches stepped in, and the election night supper was born. Today, the voting booth is generally a brief ride away, and the election results await at home, accessible with a flick of the remote. Old traditions die hard, though, and election night in the North Country still finds a number of churches and fire departments sponsoring fund-raising dinners. This listing from 1997 is typical:

Alexandria Bay, St. Cyril's Church—Ham dinner

Antwerp, First Congregational Church—turkey dinner

Barnes Corners, Barnes Corners United Methodist Church—turkey dinner

Black River, St. John's Episcopal Church—spaghetti lunch and dinner

Brownville, St. Paul's Episcopal Church—spaghetti dinner

Champion, Champion Volunteer Fire Dept.—soup & sandwich lunch

Chaumont, Lyme Youth Commission—spaghetti dinner

Croghan, Lions Club—all-you-can-eat spaghetti dinner

DePeyster, DePeyster United Methodist Church—roast beef dinner

Evans Mills, Volunteer Ambulance Squad—chicken and biscuit dinner

Fowler, Fowler Baptist Church—noon lunch and roast beef supper

Hammond, Hammond Grange—roast beef dinner

Lisbon, United Presbyterian Church—ham and scalloped potatoes dinner

Madrid, Madrid Fire Dept.—takeout cabbage roll dinner

Mannsville, United Methodist Church—soup and sandwich lunch and bazaar

Philadelphia, Philadelphia Civic League—turkey dinner

Pierrepont, Pierrepont Fire Dept.—chicken and biscuits dinner

Plessis, Plessis United Methodist Church—roast beef dinner

Russell, Russell Volunteer Fire Dept.—chicken and biscuits dinner

Tupper Lake, St. Thomas Episcopal Church—chicken and biscuits dinner

Waddington, Waddington United Methodist Church—chicken and biscuits dinner

West Stockholm, West Stockholm Fire Dept.—all day food sale, featuring cabbage rolls and homemade bread

Winthrop, Buckton United Methodist Church—take-out cabbage rolls

Winthrop, Stockholm Historical Organization—all day food sale

FIREMEN'S FIELD DAYS

Sunday, August 14th

2nd Annual

POWER BOAT REGATTA

Waddington N. Y.

SPONSORED BY

Waddington Volunteer Fire Department

CONDUCTED BY ST. LAWRENCE VALLEY BOATING & RACING ASSOCIATION, INC.

SANCTIONED BY AMERICAN POWER BOAT ASSOCIATION and CANADIAN BOATING FEDERATION

RACES START AT 1:00 P. M.

CHICKEN BAR-B-Q STARTS AT 12 NOON

Saturday, August 13th

6:30 P.M. — FIREMEN'S PARADE

8:00 P.M. — DONKEY BALL GAME

9:30 P.M. — BLOCK DANCE

A poster for the Waddington Volunteer Fire Department's annual field day and boat regatta on the St. Lawrence River promotes a parade, donkey softball game, block dance, and a popular chicken barbecue. *Courtesy of Phil McMasters, McMasters Printshop*

Firemen's Field Day

Colton

I've come on the wrong day. Oh, it's beautiful all right, with a clear blue sky full of picturesque clouds and just a haze of extremely fragrant smoke visible against the pines ringing the firemen's field. But it only takes a few minutes of conversation with Chief Scott McRobbie to make it clear that today's chicken barbecue is merely a warm-up for the really BIG event—tomorrow's ham dinner. The chicken has been part of the field day for only two or three years; the ham dinner has been a reliable fund-raiser for the fire and rescue department as long as the chief can remember—at least 50 years. He dwells in loving detail on the menu for tomorrow: the ham and raisin sauce, the mashed potatoes, the corn, and the pies—70 or 80 of them, all baked by the women of the town in pans delivered to them by the firemen earlier in the week. The hams are baking in the next building even as we speak.

But I can't smell ham over the alluring aroma of grilling chicken—250 halves. Frank Lenney and Chip Robar stand by the fire they started at 6 a.m. so it would be at the perfect point by 11:30 for the lunch crowd. The chicken halves rest on heavy metal screens with two handles. When the time comes to flip them, the two men position a second screen on top of the chicken, bend over and grasp the handles with crossed arms, then in one neat motion uncross their arms, depositing the rows of chicken halves on their backs on the new screen.

Colton has had to abandon the full-fledged traditional firemen's field day with rides for the kids and contests demonstrating the firemen's skill with their hoses. They are a small department and need to maximize the profit-per-man. You can't flip chicken and take part in contests at the same time. Still, there's plenty to do besides eat. A field of antique cars, polished to reflect the faces of admiring observers, stands beside a straggle of tents selling everything from homemade candles to garden produce to country-western tapes "direct from Nashville." I pounce on a fabulous find—an elaborately hand-turned antique wooden spurtle for stirring the chutney I'll be making in a few weeks using green tomatoes rescued from the first frost.

The chickens are now grilled to a deep brown, so I pay my money and take my place in line for the full dinner: half a chicken*, baked beans*, macaroni salad*, and a roll. I sit down at one of the long tables covered with oil-cloth and eavesdrop on the conversation of my neighbors who are reminiscing about ham dinners of the past. They were definitely THE social event of the season. Phooey, I really have blown it by coming today instead of tomorrow. Earlier the chief said, "We're still learning on the chicken, but we've got the ham down pat." I bite into my chicken. Maybe the chief is right, but graduation day can't be far off; that chicken is a winner.

Barbecued Chicken

½	gallon vinegar	¼	cup pepper
¼	gallon vegetable oil	⅛	cup salt
¼	cup poultry seasoning		

Stir this marinade together. Parboil the chicken 5 to 6 minutes in a pressure cooker. Place the chicken on the grill, cavity down. Brush with the marinade. Cook until the chicken is done (about ½ hour), flipping it occasionally and basting it with more marinade as it cooks.

Frank Lenney
Colton

Enhanced Beans

4	slices bacon	¼	cup molasses
¼	cup catsup	¼	cup barbecue sauce
1	teaspoon dry mustard	2	cans baked beans

Fry the bacon until it is crisp. Combine the catsup, mustard, molasses and barbecue sauce, then stir them into the beans. Place half the bean mixture in a greased 2-quart casserole. Break the bacon into bite-sized pieces. Lay half the bacon over the beans. Top with the rest of the beans and the remaining half of the bacon. Bake one hour at 350 degrees.

Sandy Davis
Colton

Macaroni Salad for a Crowd

15	pounds macaroni, cooked and cooled	2	dozen eggs, hard-boiled and diced
3	bunches carrots, diced	2	bunches celery, diced
	Parsley	1½	gallons mayonnaise
8	green peppers, diced		Salt and pepper to taste
6	onions, diced		

Combine all ingredients. Serve chilled.

Jerry Wilson
Colton

ICE CREAM SOCIALS

Young men and boys are among the many neighborhood fans of ice cream—especially the giant banana splits in vegetable serving bowls—at the annual Brick Chapel Ice Cream Social near Canton, St. Lawrence County. *Martha Cooper Photo/TAUNY Archives*

Ice Cream Social
Brick Chapel

The rain has stopped just long enough to let me scurry up the muddy driveway, hopping over brimming ruts and ducking to avoid tree branches heavy with water. I zip down the basement steps into a room filled with long rows of tables, colorful with a variety of plastic cloths. At 6:15 the crowd is small—partly a result of the storm and partly because the older folks who were lined up fifteen minutes before the official opening at 5 p.m. have left already, while many of the farmers have not yet finished milking. They will arrive shortly before the 8 p.m. closing. Even had the weather been more cooperative, the crowd would have stayed inside, avoiding at least those mosquitoes not enterprising enough to piggyback into the hall with new arrivals. In May we were all delighted that winter was finally over earlier than some years, but now we are paying the price in biting bugs whose larvae would have been killed by a late frost.

Inside the mood is one of low-key, comfortable festivity as lifelong friends trade quips with the cooks and the other diners. The talk is of hay, cut that afternoon in hopes that the predicted "30 percent chance of showers" would not materialize, and now lying soaked in the fields. The general outlook is cheerfully resigned—it will dry sometime. Those with scanners report that Niagara Mohawk trucks are being dispatched to Madrid to deal with storm-related power outages. Others counter with reports gleaned from the weather channel of a big storm heading for Alex Bay and Carthage—following the same route that the microburst did two years ago.

While the conversation swirls around them, the cooks—members of the Ladies Aid Society plus such children and spouses as they could dragoon— prepare and deliver a steady stream of hot dogs, hamburgers, and Italian sausage patties topped with fried peppers and onions. Customers gather up their food, then circle by a table at the entrance to the room to pay. It is clear, though, that the hot sandwiches are merely a preliminary to the delights to follow. Spaced along the ranges of tables are plates heaped with squares of every imaginable type of cake and bar cookie—angel food, chocolate* with chocolate icing, chocolate with white icing and sprinkles, brownies, chocolate chip Congo bars*. These are all-you-can eat treats, free for the taking.

But no one stops with a sandwich and a piece or two of cake. Not when a crowd of workers is busy dispensing ice cream. For the faint-of-heart there are plain scoops of vanilla, chocolate, or strawberry in bowls or cones; for the more daring, sundaes buried under frozen strawberries, real maple syrup, or homemade pineapple* or chocolate sauce*, and topped with whipped cream, nuts, and a cherry. Veterans of previous ice cream socials wave away these simple offerings with a sneer; shoulders back and chests out, they boldly announce, "I'll have a large banana split." Behind the counter, workers move into production mode, one getting out a serving dish of the size used for vegetables at church suppers, another halving a banana for the bottom, others piling on three huge mounds of ice cream—one of each flavor—and topping each with the appropriate sauce: chocolate on chocolate, strawberry on strawberry, and pineapple on vanilla. The heavy bowl now is passed on to the final station where it is crowned with whipped cream, nuts, and three cherries—one for each hummock. The annual banana split is such a tradition that one family even orders one "to go" for a father too busy to make it to the chapel to eat his prize in situ.

When the Brick Chapel Ice Cream Social began, ice cream was more of a rarity than it is today. Long-time members of the church remember hearing their fathers tell of spending the day at the church, taking turns hand-cranking five gallon containers of ice cream—five of choco-late, ten of vanilla*—made with ice they had cut from the river during the winter and piled in their ice houses to cool their summer milk and butter. The social was the one day during the busy haying season when farm families took time off to spend together, catching up on the latest news. Early in this century, the event took on a second purpose—that of fund-raiser. It was joined by the Easter pancake breakfast, the chicken barbecue in June, the ham or spaghetti dinner in September, and the chicken-and-biscuit dinner in October—all put on by the Ladies Aid Society to help maintain the church building and grounds.

From the time of its construction in 1815, Brick Chapel church has been the focal point for the community's religious and social needs. At a time when other tiny rural churches are falling into disrepair, Brick Chapel sits, an attractive little red-brick building with well-painted trim, on a small hill above a manicured lawn. Although it must now compete with hockey games, television, and a variety of restaurants for the free time of its members, it still manages to draw local residents to its doors through a potent mixture of friendliness, an offer of community—and banana splits.

Chocolate Sauce

1	cup sugar	4	tablespoons cocoa
1	cup water	1	teaspoon vanilla

Boil the sugar, water and cocoa together for 1½ hours on low heat. Add the vanilla when the sauce is cool. Makes 1 pint of sauce.

Shirley Aldous
Canton

Pineapple Sauce

This recipe was developed by Marilyn Rodee when she was first asked to provide pineapple sauce for the Brick Chapel social in the 1980s. She doubles the recipe to make six quarts of sauce every year for the ice cream social.

4	(20-ounce) cans crushed pineapple	3-4	tablespoons cornstarch, depending on the amount of juice in the pineapple
4	cups sugar		

Combine the pineapple, sugar and cornstarch. Bring them to a boil, then turn down the heat to a simmer until the sauce is thickened.

Makes 3 quarts.

Marilyn Rodee
Canton

Congo Bars

An advantage of these cookies, according to Marilyn Rodee, is that they can be put together quickly and are "a life-saver when guests drop into a home empty of cookies."

2¾	cups sifted flour	1	(1-pound) box of brown sugar
2½	teaspoons baking powder	3	eggs
⅛	teaspoon salt	1	cup chocolate chips
⅔	cup shortening, melted		Chopped nuts, optional

Grease a 15 x 10 x 1-inch jelly-roll pan. Combine all the ingredients, put them into the pan and bake at 350 degrees for 20 minutes. Be careful not to over bake.

Marilyn Rodee
Canton

Homemade Vanilla Ice Cream

Bill Rodee remembers his father's using this recipe to make ice cream for the Brick Chapel socials in the 1920s, 1930s, and 1940s. The recipe came from his great uncle, Eugene Truesdel, who made ice cream and sold it at the Saratoga race track every summer in the early 1900s.

1	quart heavy cream	1	junket tablet
4	cups sugar	1	tablespoon water
3	quarts milk	1	tablespoon vanilla

Heat the cream, sugar and milk to 100 degrees. Stir to dissolve the sugar. Crush the junket tablet and dissolve it in 1 tablespoon of water. Add the dissolved junket and the vanilla to the heated mixture and let it sit until the custard thickens. Freeze the mixture in a 6-quart ice cream freezer, following the manufacturer's instructions.

Bill Rodee
Canton

Date Shaggie Bars

This recipe won a ribbon at the 1998 St. Lawrence County Fair.

½	cup shortening	½	teaspoon salt
¼	cup white sugar	½	teaspoon vanilla
½	cup brown sugar	½	cup chopped nuts
1	egg	½	cup chopped dates
1	cup flour	1	cup crushed cornflakes,
¼	teaspoon baking soda		divided
1	teaspoon baking powder		

Cream together the sugars and shortening. Beat in the egg. Combine the flour, soda, baking powder, salt, vanilla, nuts and dates. Spread half the crushed cereal flakes in a greased 9-inch square pan. Spread the cookie batter on top of the flakes. Spread the remaining cereal flakes on top and press them into the dough. Bake at 350 degrees for 30 to 35 minutes.

Inez Beggs
Ogdensburg

Toffee Squares

This recipe won Best-of-Show in cookies at the 1998 St. Lawrence County Fair.

1	cup butter	2	cups flour
1	cup brown sugar	¼	teaspoon salt
1	egg yolk	½-¾	cup chocolate chips
1	teaspoon vanilla	½	cup chopped nuts

Combine the butter, sugar, egg yolk and vanilla. Mix in the flour and salt. Press the mixture into a 9 x 13-inch pan and bake at 350 degrees for 25 to 30 minutes. Upon removing the pan from the oven, sprinkle the chocolate chips on top. Return the pan to the oven just until the chips are melted. Spread the melted chips evenly over the cookies and top with the nuts.

Mary Hebert
Heuvelton

Chicago Crunchy Chocolate Chip Cookies

3½	cups sifted flour	1	egg
3	teaspoons baking soda	1	tablespoon milk
1	teaspoon salt	2	teaspoons vanilla
1	stick (½ cup) margarine or butter, softened	1	cup vegetable oil
		1	cup corn flakes
1	cup firmly packed light brown sugar	1	cup quick oats
		1	package chocolate chips
1	cup granulated sugar		

Sift the flour, baking soda and salt together onto a piece of waxed paper. Beat the margarine, sugars, egg, milk and vanilla in a bowl until they are well blended. Stir the flour mixture into the bowl alternately with the oil until the mixture is thoroughly combined. Stir in the corn flakes, oats and chocolate. Drop heaping teaspoonfuls of the dough onto greased cookie sheets and bake at 350 degrees for 12 minutes.

Ruth Trudell
Lisbon

Chocolate Cake

This recipe won a blue ribbon at the 1998 Jefferson County Fair.

2	eggs	2	cups sugar
1	cup milk	6	tablespoons cocoa
1	cup oil	1	teaspoon salt
2	teaspoons vanilla	2	teaspoons baking soda
3	cups flour	1	cup hot water

Combine all the ingredients except the water in a mixer bowl and blend until smooth. Gradually add the water and again blend until smooth. Grease and flour two 8-inch pans and divide the batter evenly between them. Bake at 325 degrees for 25 minutes. Remove the layers from the pans and cool on wire racks. Frost the cake with the icing of your choice.

Alexis Swan
Watertown

Oatmeal-Chocolate Chip Cake

1	cup quick oatmeal	2	large eggs
1¾	cups boiling water	1¾	cups flour
1	cup sugar	1	teaspoon soda
1	cup packed brown sugar	1	teaspoon salt
1	stick soft margarine	3	tablespoons cocoa
1	(12-ounce) package chocolate chips		

In a small bowl, mix the oatmeal and boiling water and set them aside for 10 minutes. In a large bowl, mix all the other ingredients with half of the chocolate chips. Beat the oatmeal and the flour mixtures with an electric mixer until they are well combined. Pour the batter into a greased 9 x 13-inch pan and sprinkle the remaining chips over the top. Bake at 350 degrees for 40 minutes. Does not need icing.

Ruth Trudell
Lisbon

Crumb Cake

Cake

2	cups all-purpose flour
1	teaspoon baking powder
1	teaspoon baking soda
½	teaspoon salt
½	cup butter, softened

1	cup sugar
1	teaspoon vanilla extract
3	eggs
1	cup sour cream

Topping

1 tablespoon all-purpose flour
½ cup packed brown sugar
2 tablespoons butter, softened

½ cup chopped nuts
1 (12-ounce) package (2 cups) mini-chocolate chips, divided

To make the topping, combine the flour, brown sugar and butter in a small bowl; mix them well. Stir in the nuts and ½ cup of the mini chocolate chips. Set the bowl aside.

To make the cake, combine the flour, baking powder, baking soda and salt in a small bowl. Set it aside. In a large bowl, combine the butter, sugar and vanilla extract and beat them until they are creamy. Add the eggs one at a time, beating well after each addition. Gradually add the flour mixture alternately with the sour cream. Fold in the remaining 1½ cups mini chocolate chips. Spread the batter in a greased 9 x 13-inch baking pan. Sprinkle the topping evenly over the batter. Bake at 350 degrees for 45 to 50 minutes. Cool.

Makes 24 two-inch squares.

Ruth Trudell
Lisbon

Nature's Bounty

APPLES:

Van de Water, John. "Backyard Orchards: Past and Future," *The Quarterly* [St. Lawrence County Historical Association], October, 1980, p. 7.

MAPLE SYRUP:

Gay, Kathlyn and Martin. *Encyclopedia of North American Eating and Drinking Traditions, Customs and Rituals.* Santa Barbara, CA: ABC-Clio, 1996.

Hopkinton Bicentennial Committee. *Hopkinton Maple Festival Cookbook.* Hopkinton, NY: The committee, 1976.

Rubin, Martha Adams. *Countryside, Garden and Table: A New England Seasonal Diary.* Golden, CO: Fulcrum Publishing, 1993.

WILD FOODS:

Gibbons, Euell. *Stalking the Wild Asparagus.* New York: David McKay, 1962.

Who We Are

AFRICAN AMERICANS:

Alperson, Myra and Mark Clifford. *The Food Lover's Guide to the Real New York: Five Boroughs of Ethnic Restaurants, Markets, and Shops.* New York: Prentice Hall, 1987.

Golden, John. "Blacks Have Long Had Faith in Watertown," *Watertown Daily Times,* February 26, 1995, Lifestyles and Leisure section, p. 1.

Kirlin, Katherine S. and Thomas M. Kirlin. *Smithsonian Folklife Cookbook.* Washington, DC: Smithsonian Institution Press, 1991.

Wagner, Candy and Sandra Marquez. *Cooking Texas Style: a Heritage of Traditional Recipes.* New York: Ballantine, 1983.

AMISH:

Good, Merle and Phyllis. *Twenty Most Asked Questions about the Amish and Mennonites.* Intercourse, PA: Good Books, 1995.

ARMENIAN AMERICANS:

Balakian, Peter. *Black Dog of Fate.* New York: Basic Books, 1997.

Detroit Women's Chapter of the Armenian General Benevolent Union. *Treasured Armenian Recipes.* New York: the Union, 1949.

Uvezian, Sonia. *The Cuisine of Armenia.* New York: Harper & Row, 1974.

FRENCH AMERICANS:

Clarke, T. Wood. *Emigrés in the Wilderness.* New York: Macmillan, 1941.

Pilcher, Edith. *Castorland: French Refugees in the Western Adirondacks, 1793-1814.* Harrison, NY: Harbor Hill Books, 1985.

vanLent, Peter C. *The Hidden Heritage/L'Héritage Caché: the French Folk Culture of Northern New York.* Malone, NY: the Malone Arts Council, 1988.

GREEK AMERICANS:

Rouvelas, Marilyn. *A Guide to Greek Traditions and Customs in America.* Bethesda, MD: Nea Attiki Press, 1994.

Yianilos, Theresa Karas. *The Complete Greek Cookbook: The Best from 3000 Years of Greek Cooking.* New York: Avenol Books, 1970.

HUNGARIAN AMERICANS:

Eggleston, Marcia. "History of the Hungarian People in St. Lawrence County," *The Quarterly* [St. Lawrence County Historical Association], October 1988, pp. 14-18.

Kende, Eva. *Eva's Hungarian Kitchen.* Canmore, Alberta: Try Kay Enterprises, 1984.

Dorcas Guild of Magyar United Church of Christ. *Hungarian Recipes.* Elyria, Ohio: the Guild, 1960.

ITALIAN AMERICANS:

Augustine, Frank P. *La Bella America: From the Old Country to the North Country.* Watertown, NY: Watertown Daily Times, 1989.

Parishioners of St. Anthony's Church. *A Book of Favorite Recipes.* 2nd edition. Watertown, NY: St. Anthony's Church, 1973.

JEWS:

Dobbie, Joan, Louis Greenblatt, and Blanche Levine. *Before Us: Stories of Early Jewish Families in St. Lawrence County, 1855-1920.* Potsdam, NY: Congregation Beth-el, 1981.

Spice and Spirit: The Complete Kosher Jewish Cookbook. Brooklyn: Lubavitch Women's Cookbook Publications, 1990.

Stern, Chaim. *Gates of Freedom: A Passover Haggadah.* West Orange, New Jersey: Behrman House Publishers, 1982.

KOREAN AMERICANS:

Lee, O-young and Lim, Jong-han. *Discover Korea.* Seoul, Korea: KBS Enterprises, 1986.

Rutt, Joan and Sandra Mattielli, editors. *Lee Wade's Korean Cookery.* Elizabeth, NJ: Hollym International Corp., 1996.

LEBANESE AMERICANS:

Ladies Society of St. Elijah's Orthodox Church. *The Lebanese Kitchen: a Celebration of Lebanese Cuisine.* Carp, Ontario: Gai-Garet Design & Publication Co., 1990.

Maroun, Ellen. "The Lebanese Community of Tupper Lake," *Franklin Historical Review,* vol. 23, 1986, pp. 9-13.

MENNONITES:

Friends of Croghan Mennonite Cookbook. Croghan, NY: the Friends, 1997.

Yousey, Arlene. *Strangers and Pilgrims: History of the Lewis County Mennonites.* Croghan, NY: Arlene Yousey, 1987.

MOHAWKS:

Akweks, Aren [Ray Fadden]. *History of the St. Regis Akwesasne Mohawks.* Malone, NY: Ray Fadden, 1947.

Franklin County's Senior Citizens Nutrition Program. *Grandmother's Recipes of Yesteryear.* Kansas City, KS: Cookbook Publishers Inc., 1977.

Frear, George. "The Founding of St. Regis," *The Quarterly* [St. Lawrence County Historical Association], vol. 28, October 1983, pp. 3-10.

Lazore, Carol, Christie Cook, and Carrie Jacobs, eds. *Kakhwakon (Good Food)*. Mohawk Indian Housing Corporation, 1998.

New York State Department of Social Services. *A Proud Heritage: Native American Services in New York State*. Albany, NY: the Department, 1989.

Porter, Tom. *Mohawk Marriage*. Hogansburg, NY: North American Indian Travelling College.

YANKEES:

Biondi, Mary. *"Take the Gray Basin..."* Canton, NY: Mary Hadlock Biondi, 1976.

Ellis, David Maldwyn. "The Yankee Invasion of New York, 1783-1850," in Wendell Tripp. *Coming and Becoming: Pluralism in New York State History,* Cooperstown, NY: New York State Historical Society, 1991. pp. 105-119.

Kreidberg, Marjorie. *Food on the Frontier: Minnesota Cooking from 1850 to 1900 with Selected Recipes*. St. Paul, MN: Minnesota Historical Society Press, 1975.

Landon, Harry F. *The North Country: A History*. Indianapolis: Historical Publishing Co., 1932.

Walker, Barbara. *The Little House Cookbook*. New York: Harper and Row, 1979.

Webster, Clarence. *St. Lawrence County: Past and Present*. 1945.

Building Communities

COUNTY FAIRS:

Ranlett, Judith Becker. "And Then There Was One: The Fairs of St. Lawrence County," *The Quarterly* [St. Lawrence County Historical Association], vol. 32, July 1987, pp. 3-29.

Common Measurements

3 teaspoons	=	1 tablespoon
4 tablespoons	=	¼ cup
8 tablespoons	=	½ cup
16 tablespoons	=	1 cup
5 tablespoons plus 1 teaspoon	=	⅓ cup
4 ounces	=	½ cup
8 ounces	=	1 cup
16 ounces	=	1 pound
1 ounce	=	2 tablespoons fat or liquid
2 cups fat	=	1 pound
2 cups	=	1 pint
1 pound butter	=	2 cups or 4 sticks
2 pints	=	1 quart
4 cups	=	1 quart

The Metric System

2 cups	=	473 milliliters
1 cup	=	237 milliliters
¾ cup	=	177 milliliters
⅔ cup	=	157 milliliters
½ cup	=	118 milliliters
⅓ cup	=	79 milliliters
¼ cup	=	59 milliliters
1 tablespoon	=	15 milliliters
1 teaspoon	=	5 milliliters
1 fluid ounce	=	30 milliliters

liters	x 2.1 = pints	kilograms	x 2.2	= pounds
liters	x 1.06 = quarts	grams	x .035	= ounces
cups	x .24 = liters	pounds	x .45	= kilograms
gallons	x 3.8 = liters	ounces	x 28.0	= grams

Equivalents

Ingredient	Equivalent
3 medium apples	3 cups sliced apples
3 medium bananas	2½ cups sliced, 2 cups mashed banana
1 medium lemon	2 to 3 tablespoons juice and 2 teaspoons grated rind
1 medium lime	1½ to 2 tablespoons juice
1 medium orange	⅓ cup juice and 2 tablespoons grated rind
4 medium peaches	2 cups sliced peaches
4 medium pears	2 cups sliced pears
1 quart strawberries	4 cups sliced strawberries
1 pound head cabbage	4½ cups shredded cabbage
1 pound carrots	3 cups shredded carrots
2 medium corn ears	1 cup whole kernel corn
1 large green pepper	1 cup diced green pepper
1 pound head lettuce	6¼ cups torn lettuce
8 ounces raw mushrooms	1 cup sliced cooked mushrooms
1 medium onion	½ cup chopped onion
3 medium white potatoes	2 cups cubed cooked or 1¾ cups mashed white potatoes
3 medium sweet potatoes	3 cups sliced sweet potatoes
8 slices cooked bacon	½ cup crumbled bacon
1 pound American or cheddar cheese	4 to 5 cups shredded cheese
4 ounces cheese	1 cup shredded cheese
5 large whole eggs	1 cup eggs
6 to 7 large eggs	1 cup egg whites
11 to 12 large eggs	1 cup egg yolks
1 cup quick-cooking oats	1¾ cups cooked oats
1 cup uncooked long grain rice	3 to 4 cups cooked rice
1 cup pre-cooked rice	2 cups cooked rice
1 pound coffee	40 cups perked coffee
1 pound pitted dates	2 to 3 cups chopped dates
1 pound all-purpose flour	4 cups flour
1 pound granulated sugar	2 cups sugar
1 pound powdered sugar	3½ cups powdered sugar
1 pound brown sugar	2¼ cups firmly packed brown sugar
1 cup (4 ounces) uncooked macaroni	2¼ cups cooked macaroni

4 ounces uncooked noodles . . . 2 cups cooked noodles
7 ounces uncooked spaghetti . . . 4 cups cooked spaghetti
1 pound shelled nuts . . . . 4 cups chopped nuts
1 cup whipping cream . . . . 2 cups whipped cream
1 cup soft bread crumbs . . . . . . 2 slices fresh bread
1 pound crab in shell . . . . ¼ to 1 cup flaked crab
1½ pounds fresh, ... 2 cups cooked, peeled, deveined
   unpeeled shrimp   shrimp
 1 pound fresh small shrimp . . . . . . 35 or more shrimp
 1 pound fresh medium shrimp . . . . 26 to 35 shrimp
 1 pound fresh large shrimp . . . . . 21 to 25 shrimp
 1 pound fresh jumbo shrimp . . . . less than 20 shrimp
Crackers
 19 chocolate wafers . . . . 1 cup crumbs
 14 graham cracker squares . . . 1 cup fine crumbs
 28 saltines . . . . 1 cup finely crushed crumbs
 22 vanilla wafers . . . . 1 cup finely crushed crumbs

Substitutions

Recipe Ingredients   *Substitution*

1 cup sour or buttermilk . . . . . . 1 tablespoon vinegar or lemon juice
                                    plus sweet milk to make 1 cup
1 cup commercial sour cream . . . 1 tablespoon lemon juice plus
                                    evaporated milk to equal 1 cup
1 cup yogurt . . . . 1 cup sour or buttermilk
1 whole egg . . . . 2 egg yolks plus 1 tablespoon water
1 tablespoon cornstarch . . . . . . 2 tablespoons all-purpose flour
1 teaspoon baking powder . . . . ½ teaspoon cream of tartar plus
                                    ¼ teaspoon soda
1 cup cake flour . . . . 1 cup all-purpose flour minus 2
                                    tablespoons
1 cup self-rising flour . . . . 1 cup all-purpose flour plus
                                    1 teaspoon baking powder
                                    and ½ teaspoon salt
1 cup honey . . . . 1¼ cups sugar plus ¼ cup liquid
1 ounce unsweetened chocolate . . . 3 tablespoons cocoa plus 1
                                    tablespoon butter or margarine
1 pound fresh mushrooms . . . . . 6 ounces canned mushrooms
1 tablespoon fresh herbs . . . . . . 1 teaspoon ground or crushed dry herbs
1 teaspoon onion powder . . . . . 2 teaspoons minced onion
1 clove fresh garlic . . . . 1 teaspoon garlic salt or
                                    ⅛ teaspoon garlic powder

Quantities To Serve 50 People

Coffee . . . . 1½ pounds

Lump Sugar . . . . 1½ pounds

Cream . . . . 1½ quarts

Milk . . . . 3 gallons

Tomato Juice . . . . 5 (46-ounce) cans

Soup . . . . 2½ gallons

Oysters . . . . 9 quarts

Meat Loaf . . . . 12 pounds

Ham . . . . 20 pounds

Beef . . . . 20 pounds

Roast Pork . . . . 20 pounds

Hamburger . . . . 13 pounds

Potatoes . . . . 17 pounds

Vegetables . . . . 13 pounds

Cakes 4

Ice Cream . . . . 2½ gallons

Cheese . . . . 1½ pounds

Olives . . . . 1 pound

Pickles . . . . 1½ quarts

Nuts . . . . 2 pounds

Baked Beans . . . . 2½ gallons

Bread . . . . 5 loaves

Potato Salad . . . . 6 quarts

Fruit Salad . . . . 10 quarts

Lettuce . . . . 10 heads

Salad Dressing . . . . 1½ quarts

Almond Joy cheesecake... 297
Animal cracker dessert.... 181

APPETIZERS
Baba ganouj (eggplant
   appetizer) 230
Cheddar pepper crisps ... 32
Cheese boeregs 117
Cheese tea crackers 35
Chef Locy's
   country venison pâté ... 60
Gefilte fish (stuffed fish) ... 200
Grape leaves, stuffed
   (derevi sarma)—
   meatless 118
Grape leaves, stuffed
   (yabrak anab)—
   with meat.......... 229
Head cheese
   without head (tête
   fromagée sans tête) ... 131
Hommos bi tahina
   (chick pea dip) 230
Kibbee, baked
   (kibbee bi saniyeh) ... 231
Kibbee, raw
   (kibbee nayeh) 232
Pebble Island
   pickled pike 44
Picnic rice in seaweed
   (kimpap) 217
Sesame sticks 32
Spinach pies (fatayer
   bi sabanekh) 234

APPLES
Apple brown
   Betty Baldwin 22
Apple cider pie 20
Apple cinnamon muffins ... 20
Apple dumplings 18

Apple fritters 245
Apple pie,
   Just like Grandma's 19
Apple walnut cake 21
Applesauce cake...... 247
Baked apples
   with Maple Sugar 21
Cider apple butter 109
Craisin-apple pie...... 309
Crow's nest 17
Indian Relish.......... 23
Microwave apple crisp
   for one 22
Scalloped sweet potatoes
   and apples.......... 24
Applesauce cake 247
Arni meh prassa Mahala
   (lamb and leeks
   Mahala)............ 147
Baba ganouj
   (eggplant appetizer) 230
Baccala (codfish in sauce) ... 189
Baked beans, quick 68
Baklawa 238

BANANAS
Banana cake 99
Frozen chocolate-coated
   banana 280

BARBECUE SAUCES
Barbecued ribs 93
Black Jack
   barbecue sauce 58
Chicken barbecue sauce,
   Colton Fire Dept. 315
Chicken barbecue sauce,
   Ezra Widrick's 243
Bean curd, fried
   (tubu puch'im)........ 216

BEANS

Baked Romano beans . . 161

Bean soup 107

Creamed string bean soup
(habart
zöldbab leves) 173

Dilly beans 162

Enhanced beans 315

Kidney bean casserole. . . 23

Milk beans 161

Quick baked beans 68

Three-bean salad 294

BEEF

Boiled dinner 267

Bulgogi (Korean
broiled beef) 219

Carbonada criolla (meat
and vegetable stew) . . . 162

Corned beef and
cabbage casserole . . . 293

Cranberry pot roast 201

Croghan bologna,
homemade 108

Easter meatloaf
(vagdalt hús) 175

Goulash soup
(gulyás leves) 174

Hungarian goulash
(pörkölt) 174

Kibbee, baked
(kibbee bi saniyeh) . . . 231

Kibbee, raw
(kibbee nayeh) 232

Meat stew (cholent) 198

Michigans 280

Mincemeats (Italian) . . . 188

Mincemeat
(Mennonite) 246

Noodles with meat
and vegetables
(chapch'ae) 220

Shepherd's pie 295

Stew of meat balls and
pig hocks (Ragoût
de boulettes) 131

Stuffed cabbage 202

Tomato-beef casserole . . . 294

Wedding hash 259

BEETS

Beets in tangy sauce . . . 159

Maple pickled beets 68

Pickled beets 260

BEVERAGES

Dandelion wine 76

Hot buttered rum 67

Sumac drink 79

Switchel 269

Tahn (chilled
yoghurt drink) 123

BISCUITS

Baking powder
biscuits 284

Cheese-topped
biscuits 30

Black Jack
barbecue sauce 58

BLACKBERRIES

Blackberry cake 80

Blackberry pudding 80

Blintzes 209

BLUEBERRIES

Blueberry batter cake . . . 260

Blueberry pie 307

Boiled dinner 267

Bologna 107

Bologna, homemade
   Croghan 108

Bon-bons, coconut. 111

Bread pudding, "By guess
   and by gosh" 270

BREADS

(See also doughnuts and fritters)

Apple cinnamon muffins . . . 20

Baking powder biscuits . . . 284

Brown bread 268

Cattail pollen muffins 78

Cheese-topped biscuits. . . 30

Coffee time doughnuts . . . 308

Cornmeal potatoes 258

Easter bread
   (cheoreg) 121

Fried bread 258

Funnel cakes. 281

Golden corn bread 97

Healthy
   homemade rolls 308

Holiday challah
   (bread) 207

Honey graham
   nut loaf 286

Hush puppies 96

Johnnycake 267

Kuchen bread 248

Lebanese bread
   (khubis talameh) 235

Maple johnnycake. 66

Ola Lowe's doughnuts . . . 310

Pumpkin muffins 281

Sunday bread, Greek
   (tsoureki) 149

BROCCOLI

Broccoli-cheddar soup . . . 304

Broccoli special
   casserole 296

Brown bread 268

Brownies, Passover 204

Bûche de Noël (Yule log) . . . 132

Buckwheat pancakes
   (galettes de sarrasin) . . . 134

Bulgogi (Korean
   broiled beef) 219

Bullhead, deep-fried 305

Burdock roots 78

CABBAGE

Cabbage noodles
   (káposztas kocka) 175

Cabbage rolls, lemon (yabrak
   malfouf bi hamith) 233

Coleslaw 306

Corned beef and
   cabbage casserole . . . 293

Napa cabbage kimch'i
   (paech'u kimch'i) 218

Stuffed cabbage, Hungarian
   (töltöttkáposzta) 177

Stuffed cabbage,
   Jewish 202

CAKES

Apple walnut cake 21

Applesauce cake. 247

Banana cake 99

Blackberry cake 80

Blueberry batter cake. . . 260

Bûche de Noël
   (Yule Log) 132

Carrot cake 283

Chocolate cake. 323

Coffee cake 284

Crumb cake 324

Mémère Montpetit's
    Mokas 133

Oatmeal chocolate
    chip cake 323

Open-faced
    raspberry pie 82

Passover sponge torte 205

Striped cake (torte) 180

CANDY
Coconut bonbons 111

Ingberlach
    (ginger candy) 205

Jack wax 65

Maple popcorn 66

Maple syrup squares 67

Peanut brittle 111

Pralines 67

Carbonada criolla (meat
    and vegetable stew) 162

CARROTS
Carrot cake 283

Carrot soup 159

Sweet Potato and Carrot
    Tzimmes 203

Cattail pollen 78

Cauliflower, Greek
    (kounoupidi) 142

Challah, holiday
    (bread) 207

Chapch'ae (noodles with
    meat and vegetables) 220

Cheddar pepper crisps 32

CHEESE
Almond Joy
    cheesecake 297

Blintzes 209

Broccoli-cheddar soup . . . 304

Cheddar pepper crisps 32

Cheese boeregs 117

Cheese hash browns 33

Cheese pudding with
    Creole sauce 31

Cheese sauce
    (krema meh teree) 152

Cheese strata 34

Cheese tea crackers 35

Cheese-topped biscuits . . . 30

Crêpes with
    cottage cheese
    (turós palacsinta) 178

Fish and
    cheese chowder 30

Four-cheese macaroni . . . 34

Italian three-cheese
    macaroni 35

Matzoh-cheese kugel
    for Passover 204

Noodle kugel 206

Ricotta balls 187

Ricotta gnocchi 190

Sesame sticks 32

Southern macaroni
    and cheese 94

Welsh rarebit 33

Chef Locy's
    country venison pâté 60

Cheoreg (Easter bread) 121

Chicago crunchy chocolate
    chip cookies 322

CHICK PEAS
Chick pea dip (hommos
    bi tahina) 230

Macaroni and chick peas
    (pasta a ceci) 187

CHICKEN
Barbecued chicken, Colton
Fire Department 315
Barbecued chicken,
Ezra Widrick 243
Chicken breasts
with cheese 36
Chicken paprikas
(csirkepaprikás) 176
Chicken pilaf
(havov pilav) 120
Chicken soup
(takkogiguk) 216
Chicken soup
with matzoh balls 199
Chicken soup with meatballs
and escarole 192
Fried chicken 92
Lemon chicken oregano
(psiti kota meh
lemoni kai rigani) 143
Chili, wild game 54

CHOCOLATE
Almond Joy
cheesecake 297
Animal cracker dessert . . . 181
Chicago crunchy chocolate
chip cookies 322
Chocolate cake 323
Chocolate-mint tart 298
Chocolate sauce 320
Congo bars 320
Crumb cake 324
Frozen chocolate-coated
banana 280
Oatmeal
chocolate chip cake 323
Passover brownies 204
Striped cake (torte) 180

Whoopie pies 244
Cholent (meat stew) 198
Cider apple butter 109
Cider pie 20
Clam chowder, Manhattan . . . 48
Clam sauce, white,
with linguine 190

COBBLERS
Blueberry batter cake . . . 260
Peach 98
Raspberry 81
Rhubarb pudding 167
Coconut bonbons 111
Codfish in sauce
(baccala) 189
Coffee cake 284
Coffee time doughnuts 308
Coleslaw 306
Collard greens with ham . . . 95
Congo bars 320

COOKIES
Chicago crunchy chocolate
chip cookies 322
Congo bars 320
Date shaggie bars 321
Filled cookies 285
Kifli
(crescent cookies) 179
Kurabia 123
Lemon crackers 271
Passover brownies 204
Sweet koulourakia 150
Tarales 186
Toffee squares 322
Venetian honey cookies
(fenekia) 148
Whoopie pies 244

CORN

Corn bread, golden 97

Corn chowder 266

Cornmeal potatoes 258

Corn pudding 266

Corn relish 288

Corn soup 257

Hulled Indian corn,
old method 256

Hulled Indian corn,
modern method 256

Hush puppies 96

Johnnycake 267

Maple johnnycake 66

Corned beef and cabbage
casserole 293

Cottage pudding, Nana's . . . 269

Cowslips 77

Craisin-apple pie 309

Cream of basil soup 160

Crêpes with cottage cheese
(turós palacsinta) 178

Crescent cookies (kifli) 179

Croghan bologna,
homemade 108

Crow's nest 17

Crumb cake 324

Csirkepaprikás (chicken
paprikas) 176

Cucumber and yoghurt
salad (jajik) 124

Custard pie 309

DANDELIONS

Dandelion greens 76

Dandelion green salad 76

Dandelion wine 76

Date shaggie bars 321

Derevi Sarma (stuffed
grape leaves) 118

DESSERTS *(See also cakes, candies, cobblers, cookies, doughnuts and fritters, pies, puddings)*

Almond Joy
cheesecake 297

Animal cracker dessert . . . 181

Apple brown
Betty Baldwin 22

Apple crisp for one,
microwave 22

Apple dumplings 18

Baked apples
with Maple Sugar 21

Baklawa 238

Chocolate sauce 320

Crêpes with cottage cheese
(turós palacsinta) 178

Crow's nest 17

Dumplings in maple syrup
(Grand-pères
au sirop d'Érable) 66

French toast 44

Fried dough 282

Fried honey-cakes
(yakkwa) 223

Frozen chocolate-coated
banana 280

Funnel cakes 281

Matzoh cheese kugel
for Passover 204

Mincemeats
(fried tarts) 188

Noodle kugel 206

Peach cobbler 98

Pineapple sauce 320

Raspberry cobbler 81

Raspberry crisp 82

Sweet spiced rice
(yakshik) 223

Tell kadayif 122

Vanilla ice cream,
homemade. 321

Walnut crescents
(sambusak). 237

Dilly beans. 162

Diples (Greek crullers) 147

DOUGHNUTS AND FRITTERS

Apple fritters. 245

Buckwheat pancakes
(galettes de Sarrasin) . . . 134

Coffee time doughnuts . . . 308

Diples
(Greek crullers) 147

French toast 44

Fried bread 258

Fried dough 282

Fried honey-cakes
(yakkwa) 223

Funnel cakes. 281

Mincemeats (Italian) . . . 188

Mincemeat
(Mennonite) 246

Ola Lowe's doughnuts . . . 310

Duck, Magnolia Lane roast . . . 55

DUMPLINGS

Apple dumplings 18

Cornmeal potatoes 258

Csipetke (dumplings). . . . 174

Dumplings in maple syrup
(Grand-pères
au sirop d'Érable) 66

Easter bread (cheoreg) . . . 121

Easter meatloaf
(vagdalt hús). 175

Egg and lemon sauce
(saltsa avgholemono) . . . 152

Egg Noodles 112

EGGPLANT

Baked eggplant
(moussaka). 144

Eggplant appetizer
(baba ganouj) 230

Eggplant Byzantine
(melitzanes vizantiou). . . 142

Fried eggplant with Greek
sauces (tiganites melitzanes
meh saltses) 143

Enhanced beans 315

Fatayer bi sabanekh
(spinach pies) 234

Fatback sandwich. 43

Fenekia (Venetian
honey cookies) 148

Fiddleheads 76

Filled cookies 285

FISH

Baccala
(codfish in sauce) 189

Baked fish Mykonos
(psito psari) 145

Baked fish Salonika
(plaki) 145

Black Lake pan fish
with almonds 45

Deep-fried bullhead 305

Dilled pike
and pea pods. 49

Fish and
cheese chowder 30

Fish chowder 46

Fried fish 43

Gefilte fish
(stuffed fish) 200

Lake Champlain smelt . . . 46

Lawrence Senecal's
fish chowder 47

Manhattan
clam chowder 48

New Orleans-style
pike fillets 47

Pebble Island
pickled pike 44

Trout with vegetables 48

Zesty grilled fillets 45

Four-cheese macaroni 34

French toast 44

Fried bean curd
(tubu puch'im) 216

Fried bread 258

Fried dough 282

Fried fish 43

FRITTERS *(See doughnuts)*

Frosting, maple fluff 69

FRUIT SALAD
Maple fruit salad 69

Yoghurt fruit salad 24

Funnel cakes 281

Galettes de sarrasin
(buckwheat pancakes) . . . 134

Garlic, wild 78

Garlic dressing
(skordalia) 151

Gefilte fish (stuffed fish) . . . 200

Ginger candy
(ingberlach) 205

Gnocchi, ricotta 190

Goulash, Hungarian
(pörkölt) 174

Goulash soup
(gulyás leves) 174

Grand-pères au sirop
d'Érable (dumplings
in maple syrup) 66

GRAPE LEAVES, STUFFED
Derevi sarma—
meatless 118

Yabrak anab—
with meat 229

Grape nuts 110

Greek-style vegetables
(salatica ladolemono) 141

Greens, wild 76

Gulyás leves
(goulash soup) 174

Habart zöldbab-leves
(creamed
string bean soup) 173

HAM
Maple ham loaf 69

Raisin sauce for ham . . . 293

Hash, wedding 259

Hash browns, cheese 33

Head cheese
without head (tête
fromagée sans tête) 131

Havov pilav
(chicken pilaf) 120

Hommos bi tahina
(chick pea dip) 230

Honey-cakes, fried
(yakkwa) 223

Honey graham nut loaf 286

Hoppin' John 94

Hot buttered rum 67

Hulled Indian corn,
modern method 256

Hulled Indian corn,
old method 256

Hush puppies 96

Hutsput 166

Ice cream, vanilla 321

Indian Relish 23

Ingberlach
(ginger candy) 205

Italian three-cheese
macaroni 35

Jack wax 65

Jajik (cucumber and
yoghurt salad) 124

JELLY *(See preserves)*

Jerky, original Stillwater
first and last weekend
venison 59

Johnnycake 267

Johnnycake, maple 66

Káposztas kocka
(cabbage noodles) 175

Kasha varnishkas 208

Khubis talameh
(Lebanese bread) 235

Kibbee bi saniyeh
(baked kibbee) 231

Kibbee nayeh
(raw kibbee) 232

Kidney bean casserole 23

Kifli (crescent cookies) 179

Kimch'i, Napa cabbage
(paech'u kimch'i) 218

Kimpap (picnic rice
in seaweed) 217

Koulourakia, sweet 150

Kounoupidi
(Greek cauliflower) 142

Krema meh teree
(cheese sauce) 152

Kuchen bread 248

KUGELS
Matzoh cheese
kugel for Passover 204

Noodle kugel 206

Potato kugel 201

Kurabia 123

Ladolemono (oil and
lemon dressing) 151

LAMB
Baked kibbee
(kibbee bi saniyeh) . . . 231

Lamb and leeks
mahala (arni meh
prassa mahala) 147

Lamb and okra stew
(missov bami) 119

Lemon cabbage rolls
(yabrak malfouf
bi hamith) 233

Raw kibbee
(kibbee nayeh) 232

Shish kebab
(barbecued lamb) 124

Latkes
(potato pancakes) 201

Lebanese bread
(khubis talameh) 235

Leeks, wild 78

Lemon cabbage rolls (yabrak
malfouf bi hamith) 233

Lemon chicken oregano
(psiti kota meh
lemoni kai rigani) 143

Lemon crackers 271

LETTUCE
Greek lettuce salad
(maroulosalata
anamikti) 140

Lettuce bundles
(sangch'ussam) 222

Linguine with
white clam sauce 190

MACARONI
Four-cheese macaroni . . . 34

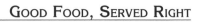

Italian three-cheese
macaroni 35

Macaroni and chick peas
(pasta a ceci) 187

Macaroni salad 316

Southern macaroni and
cheese 94

MAIN DISHES WITH MEAT
(See also fish, stews)
Barbecued chicken, Colton
Fire Department 315

Barbecued chicken,
Ezra Widrick's 243

Barbecued ribs 93

Boiled dinner 267

Bologna 107

Bulgogi (Korean
broiled beef) 219

Chicken breasts
with cheese 36

Chicken paprikas
(csirkepaprikás) 176

Chicken pilaf
(havov pilav) 120

Corned beef and
cabbage casserole . . . 293

Cranberry pot roast 201

Croghan bologna 108

Easter meatloaf
(vagdalt hús) 175

Fatback sandwich 43

Fried chicken 92

Grandma's New Year
pork pie (tourtière) 130

Ham, raisin sauce for . . . 293

Kidney bean casserole . . . 23

Lemon cabbage rolls
(yabrak malfouf
bi hamith) 233

Lemon chicken oregano
(psiti kota meh
lemoni kai rigani) 143

Magnolia Lane
roast duck 55

Maple ham loaf 69

Meatballs di Plati 191

Michigans 280

Moussaka
(baked eggplant) 144

Mung bean pancake
(pindaettok) 221

Noodles with meat
and vegetables
(chapch'ae) 220

Original Stillwater
first and last weekend
venison jerky 59

Partridge or pheasant
in wine sauce 56

Rabbit baked
in tarragon mustard,
garlic and cream 57

Rabbit casserole,
Good and easy 56

Rabbit stew 55

Shepherd's pie 295

Shish kebab 124

Stuffed cabbage,
Hungarian
(töltöttkáposzta) 177

Stuffed cabbage,
Jewish 202

Tomato-beef casserole . . . 294

Tourtière (meat pie) 130

Wedding hash 259

Wild game chili 54

Wild game meatballs . . . 53

MAIN DISHES, MEATLESS
(See also fish)
Blintzes 209

Broccoli special
casserole 296

Cheese pudding with
Creole sauce 31

Cheese strata 34

Fried bean curd
(tubu puch'im) 216

Four-cheese macaroni . . . 34

Italian three-cheese
macaroni 35

Kasha varnishkas 208

Latkes
(potato pancakes) 201

Linguine with
white clam sauce 190

Milk beans 161

Pasta a ceci (macaroni
and chick peas) 187

Pizza alla Napoletana
(Neopolitan pizza) . . . 189

Ricotta balls 187

Ricotta gnocchi 190

Southern macaroni
and cheese 94

Spanakopita
(spinach pie) 146

Tummybuster summer
squash casserole. 163

Welsh rarebit 33

MAPLE

Dumplings in maple syrup
(Grand-pères au sirop
d'Érable) 66

Maple cream 65

Maple fluff frosting 69

Maple fruit salad. 69

Maple ham loaf 69

Maple hard sauce 270

Maple johnnycake. 66

Maple pecan pie 65

Maple pickled beets 68

Maple popcorn 66

Maple syrup squares 67

Pralines 67

Wax on snow 65

MARMALADE (See preserves)

Maroulosalata anamikti
(Greek lettuce salad) . . . 140

Matzoh cheese kugel
for Passover 204

Meat pie (tourtière) 130

Meatball and pig hock stew
(ragoût de boulettes et de
pattes de cochon) 131

Meatballs di Plati 191

Meatballs, wild game 53

Meatloaf, Easter
(Vagdalt hús) 175

Melitzanes vizantiou
(eggplant Byzantine) . . . 142

Michigans 280

Milk beans. 161

Milkweed 77

Mincemeat. 246

Mincemeats
(fried tarts) 188

Minestrone Genoa 158

Missov bami
(lamb and okra stew) . . . 119

Mixed pickles (titvash) 119

Miyŏkkuk
(seaweed soup). 215

Mokas, Mémère
Monpetit's 133

Moussaka
(baked eggplant). 144

Mung bean pancake
(pindaettok) 221

Mushrooms, wild 79

Neopolitan pizza (pizza
alla Napoletana) 189

Noodles, Egg 112

Noodle kugel 206

Noodles with meat
and vegetables
(chapch'ae) 220

Oatmeal
chocolate chip cake 323

Oil and lemon dressing
(ladolemono) 151

Olives, marinated
(zeitoun) 236

Palacsinta, turós
(crêpes with
cottage cheese) 178

Pan fish with almonds,
Black Lake 45

PANCAKES
Blintzes 209
Buckwheat pancakes
(Galettes de Sarrasin) . . . 134
Crêpes with cottage cheese
(turós palacsinta) 178
Mung bean pancakes
(pindaettok) 221
Potato pancakes
(latkes) 201
Parsley-wheat salad
(taboulleh) 236

PARSNIPS
Baked parsnips 165
Fried parsnips 268
Partridge or pheasant
in wine sauce 56
Passover brownies 204

Passover sponge torte 205

PASTA
Egg noodles 112
Four-cheese macaroni . . . 34
Italian three-cheese
macaroni 35
Kasha varnishkas 208
Linguine with
white clam sauce 190
Macaroni and chick peas
(pasta a ceci) 187
Macaroni salad 316
Noodle kugel 206
Noodles (tarhonya) 176
Noodles with meat
and vegetables
(chapch'ae) 220
Ricotta gnocchi 190
Southern macaroni
and cheese 94
Pasta a ceci (macaroni and
chick peas) 187

PEAS
Pea soup
(soupe aux pois) 134
Scalloped peas
and onions 248

PEACHES
Peach cobbler 98
Peach marmalade 287
Peach pie, Amish 106
Peach pie 296
Peanut brittle 111
Pecan pie, maple 65
Pesto 166
Pheasant (or partridge)
in wine sauce 56

PICKLES *(See also relishes)*
Dilly beans 162
Maple pickled beets 68
Marinated olives
  (zeitoun) 236
Pickled beets 260
Pickled pusley
  (purslane) 76
Pickled turnips
  (lift makbous) 234
Thirteen-day
  sweet pickles 110
Titvash (mixed pickles) . . . 119
Picnic rice in seaweed
  (kimpap) 217

PIES
Apple cider pie 20
Blueberry pie 307
Chocolate-mint tart 298
Craisin-apple pie 309
Custard pie 309
Grandma's New Year
  pork pie (tourtière) . . . 130
Just like Grandma's
  apple pie 19
Maple pecan pie 65
Peach pie, Amish 106
Peach pie 296
Pie plant (rhubarb) pie . . . 246
Raisin-nut pie 244
Shoo-fly pie 245
Spinach pies (fatayer bi
  sabanekh) 234
Sugar pie
  (tarte au sucre) 133
Sugar-free
  strawberry pie 296
Sweet potato pie 97

Tourtière (meat pie) 130
Vinegar pie 271
Pie plant (rhubarb) pie 246
Pigweed 76

PIKE
Dilled pike
  and pea pods 49
New Orleans-style
  pike fillets 47
Pebble Island
  pickled pike 44
Pindaettok (mung
  bean pancake) 221
Pineapple sauce 320
Pizza alla Napoletana
  (Neopolitan pizza) 189
Plaki (baked fish
  Salonika) 145
Pollen muffins, cattail 78
Popcorn, maple 66

PORK
Barbecued ribs 93
Grandma's New Year
  pork pie (tourtière) . . . 130
Head cheese
  without head (tête
  fromagée sans tête) . . . 131
Meatballs di plati 191
Salt pork soup 257
Stew of meatballs and
  pork hocks (ragoût
  de boulettes) 131
Tourtière 130
Pörkölt
  (Hungarian gulash) 174
Pot roast, cranberry 201

POTATOES
Cheese hash browns 33

Hutsput 166

Potato pancakes
(latkes). 201

Potato pudding (kugel) . . . 201

Scalloped potatoes 306

Pralines 67

PRESERVES
Cider apple butter 109

Peach marmalade 287

Red raspberry jelly 286

Psiti kota meh lemoni
kai rigani (lemon
chicken oregano) 143

Psito psari (baked fish
Mykonos) 145

PUDDINGS
Blackberry pudding 80

"By guess and by gosh"
bread pudding 270

Corn pudding 266

Matzoh cheese kugel
for Passover 204

Nana's
cottage pudding 269

Noodle kugel 206

Rhubarb pudding 167

Steam Pudding 272

Puffballs. 79

Pumpkin muffins 281

Purslane (pusley) pickles . . . 76

Pusley (purslane) pickles . . . 76

RABBIT
Rabbit baked in
tarragon mustard,
garlic, and cream 57

Rabbit casserole,
good and easy 56

Rabbit stew 55

Ragoût de boulettes et de
pattes de cochon (Meat ball
and pig hock stew) 131

RAISINS
Raisin nut pie 244

Raisin sauce for ham . . . 293

RASPBERRIES
Open face raspberry pie . . . 82

Raspberry cobbler 81

Raspberry crisp 82

Raspberry jelly, red 286

RELISHES *(See also pickles)*
Corn relish 288

Indian Relish 23

Sandwich spread 108

Zucchini relish 164, 288

RHUBARB
Pie plant (rhubarb) pie . . . 246

Rhubarb pudding 167

Ribs, barbecued 93

RICE
Picnic rice in seaweed
(kimpap) 217

Sweet spiced rice
(yakshik) 223

Ricotta balls 187

Ricotta gnocchi 190

Rolls,
healthy homemade 308

Romano beans, baked . . . 161

Rum, hot buttered 67

SALADS
Coleslaw 306

Cucumber and
yoghurt salad (jajik) 124

Dandelion green salad 76

Greek lettuce salad
(maroulosalata
anamikti) 140

Greek-style vegetables
(salatica ladolemono) . . . 141

Macaroni salad 316

Maple fruit salad 69

Sauerkraut salad 247

Taboulleh
(parsley-wheat salad) . . . 236

Three-bean salad 294

Yoghurt fruit salad 24

Salatica ladolemono
(Greek-style
vegetables) 141

Salt pork soup 257

Saltsa avgholemono (egg
and lemon sauce) 152

Saltsa domata
(tomato sauce) 152

Sambusak
(walnut crescents) 237

Sandwich spread 108

Sangch'ussam
(lettuce bundles) 222

Sauces

Black Jack
barbecue sauce 58

Barbecued chicken, Colton
Fire Department 315

Barbecue sauce for chicken,
Ezra Widrick's 243

Cheese sauce
(krema meh teree) 152

Chocolate sauce 320

Egg and lemon sauce
(saltsa avgholomono) . . . 152

Garlic dressing
(skordalia) 151

Maple hard sauce 270

Oil and lemon dressing
(ladolemono) 151

Pesto 166

Pineapple sauce 320

Raisin sauce for ham . . . 293

Sesame dressing
for chard,
spinach or kale 163

Tomato sauce
(saltsa domata) 152

Yogurt salad dressing
(yaourti mayoneza) . . . 151

Sauerkraut salad 247

Seaweed soup
(miyŏkkuk) 215

Sesame dressing for chard,
spinach or kale 163

Sesame sticks 32

Shaggy manes 79

Shepherd's pie 295

Shish kebab 124

Shoo-fly pie 245

Skordalia
(garlic dressing) 151

Smelt, Lake Champlain 46

Soupe au pois
(pea soup) 134

Soups

Bean soup 107

Broccoli-cheddar soup . . . 304

Carrot soup 159

Chicken soup
(takkogiguk) 216

Chicken soup
with matzoh balls 199

Chicken soup
  with meatballs
  and escarole 192
Corn chowder 266
Corn soup 257
Cream of basil soup ... 160
Creamed string bean
  soup (habart
  zöldbab-leves) 173
Fish and
  cheese chowder 30
Lawrence Senecal's
  fish chowder 47
Fish chowder 46
Goulash soup
  (guylas leves) 174
Manhattan
  clam chowder 48
Minestrone Genoa 158
Pea soup
  (Soupe au pois) 134
Salt pork soup 257
Seaweed soup
  (miyŏkkuk) 215

SPINACH
Spanakopita
  (spinach pie) 146
Spinach pies (fatayer
  bi sabanekh) 234
Spinach soufflé 295
Sponge torte, Passover 205

SQUASH
Spiced winter squash... 259
Tummybuster summer
  squash casserole..... 163
Steam Pudding 272

STEWS
Carbonada Criolla 162

Cholent (Meat Stew).... 198
Hungarian goulash
  (pörkölt)........... 174
Lamb and leeks
  Mahala (arni meh
  prassa mahala)...... 147
Lamb and okra stew
  (missov bami) 119
Rabbit stew 55
Stew of meatballs and
  pork hocks (ragoût de
  boulettes) 131
Wild game stew 54
Strawberry pie,
  sugar-free........... 296
String bean soup,
  creamed (habart
  zöldbab-leves) 173
Striped cake (torte) 180
Stuffed fish
  (gefilte fish).......... 200
Sugar pie
  (tarte au sucre) 133
Sumac drink........... 79
Sunday bread,
  Greek (tsoureki) 149

SWEET POTATOES
Candied yams 95
Maple candied
  sweet potatoes 68
Scalloped sweet potatoes
  and apples.......... 24
Sweet potato and
  carrot tzimmes 203
Sweet potato pie....... 97
Switchel.............. 269
Taboulleh
  (parsley-wheat salad)... 236
Tahn (chilled
  yoghurt drink) 123

Takkogiguk
(chicken soup) 216

Tarales 186

Tarhonya (noodles) 176

Tarte au sucre
(sugar pie) 133

Tell kadayif 122

Tête fromagée
sans tête (head cheese
without head) 131

Thirteen-day
sweet pickles 110

Three-bean salad 294

Tiganites melitzanes
meh saltses (fried eggplant
with Greek sauces) 143

Titvash (mixed pickles) 119

Toffee squares 322

Töltöttkáposzta
(stuffed cabbage) 177

Tomato-beef casserole 294

Tomato sauce
(saltsa domata) 152

Tomatoes, stewed 96

Tourtière (meat pie) 130

Trout with vegetables 48

Tsoureki (Greek
Sunday bread) 149

Tubu puch'im
(fried bean curd) 216

Tummybuster summer
squash casserole 163

Turnips, pickled
(lift makbous) 234

Turós palacsinta (crêpes
with cottage cheese) . . . 178

Tzimmes, sweet potato
and carrot 203

Vagdalt hús
(Easter meatloaf) 175

VEGETABLES

Baked parsnips 165

Baked Romano beans . . . 161

Beets in tangy sauce . . . 159

Burdock roots 78

Cabbage noodles
(káposztas kocka) 175

Candied yams 95

Chard, spinach
or kale with
sesame dressing 163

Cheese hash browns 33

Coleslaw 306

Collard greens
with ham 95

Corn pudding 266

Cowslips 77

Dandelion greens 76

Eggplant Byzantine
(melitzanes
vizantiou) 142

Enhanced beans 315

Fiddleheads 76

Fried eggplant with
Greek sauces
(tiganites melitzanes
meh saltses) 143

Fried parsnips 268

Greek cauliflower
(kounoupidi) 142

Hoppin' John 94

Hutsput 166

Lettuce bundles
(sangch'ussam) 222

Maple candied
sweet potatoes 68

Maple pickled beets 68

Milk beans 161

Milkweed 77

Napa cabbage kimch'i
(paech'u kimch'i) 218

Pesto 166

Pigweed 76

Potato pudding (kugel) . . . 201

Puffballs 79

Pusley (purslane) 76

Quick baked beans 68

Scalloped peas
and onions 248

Scalloped potatoes 306

Scalloped sweet potatoes
and apples 24

Shaggy manes 79

Spanakopita
(spinach pie) 146

Spiced winter squash . . . 259

Spinach soufflé 295

Stewed tomatoes 96

Stir-fried watercress 77

Sweet potato
and carrot tzimmes . . . 203

Tummybuster summer
squash casserole 163

Watercress sandwiches . . . 77

Wild garlic 78

Wild leeks 78

Wintercress 76

Venetian honey cookies
(fenekia) 148

Venison jerky, original
Stillwater first and
last weekend 59

Venison pâté,
Chef Locy's country 60

Vinegar pie 271

Walnut crescents
(sambusak) 237

WATERCRESS
Stir-fried watercress 77
Watercress sandwiches . . . 77

Wax on snow 65

Wedding hash 259

Welsh rarebit 33

Whoopie pies 244

WILD GAME
Wild game chili 54
Wild game meatballs . . . 53
Wild game stew 54

Wine, dandelion 76

Wintercress 76

Yabrak anab
(stuffed grape leaves) . . . 229

Yabrak malfouf bi hamith
(lemon cabbage rolls) 233

Yakkwa (fried
honey cakes) 223

Yakshik
(sweet spiced rice) 223

Yams, candied 95

Yaourti mayoneza (yoghurt
salad dressing) 151

YOGHURT
Cucumber and yoghurt
salad (jajik) 124
Yoghurt drink,
chilled (tahn) 123
Yoghurt fruit salad 24
Yoghurt salad dressing
(yaourti mayoneza) . . . 151

Yule Log
(Bûche de Noël) 132

Zeitoun
(marinated olives) 236

Zucchini relish 164, 288

Good Food, Served Right
Traditional Arts in Upstate New York

Quantity	Book			Total
_____	*Good Food, Served Right*	@	$19.95 each	_____
	Shipping & Handling	@	$ 4.50 each	_____
	NYS residents add 7% sales tax			_____
			Total enclosed	_____

Please send the above cookbooks to:

Name_____

Address _____

City _____ State_____ Zip_____

Telephone_____

I want to pay my order by:

☐ Check made out to Traditional Arts in Upstate New York

☐ Credit Card

    ☐ VISA   ☐ MasterCard   ☐ Discover   ☐ American Express

Card # _____ Expiration Date_____

Signature _____

Mail orders to Traditional Arts in Upstate New York, P.O. Box 665, Canton, NY 13617

You may also order by calling 315-386-4289 or by e-mailing us at **tauny@northnet.org**. If you order via e-mail, include a daytime phone number so that we can call to get your credit card information. DO NOT SEND YOUR CREDIT CARD INFORMATION TO OUR E-MAIL ADDRESS.

Good Food, Served Right
Traditional Arts in Upstate New York

Quantity	Book			Total
_____	*Good Food, Served Right*	@	$19.95 each	_____
	Shipping & Handling	@	$ 4.50 each	_____
	NYS residents add 7% sales tax			_____
			Total enclosed	_____

Please send the above cookbooks to:

Name_____

Address _____

City _____ State_____ Zip_____

Telephone_____

I want to pay my order by:

☐ Check made out to Traditional Arts in Upstate New York

☐ Credit Card

    ☐ VISA   ☐ MasterCard   ☐ Discover   ☐ American Express

Card # _____ Expiration Date_____

Signature _____

Mail orders to Traditional Arts in Upstate New York, P.O. Box 665, Canton, NY 13617

You may also order by calling 315-386-4289 or by e-mailing us at **tauny@northnet.org**. If you order via e-mail, include a daytime phone number so that we can call to get your credit card information. DO NOT SEND YOUR CREDIT CARD INFORMATION TO OUR E-MAIL ADDRESS.